Adolescents after Divorce

Adolescents after Divorce

Christy M. Buchanan

Eleanor E. Maccoby

Sanford M. Dornbusch

HARVARD UNIVERSITY PRESS

Cambridge, Massachusetts • London, England • 1996

Copyright © 1996 by the President and Fellows of Harvard College
All rights reserved
Printed in the United States of America

Library of Congress Cataloging-in-Publication Data

Buchanan, Christy M.
  Adolescents after divorce / Christy M. Buchanan, Eleanor E.
Maccoby, Sanford M. Dornbusch.
    p. cm.
  Includes bibliographical references and index.
  ISBN 0-674-00517-1 (alk. paper)
  1. Children of divorced parents—United States—Attitudes.
2. Teenagers—United States—Attitudes. 3. Divorce—United States.
4. Divorce—Psychological aspects. I. Maccoby, Eleanor E., 1917– .
II. Dornbusch, Sanford M. III. Title.
HQ777.5.B796 1996
306.874—dc20   96-11882

To the adolescents who trusted us
with their feelings and
experiences,
and who responded so thoughtfully
and candidly to our questions

92116

CONTENTS

PREFACE

The decision to divorce is grueling for most parents, who often worry heavily about the impact of divorce on their children. Like other parents, those who divorce want to provide their children with the opportunities to develop into well-functioning, happy, responsible, independent adults. And despite doomsayers' predictions concerning the impact of divorce and "broken families" on children and society, research clearly shows that many children adapt quite well after their parents' divorce. Perhaps even more children would thrive if more information and more support were provided for divorcing parents and the professionals who work with them.

This book was written in an effort to help those parents whose best or only option is divorce. Our research was conducted under the assumption that, for good or ill, divorces will continue to happen. Our aim was never to argue for or against divorce. Rather, we wanted to find out what circumstances of family life after divorce were associated with good adjustment on the part of children, so that both parents and professionals could enhance children's development. With the indispensable help of over five hundred adolescents, we discovered much about what matters—and what does not matter—with respect to adolescents' well-being after divorce. Our hope is that making this information available will aid and encourage parents in this difficult situation, and ultimately improve the lives of their children.

Some of the findings reported in Chapters 4, 5, and 6 were previously reported in Buchanan, Maccoby, and Dornbusch (1992). Certain findings in Chapter 11 previously appeared in Buchanan, Maccoby, and Dornbusch (1991).

We are tremendously grateful for the generous support of the W. T. Grant Foundation (grant no. 88119688 to Eleanor E. Maccoby and Sanford M. Dornbusch) and of the Center for the Study of Families, Children, and Youth at Stanford University. Our thanks also go to Wake Forest University, whose summer support for faculty and other resources contributed in important ways to the completion of this book. We are indebted to Sue Dimicelli and Patricia Weaver, who demonstrated extraordinary commitment to this project, helping with a wide variety of tasks ranging from endless typing to data analysis. Their hard work, as well as their support and encouragement, made our lives less stressful throughout every phase of this endeavor. We are also grateful for the good work of the interviewers, for the research assistance of Sue Monahan, and for the advice and comments of our colleagues Lee Cronbach and Kate Funder and two reviewers. Finally, this project would not have been possible without the patience and enduring support of our families. We especially want to thank Jeff, Kelly, Riley, Brady, Mac, and Red.

February 1996

Concepts and Methods

1

Introduction

Each year, a large new group of children joins the growing number of those whose parents have divorced. For at least some period of time, these children must adapt to life in a single-parent family. From the child's standpoint, the loss of the familiar everyday presence of the parent who has left the household is often a major event that initiates a cascade of consequences. Although many families attempt to make up for this loss by arranging visitation with the "outside" parent, it is a very different situation for the child to spend time with the two parents in two different households than it was to see them together in the same setting. In addition, the child's new life may involve a change in neighborhood or school, new caretakers while the custodial parent works longer hours, and a substantial drop in standard of living.

Much has been written concerning the adjustment of children whose parents have divorced. These children have been compared with children in nondivorced families to see what kinds of adjustment problems, if any, occur when parents have separated. There is evidence that parental divorce does, indeed, increase the risk of several forms of maladaptation in children. But popular articles on the subject (for example, Whitehead, 1993) not only exaggerate the risks but oversimplify the issues. For example, we now know that many of the problems seen in children from divorced families were evident before the parents separated (Block, Block, and Gjerde, 1986; Cherlin et al., 1991), so that the problems cannot be attributed simply to the divorce itself. Furthermore, the dictum "Two parents are better than one," while generally true, needs to be qualified to read "Two *allied* parents are better than one" (Amato and Keith, 1991; Emery, 1982; Peterson and Zill, 1986). And popular writings tend to lose sight of the fact that many children with divorced parents function adequately or even exceptionally well, especially after the initial disrupted period following parental separation has passed (Amato and Keith, 1991; Chase-Lansdale, Cherlin, and Kiernan, 1995).

The first central fact that needs to be understood is the enormous diversity in postdivorce family life (Amato, 1993; Barber and Eccles, 1992; Furstenberg, 1990). The second is the dynamic quality of the postdivorce period—the fact that divorce is not just one event, but part of a set of changes that unfold over time. Some children adapt well to these changes, and get on with their developmental agendas. Others falter or even regress. Our purpose in this book is not to pursue the question of whether divorce is good or bad for children. We take seriously the fact that there is a great deal of variability in how children adjust to divorce. Thus we seek to understand the conditions that make divorce more or less difficult for children—that enable some to cope with their new and changing life situation in positive ways and that interfere with positive adaptation for others. We have no wish to downplay the grief, the sense of betrayal, the disorientation, that children experience when their parents separate. We believe that the optimal situation for children's development is, in most cases, living in a single household with two parents, both of whom are committed to the children's welfare and who are able to cooperate with each other—when such a family setting is a real possibility. But the main question we are asking is not how marriages might be made more stable—important though that issue is—but how to optimize the life chances of children whose parents do divorce.

Factors That May Affect Children's Postdivorce Functioning

Analysts of family structure have pointed to a number of conditions that may account for the tendency for children of divorce to exhibit more problems, on average, than children whose parents have not divorced. The variability in these factors among divorced families may help us to understand the variability we see in children's adjustment. Some of the conditions most commonly thought to be important can be classified as follows (see also Amato, 1993).

1. *Loss of a parent.* Children's parents are their anchors. Parents provide the structure for children's daily lives, and even when parents are not functioning very well, children depend on them for a sense of security that enables them to cope with their developmental tasks. When one parent leaves the home, the child realizes a shattering possibility: parents are not always there. If one leaves, the other might too. But at the time

of divorce, families differ greatly in the degree to which a parent disappears from the child's life. In a few cases, both parents remain completely accessible, in others partly accessible, and in other cases only one continues to be part of the child's life. The hypothesis is that children's powerful anxiety over losing one or both parents will be considerably mitigated by ensuring continuing contact and a continuing emotional bond with both.

2. *Interparental conflict.* Previous research has indicated that conflict between parents can be seriously harmful to children, particularly if they are directly exposed to the conflict (Camara and Resnick, 1988; Cummings and Davies, 1994; Emery, 1982; Johnston and Campbell, 1988). Presumably there is a build-up of conflict between parents before the decision to divorce is made. Moving into separate residences ought to mean that episodes of conflict occur less frequently, and by virtue of the separation of the warring parties, all family members may experience some relief from the intense levels of conflict surrounding the divorce itself. Still, in many families, conflict between the parents continues at some level (Maccoby and Mnookin, 1992). It is reasonable to expect that children's adjustment in the postdivorce period will depend, at least to some extent, on the level of conflict that is maintained between their parents or, alternatively, on the extent to which parents can moderate their conflict or shield the children from exposure to it. In an extensive review of the literature on children's adjustment to divorce, Amato (1993) concluded that the level of continuing interparental conflict was the most well-documented predictor of outcomes following divorce.

3. *Diminished parenting.* Many believe that when children from divorced families exhibit problems, this happens primarily because the divorce has brought about a deterioration in the quality of parenting provided by the custodial parent (with the custodial parent typically being the mother). Indeed, considerable evidence exists that a period of "diminished parenting," at least during the first two years following divorce, does occur. Studying single divorced mothers in the first two postdivorce years, Hetherington and colleagues reported that the emotional distress being experienced by these mothers was in many cases translated into a lowered level of responsiveness to their preschool-aged children, lessened vigilance for their safety and emotional states, less patience, and a more peremptory style of discipline and control (Hetherington, Cox, and Cox, 1982). The mothers were also less able to maintain organized household routines: to provide meals on time, monitor bedtimes, and the like. This diminished quality of parenting seemed to be directly responsible for some of the children's behavior problems, and

when the quality of parenting recovered—as it did in many cases within two years—the children's behavior also improved. Others have noted that single mothers are less likely to have a participatory parenting style than are mothers who have not been divorced or mothers who have remarried—in other words, single mothers are more likely to let their adolescent children make decisions without parental input (Dornbusch et al., 1985).

More recent work by Hetherington and colleagues (Hetherington and Clingempeel, 1992) with early adolescent children (average age: eleven years) whose parents had been divorced for a longer time than had parents in Hetherington's earlier studies did not implicate diminished parenting as a major reason for poorer adjustment in divorced compared with nondivorced families, but did point to the importance of quality of parenting in children's adjustment within each type of family structure (nondivorced, divorced, remarried). We expect, then, that children's success or failure in coping with the postdivorce situation depends at least in part on the quality of parenting maintained by the primary custodial parent.

Widespread recognition of these factors[1] as potentially affecting the postdivorce lives of families has led to (or been accompanied by) changes in the statutes governing divorce and the legal processes that surround it. Certain of these changes appear to be designed to mitigate some of the risks just listed. We believe that research on conditions that may soften or exacerbate the effects of divorce on children must continue to focus on these factors, but that the new legal context must now be taken into account as well, as changing arrangements for custody and visitation may interact with the interpersonal factors that have proved to be important to date.

The Changing Legal Context for Divorce

The past two decades have seen great changes in the legal context of divorce. In the United States and most other industrialized nations, "fault-based" statutes have all but disappeared. There has also been a change in presumptions about which parent will get custody. Although the custody of children almost automatically went to mothers earlier this century (unless the mother was proved "unfit"), divorce statutes are now carefully couched in gender-neutral terms. Neither fathers nor mothers are to be given preference in custody awards; rather, custody decisions are to be made individually, case by case, in accordance with what appears to be the best interests of the child. And the courts, more and more, have been withdrawing from the decision process, leaving custody decisions to the two parents whenever possible and turning to mandatory mediation when parents cannot agree.[2] Presumably these changes are intended to make divorce procedures less adversarial, and to minimize postdivorce conflict by helping parents to formulate agreed-upon plans for the children's lives.

In practice, it has proved difficult to determine what custodial arrangements are in the best interests of children. There is no clear consensus among family-law attorneys, judges, or mediators concerning how children's time should be divided between the two parents. Still, a basic premise of the new legal context for divorce is that children should have access to both parents—presumably to soften the child's sense of being abandoned by a parent. Although there were early claims that the custodial parent ought to have veto power over whether and under what conditions children would see the "outside" parent (Goldstein, Freud, and Solnit, 1979), this point of view has not prevailed. Current laws generally embody provisions that encourage visitation with noncustodial parents and impose costs on custodial parents who attempt to impede visitation. Furthermore, joint custody arrangements have been recognized or even given preference. These changes have been justified in terms of the presumed benefits to children of maintaining relationships with both parents, but they also reflect strong pressure from fathers' rights groups, who have claimed that fathers and mothers should have equal rights of access to their children.

Whether because of the current legal climate or because of changes in the climate of public attitudes or both, there is evidence that children now maintain contact with noncustodial parents at higher rates than was formerly the case. For example, quite high rates of "father dropout" were reported by Furstenberg and colleagues (1983), who studied children for whom parental divorce occurred mainly in the early 1970s. Higher rates of contact between children and their noncustodial fathers, however, have been reported for more recent divorces (Braver et al., 1991; Bray and Berger, 1990; Maccoby and Mnookin, 1992; Seltzer, 1991), and the little information available on noncustodial mothers indicates that they maintain even higher rates of contact with their children than do noncustodial fathers (Furstenberg et al., 1983; Maccoby and Mnookin, 1992). The more recent data thus indicate that large numbers of children are now spending time in two different parental households. We may speculate about what this means for their lives. It seems obvious that they must face greater exposure to conflicting parental standards and expectations than they would if they lived in only one household. Their divided lives may also involve greater exposure to interparental conflict, along with the loyalty conflicts that can stem from maintaining relationships with two parents who continue to harbor hostility toward each other. These negative factors might, of course, be offset by the presumed value of receiving support and guidance from two parents rather than one. The fact is, though, that we know next to nothing concerning how children integrate—or fail to integrate—their experiences in two households. It is a major purpose of this book to explore this question.

The state of California was among the first to reform its divorce laws, and following the changes, there was an increase in the number of families awarded joint physical custody. California was, therefore, a promising locale in which to study the postdivorce lives of parents and children in the context of the new legal climate.

The Stanford Custody Project

The Stanford Custody Project has followed a diverse group of divorcing families in two northern California counties. Families were initially enrolled in the study approximately five years after the major revisions of California divorce law went into effect (the intake period for the study was from September 1984 to April 1985). Approximately 1,100 families, all having at least one child under sixteen years of age, were enrolled. Although the mothers were awarded physical custody of the children in a substantial majority of these families, there were nevertheless sizable subgroups in which the fathers had primary custody or in which parents were sharing custody. The sample thus presents an opportunity to contrast three different custodial arrangements.

The research has been conducted in two phases: in the first (Study 1), parents were interviewed on three successive occasions, covering a period of approximately three and a half years from the time of parental separation. That phase of the study dealt focally with the residential and visitation arrangements for the children—how these arrangements were arrived at, whether they were stable over time, and if not, how and why they changed. Both legal and physical custody (or "residence")[3] were considered. A second major focus was on co-parenting: how the parental responsibilities were divided between the two parents, how (and whether) parents communicated, whether they were able to cooperate in matters concerning the children, and how much interparental conflict existed. The findings of the first phase of the research have been reported in *Dividing the Child: Social and Legal Dilemmas of Custody* (Maccoby and Mnookin, 1992).

All of the information in that book represents the parents' perspectives, and it told us little about how the children were weathering the many changes and stresses in their lives. We felt it important to get the perspective of the children themselves, and therefore undertook the second phase of the research (Study 2): a follow-up study of the adolescent children in the families included in phase 1. Although it would have been interesting to learn about the children of all ages, we limited ourselves to interviews with children aged ten to eighteen, who had been six years old or older at the time their parents separated. Many of the children in the families included in the parent study—indeed, the majority of children in those families—were toddlers or preschoolers at the time of their parents' divorce, and we recognize that our findings in the present study may not apply in some respects to these younger children. The advantage of focusing as we did on the older children is that, by the age of ten and older, children were able to describe their lives in detail, and they were capable of reflecting on their own perceptions and reactions to the events in their families. Telephone interviews with these children produced a wealth of data on life inside diverse households. The adolescents' experiences and the quality of their adjustment are the subject of the chapters that follow.

The fact that the families of our adolescents were studied longitudinally during the first three and a half years following the parents' separation provided us with a unique opportunity. We were able to link information obtained from the adolescents to information obtained from their parents during the preceding several years. In particular, we could contrast the adjustment of adolescents whose parents maintained a cooperative co-parental relationship with those whose parents were conflicted. And we could see whether adolescent adjustment was related to the history of an adolescent's residential arrangements. In the earlier study, we found that residential arrangements were often unstable and in a number of cases did not correspond to the form of physical custody specified in the divorce decree. Substantial numbers of children moved from one parental household to another, or into or out of joint custody. We could ask not only about the impact of each of the three residential arrangements on a child's adjustment, but also about the impact of a history of residential instability.

The Focus of the Adolescent Study

As we noted earlier, previous research on the adjustment of children whose parents have divorced has pointed to the processes within the primary residential home as being especially important. In particular, the closeness of the emotional relationship between the residential parent and the child, the amount of conflict between them, and the presence of firmly established standards of behavior—along with careful monitoring by the parent of the child's performance in meeting these standards—have emerged as significant factors for children's adjustment.[4] We assessed the kind of parent-child interactions that occurred within our adolescents' primary residence (as seen from the adolescents' perspective), and then examined how these processes were related to adolescent adjustment.

Although parent-child interactions in the nonresidential household have seldom been examined, we believed that they might matter too, at least for children who spent substantial amounts of time with the other parent. We therefore examined a variety of processes in both parental households, as reported by the adolescents experiencing them.

Given the changing views and practices about who should have custody of children after divorce, we were also interested in how processes and interactions in each home varied as a function of residential arrangement. In families that have not divorced, fathers and mothers often assume somewhat different parental roles and display somewhat different parenting styles (Maccoby, 1995). Little is known concerning whether this differentiation survives when mothers or fathers become single parents. Do single parents become "both father and mother" to the children, adding to their own accustomed roles the functions and styles formerly characterizing the ex-spouse? Or do they continue to function primarily in their accustomed ways? If the latter, then the family processes prevailing in father-headed households might be somewhat different from those in mother-headed households, and these differences might have consequences for children's adjustment.

Specific Objectives

As noted, a central concern of this book is to compare and contrast the three major residential arrangements: primary mother residence, primary father residence, and dual residence (an arrangement in which the child's residential time is fairly equally shared between the two parental house-holds). We compared these three residential arrangements with respect to the experiences and adjustment of the adolescents in each. Our first set of questions was as follows:

1. Does the adjustment of adolescents depend in any degree on their current residential arrangement? And is adjustment related to how stable this arrangement has been since the parents separated?
2. Do processes such as rule-setting, emotional support, or parent-child conflict differ between mothers' and fathers' households? Is it more difficult for a parent to monitor children, maintain predict-able household routines, or achieve emotional closeness when chil-dren are in joint custody (dual residence) rather than living primarily in one parental household?
3. What factors are linked to adjustment of adolescents within each residential arrangement? Can differences in within-household processes between residential arrangements explain any differ-ences in adolescent adjustment that occur?

Of course, the situation an adolescent faces in a parent's household may be affected by whether the parent has a new partner and how serious that relationship is. As just one possible example, we know that the advent of new partners may affect the amount of conflict between the two divorced parents (Maccoby and Mnookin, 1992), which may in turn redound upon the relationship between the parents and the adolescent. We also know relatively little about the conditions under which adoles-cents are willing to accept the authority of a new parental figure in their lives. These considerations led to an additional set of questions:

1. Is adolescent adjustment related to whether the residential parent has a new partner? Does it matter whether the new partner merely lives with the parent and adolescent, or whether a remar-riage has occurred?
2. Is the impact of a residential father's new partner similar to that of a residential mother's new partner?
3. Does the existence of a new partner for the residential parent af-fect adolescents' relationships with nonresidential parents?
4. What factors are related to adolescents' acceptance of their par-ents' new partners?

Another major objective of our study was to examine what it means to adolescents to spend time in two different parental households. Although dual-resident adolescents are faced with this experience most intensively, it is also faced by young people who live primarily with one parent and visit the other. For adolescents who had their primary residence with one parent, several questions were pertinent:

1. What patterns of visitation are maintained between adolescents and nonresidential parents? How is visitation experienced by adolescents, and how much voice do they feel they have in visitation schedules?
2. To what extent does the quality of the relationship with a nonresidential parent depend on the frequency of contact? What other factors predict the quality of that relationship?
3. Do large amounts of visitation with the nonresidential parent interfere in any way with processes in the residential home? with the relationship between child and residential parent?
4. Is adolescent adjustment related to how much contact the adolescent has with the nonresidential parent? to the quality of the relationship with the nonresidential parent?

For both the adolescents in dual residence and those who lived primarily with one parent and visited the other, two major questions were posed:

1. Does having a close relationship with one parent make it more or less difficult to maintain a close relationship with the other? Is it beneficial for adolescents to maintain a close relationship with both parents after divorce, or is a close relationship with one parent "enough" to facilitate good adjustment?
2. In terms of the adolescent's adjustment following divorce, does it matter how consistent the rules and standards of the two households are?

As we noted earlier, there is every reason to believe that adolescent adjustment will be related to whether the two parents continue to be in conflict with each other. The fact that the parents must maintain some sort of contact if the children are to go back and forth between households must mean that there are continuing opportunities for interparental conflict to occur. At the same time, we know that there are some parents who manage to do business together in a reasonably cooperative fashion, and others who are neither cooperative nor conflicted in their co-parental relationship but, rather, simply stay disengaged from each other even though the children are members of both parental households (Maccoby and Mnookin, 1992). We were concerned with how the levels of co-parental conflict or cooperation that had prevailed since the divorce were related to adolescent adjustment. In addition, there are many references in the divorce literature to the potential problem of loyalty conflicts for children of divorce. According to Emery (1988), "most children . . . feel the pressures created by torn loyalties even when parents cooperate relatively well" (p. 13). We wanted to examine the extent to which adolescents reported torn loyalties or feelings of being "caught" between their parents, the conditions under which these feelings were likely to occur, and the relation of such feelings to adolescent adjustment.

We recognized that the answers to some or all of our questions would not be the same for adolescents of the two sexes. Some studies have indicated that children adjust better when living with the same-sex parent, but several of these studies have utilized very small samples, and the hypothesis needs examining with a larger and more diverse group of divorcing families. Also, it was quite possible that the younger adolescents in our sample would react differently than the older ones to their parents' breakup and the events that have followed it. Many changes occur over the adolescent years: children become more and more independent, less concerned and more comfortable with the physical changes of puberty, and more susceptible to risky behaviors and several kinds of adjustment problems (for example, depression and deviance). Thus for most of the questions we examined, we looked at whether the answers differed depending on whether we were talking about boys versus girls, or younger versus older adolescents.

Overview of the Book

The book is divided into three parts. Part I (Chapters 1–3) sets out the goals and methods of the study and discusses the assessment of family processes, interparental relationships, and adolescent adjustment. In addition, the contexts of our adolescents' lives are described: their residential history, the characteristics of their households, and major events that have occurred recently in their lives. We also provide a general picture of the adjustment and well-being of our adolescents as a group.

In Part II (Chapters 4–7), the three residential arrangements are compared with respect to the adjustment of the adolescents living in them, as well as the contextual factors, interpersonal relationships, and forms of parental control and management that prevail in each. Subsequently, within each residential group, the connections between characteristics of the family and adolescent adjustment are examined. A comparison of the predictors of adjustment in each residential group allows us to consider whether adjustment is linked to the same or different family processes within each. We are also able to address whether differences in adjustment among residential groups have to do with differences among arrangements in the family environment. Finally, the impact of parents' new partners on adolescents' experience and adaptation is explored, as is the adolescent's acceptance of a new partner.

In Part III (Chapters 8–12), we explicitly examine the experience of participating in two different parental households. Visitation and the nature of the adolescent's relationship with the nonresidential parent are explored, focusing on the way in which they relate to characteristics of household and family functioning, and to adjustment. Adolescents' feelings of being caught between their parents are studied, as are the effects of inconsistency between the two households in patterns of control and management.

In Chapter 13, we summarize our main findings and consider their implications.

2

Methods

This book is about the way adolescents were adjusting to their post-divorce lives approximately four and a half years after their parents separated. All of the adolescents in our study were members of families who had experienced a divorce, and whose parents had participated in a previous phase of this research (Study 1). Study 1 began at the time the parents filed for divorce, during 1984–1985. Our interviews with the adolescents took place between November 1988 and June 1989. For Study 1, during the period between the divorce filing and the adolescent interview, we talked to at least one of the adolescent's parents—and often both—on several (up to three) occasions.[1] The first parent interview (Time 1, or T1) took place at six months after the separation, the second (T2) at one and a half years after the separation, and the third (T3) at three and a half years after the separation. Thus we had a good deal of information about recent family history—the amount of conflict that had been involved in the divorce process, where the adolescent had lived, parental remarriage, residential moves, the relationship between the parents—before we talked to the adolescents themselves in Study 2 (or T4). The research reported in this book thus concerns the adolescent children in the Study 1 families, and it links the children's adjustment to the conditions of their parents' divorce and custody arrangements as well as to concurrent family functioning and circumstances.

The Sample

There were 1,500 children whose parents remained in Study 1 throughout the three-year postdivorce period. Ideally, we would have conducted in-depth assessments (including, for example, behavioral observations and reports by teachers or parents) on at least a random subset of these children. Such in-depth assessments are expensive and time-consuming, however, and to undertake them would have meant severely restricting our sample size. Using a small subsample would have kept us from achieving some of the most important objectives of our work, for example, comparisons of children living in different residential arrangements, or comparisons of children from high-conflict versus low-conflict divorces. The limitations of taking a small random sample would have been especially great given the large age range of the children from Study 1 (0–16 at parental separation) and the fact that predictors of adjustment to divorce vary for children of different ages.

As noted in Chapter 1, our main objective in Study 2 was to go beyond the information and viewpoints provided by parents in Study 1 by exploring the perspective of the children themselves. We wanted a sample of substantial size, sufficient to represent the diversity of family circumstances that was evident in Study 1. We decided, therefore, to rely on interviews rather than on in-depth clinical assessments, and to focus on the older children among our Study 1 families—those old enough to take part in a telephone interview. Some pilot work, and our reading of the research literature, led us to choose the age range from ten to eighteen (inclusive). We believed (rightly, as it turned out) that it would be possible for children in this age range to talk to us cogently about their current life situations and their experiences in their maternal and paternal households. Hoping to obtain a sample large enough for the needed comparisons of subgroups, we elected to interview all of the children in our Study 1 families who met the age criterion.

The target sample for the adolescent study thus consisted of children at or between the ages of ten and eighteen. Ten-year-olds were interviewed if they were in fifth grade and would be eleven by June 1, 1989. In cases where adolescents were already eighteen years old when we began interviewing in the fall of 1988, we tried to recruit that family as early in the data collection period as possible. This was done for two reasons: to reach these older children before they turned nineteen, and to catch those children who had moved after high school before they had been out of the home for very long. By interviewing these adolescents early in the data collection period, we were able to obtain information about their recent past—when they were still living with one or both parents—and to classify them according to their prior residential arrangement.

There were 647 children within our target age range in the Study 1 families. Ultimately we interviewed 522 adolescents from 365 families, or

81 percent of our intended group. In 12 percent of the target cases, a parent or child refused to participate. Five percent of the cases were not locatable, and 2 percent were not eligible for the study owing to the parents' reconciliation, the death of a parent or the child, or a mental handicap that precluded participation. In 229 of the families that agreed to participate (63 percent), only one adolescent was interviewed; in 118 families (32 percent), two adolescents were interviewed; in 18 families (5 percent), three or four children were interviewed.

How Representative Is Our Sample?

The adolescents in our study were all members of families who lived in two counties in Northern California at the time the parents divorced. The children's residences had fanned out geographically somewhat since the beginning of Study 1 because of residential moves on the part of the parents, but the large majority of our adolescents still lived within or close to the original two counties. We do not know in what respects they are representative of young people who live in other parts of the country. We know that teenage cultures do vary by geographical region. Analysis of population statistics indicated that the parents in our Study 1 families were better educated and had higher incomes than the national average (Maccoby and Mnookin, 1992), although the sample was diverse, ranging from people on public assistance to people of some wealth. Similarly, although the adolescents in our sample were living in somewhat more affluent circumstances on the average than might be true of a sample taken elsewhere in the country, conditions in the neighborhoods in which our adolescents lived varied from comfortable suburbia to inner-city crowding and shabbiness. As might be expected from a California sample, fewer of our adolescents were African-American, and more were ethnically Hispanic, than would be found in a national sample. In addition, because of California laws in the early 1980s that favored joint custody and liberal visitation rights, our sample may not be fully representative of other geographic regions with respect to the families' custody and visitation arrangements. Our adolescents were probably more likely than those in states not favoring joint custody or liberal visitation to maintain relatively high levels of contact with both parents (see Chapters 3 and 9).

How representative were our sample families of all families from the two California counties that filed for divorce during this time? The families in Study 1 were originally selected from the court records of divorce filings over a specified intake period. Although not all the families whose names appeared in the court records could be reached and interviewed, both recruitment and maintenance rates were high in Study 1. The attrition that did occur in recruitment and maintenance over the three-year span of Study 1 did not change the composition of the sample materially, with the exception that families retained in the study included a higher proportion of people with joint custody than was the case for the families not successfully recruited. Study 1 families (and their children) were thus reasonably representative of the families in which divorce occurred during the specific time period when sample selection occurred (Maccoby and Mnookin, 1992).

Finally, how well do the adolescents we interviewed in Study 2 represent all adolescents we could have recruited? Very well, it appears. Analyses comparing the families of adolescents we interviewed with the families in which either the parent or the adolescent refused to participate, or who were not located, indicated that we were somewhat more successful in recruiting families in which parents had more education. The two groups of families did not differ with respect to income, ethnicity, the amount of conflict or cooperation between parents, parents' hostility, or parents' satisfaction with the residential arrangement as measured in the three parental interviews. At the level of the individual child, there were no differences between adolescents we interviewed and adolescents we did not in parents' reports of child unhappiness (measured at T2), irritability, independence, or being difficult to manage (measured at T2 and T3). There were also no differences in age or sex of adolescents between the interviewed and noninterviewed groups. We were slightly less successful in recruiting adolescents who had been living with their fathers at the time of the last parent interview than adolescents who had been living with their mothers or with both parents. On the whole, then, our sample of adolescents was not distorted by the loss of 19 percent of our original target group: the adolescents not recruited were very similar to those who participated in the study. More detailed information on the participants in Study 2 can be found in Chapter 3.

Interviewing More than One Adolescent per Household

A crucial issue we faced was how to handle families in which more than one child fell within our target age range. In the past, many researchers have limited their samples to one sibling per family. They have reasoned that siblings, in some respects, are not independent cases, so that the usual statistical tests of significance would not be valid if more than one sibling were included in a sample. We knew that we would face this problem if we gathered data from more than one child per family: siblings in a given family obviously always have the same score on family-level variables such as parental income or education; they almost always live in the same residence, and almost always share the same schedule of visits to the nonresidential parent; and they share the same divorce history, as reflected in the data obtained from parental interviews during the first three years after the divorce.

We were reluctant, however, to limit our sample to only one sibling per family. For one thing, this would seriously underrepresent children who had siblings within our age range. That is, children with no such siblings would have a 100 percent chance of being in the sample, those with one target sibling would have a 50 percent chance, children with two target siblings would have a 33 percent chance, and so forth. For any outcome on which children with siblings might differ from those without them, such a sampling strategy introduces distortion.

An additional problem with the strategy of selecting one adolescent per family involved choosing the adolescent to be included. To follow the strategy of taking only the oldest child would overrepresent older children and restrict the age range. Even choosing a child at random—a popular solution—raises the question of which random choice to use (since different random samples will, by chance, sometimes produce different results).

Another, perhaps more important, reason for our reluctance was that correlations between siblings on most of our outcome variables were expected to be (and were) low. Current research on siblings (for example, Dunn, 1990) makes it clear that siblings often respond quite differently to the antecedent conditions we used as predictors. Siblings also differ in a number of ways that were pertinent to our analyses: on sex and age, and on the relationship with each parent (for example, closeness to parents or feelings of being caught between parents). In these respects, siblings are, in fact, independent cases.

For these reasons, we chose to interview all eligible adolescents in a family. In our analyses, we considered two solutions that would allow us to use all of the data we had gathered: (1) using data from all children but using the number of families as our degrees of freedom in statistical analyses, and (2) weighting each individual's scores by the inverse of the number of siblings in the sample. Both of these solutions had the potential to become unwieldy, however, as we carried out the complex analytic tasks planned for the study. Furthermore, we were not convinced that either of them actually solved the problem of correlated error among our cases.

In the end, we took the following approach in the vast majority of our analyses. We conducted each analysis at least twice: once using all cases and once using a subsample consisting of all adolescents in families where only one was interviewed, but only one adolescent per family, chosen on a random basis, in families where more than one adolescent was interviewed. When the results of these two analyses agreed with regard to direction and statistical significance, we have reported the statistics from the full sample. When results differed, we repeated the analyses on at least one, possibly two, additional random subsamples. On the basis of these analyses, we identified those relations that seemed to be robust versus those that appeared borderline through examination of both the magnitude of differences between means and tests of statistical significance. Our discussion of results in such cases reflects our subsequent judgment.

There were two instances where this strategy was not used. First, if an analysis used only or primarily "family-level" factors (for example, interparental conflict at any point during Study 1 or parental remarriage status in Study 2) as either the predictor (independent) variables or the predicted (dependent) variable, analyses were almost always conducted using random subsamples (in other words, only one adolescent per family) rather than all cases (see Chapter 7 for an exception). In such instances, as we have noted, siblings are clearly nonindependent cases because their scores on these measures are exactly the same. Second, in Chapter 6, where a series of quite complicated analyses involving large numbers of factors was conducted, each analysis building on the results of a previous analysis, it was virtually impossible to follow the usual strategy. The results of the Chapter 6 analyses are therefore based on all cases. Our experience using both the full sample and the random samples in the many analyses reported in other chapters leads us to believe, however, that the results of analyses using all cases are almost always supported using random subsamples. Especially because we emphasize the strongest and most consistent results throughout Chapter 6, we feel confident that the results reported are trustworthy.

The Telephone Interview

We initially planned to conduct face-to-face interviews with our adolescent subjects, but we quickly encountered several impediments to such a plan. First, the adolescents were geographically scattered, and some had moved away from the Bay Area. Second, even those who lived near enough for us to visit proved difficult to catch at home. This problem was

especially common for adolescents who were spending time in both parental households, but even those who were not were involved in a variety of extracurricular activities that meant inconsistent schedules from one day to another. We were forced to consider telephone interviews, which could be more easily done in the evening, and which would permit repeated call-backs to locate adolescents at home. Existing evidence on the reliability and validity of telephone interviews was encouraging. Among adults, the amount and type of information disclosed over the telephone is comparable to that obtained in face-to-face interviewing when good interviewing techniques are employed (Groves and Kahn, 1979; McCormick et al., 1993). In addition, investigators who have used this method with adolescent populations find that adolescents are comfortable with the telephone as a mode of communication, and that information obtained in this manner is reliable and valid (Furstenberg et al., 1983; Montemayor and Brownlee, 1987).

Although establishing rapport may be somewhat more difficult than in face-to-face interviews, using telephone interviews with our adolescent subjects had potential advantages. First, recruitment and scheduling were easier and less costly, allowing us to achieve our goal of recruiting larger numbers of adolescents in the less common residential arrangements. Second, adolescents may feel less inhibited about discussing sensitive issues over the phone; in particular, the telephone makes it possible to reduce the salience of talking with an older person.

In order to recruit participants into the study, a packet of information was mailed to one parent in each family with eligible adolescents. The parent chosen to receive the initial mailing was the person who had participated in Study 1. If both parents had participated in the earlier study, the mailing, with rare exceptions, was sent to the parent with whom the child was living.

In order to maximize the reliability and validity of the information we collected, interviewers went through a minimum of thirty-five hours of training, much of which focused on developing and maintaining rapport with the adolescents. Interviews averaged one hour in length. At the conclusion of the interview, adolescents were sent a check for ten dollars and a letter thanking them for participating.

Measures

Our objectives called for devising questions that would assess two major areas: adolescent adjustment and the factors that might lead an adolescent to adjust well or poorly following parental divorce. Here we summarize the measures under their major categories.[2] More detailed information about the questions asked and scales constructed is provided in subsequent chapters, where findings concerning specific scales are discussed. In addition, statistics for each scale, including average scores, range of scores, and scale reliability can be found in Appendix Table B.1.

Adolescent Adjustment

"Problem behaviors." In previous research on adolescent adjustment, investigators have often distinguished between two forms of adjustment difficulties: the "externalizing" forms—including aggression, substance use, truancy, and a variety of delinquent or antisocial acts—and the "internalizing" forms, including depression, anxiety, withdrawal, and suicidal impulses. These two kinds of problem behavior are not mutually exclusive, of course, and in cases of severe maladjustment individuals are likely to display both. In our battery of adjustment measures, we included a measure of depression/anxiety and measures of several aspects of deviance (for example, substance use; antisocial acts such as destroying property or carrying a weapon; and various kinds of rule-breaking at school, including truancy, copying others' work, and cutting classes).

School adjustment. We asked the adolescents about the grades they were getting in school and about the amount of effort they were putting into their schoolwork, as indexed by the time they spent on homework and their level of attention to schoolwork in class.

"Worst problem." Although scores on the outcomes of depression, deviance, and school adjustment were moderately correlated (correlations among depression, deviance, and either grades or school effort ranged from .14 to .38 in absolute value), the correlations were not so high as to rule out the possibility that individual adolescents exhibit adjustment problems in different ways. For example, one adolescent might become depressed while another acts out, while yet another slacks off in school. For this reason, we also constructed a score that represented an adolescent's worst problem—his or her worst score on depression/anxiety, deviance, or school effort.

Personal resources. Adjustment is not only a matter of the presence or absence of problems. Also pertinent are the positive skills and resources adolescents can bring to bear on solving the problems they face. We assessed several such personal resources. These included conflict resolution styles, close relationships with peers, and interests in a range of recreational and other extracurricular activities.

Factors That May Affect Adjustment

Demographic factors. We assessed the usual battery of demographic factors—parental income and education, family size, and age and sex of child—and we added information on the out-of-home working hours of both parents. In addition, we inquired about the composition of both parental households: the presence of parents' new partners, stepsiblings, and half-siblings.

Arrangements for residence and visitation. It was central to our objectives to consider adolescents' adjustment in relation to the amount of contact they had with each of the two parents. We therefore asked in detail about residence and visitation: which parent the adolescent lived with most of the time, how often overnight or daytime visits to the nonresidential parent occurred during regular portions of the school year, and how much contact there was with each parent during vacations. In Study 1, we had learned that there was substantial shifting in these arrangements as time passed; given the data on residence obtained from T1–T4, therefore, we created an index of the stability of each adolescent's residential arrangement over the span of time since the parents had separated.

Life stresses. A substantial literature indicates that adjustment is affected by the incidence of a variety of life changes, such as residential moves, loss of a pet, or illness of a family member. When many changes happen at the same time, stress factors cumulate, and stressors with which an adolescent might cope successfully if taken one at a time may be much more difficult to handle. Although we knew that all of our adolescents had had to cope with the stress of their parents' divorce, we needed to consider the context of other stressors—related and unrelated to the divorce—in our adolescents' lives. We therefore included a "life stress" inventory in our measures.

Interparental relationships. Especially for adolescents who continue to spend some time with each parent, the relationship between the two divorced parents can be crucial. We wanted to know whether the parents had developed a modus operandi that enabled them to do necessary business together and whether they were able to cooperate in matters concerning the children. We relied in part on measures of interparental hostility, and co-parental discord or cooperation, that had already been derived from Study 1 data. In addition, we asked the adolescents in Study 2 for their perceptions of parental discord and cooperation, both generally and on matters that specifically concerned the adolescents' lives.

Parent-child relationships. We assessed the quality of the adolescents' relationships with each parent, including feelings of closeness and trust, desire to be like the parent (what we call "identification with" a parent), and how many joint activities adolescents engaged in with each parent. Negative aspects of the relationship, such as the amount of conflict between parent and child, and children's feelings of disengagement from the home (feelings of not wanting to be there, or not feeling at home there) were also measured. In addition, we asked about "role reversal"—the extent to which adolescents felt they needed to take care of a parent and the frequency of parents' confiding in their children and relying on them for emotional support.

Parental control and management. Households differ with respect to the amount of structure they provide for their adolescent children. In some households, there are regular routines for activities like meals, chores, bedtimes, or television watching, and adolescents are expected to conform to—and participate in—the family routines. In other households, adolescents have much more autonomy and can function fairly independently of the activities of other household members. In addition, some parents insist on being involved in decisions concerning their children's lives (how they spend their money, where they can go after school, when they must be home); other parents leave such decisions up to the child. To assess these dimensions of management and control, we asked about decision-making practices between parents and adolescents, about the presence or absence of predictable household routines, about rules concerning the adolescent's activities inside and outside the home, and about the chores adolescents were expected to do in each household. In addition, we asked how successfully each parent monitored the adolescent, that is, the extent to which parents knew of the adolescent's whereabouts and activities.

Feelings of being caught between one's parents. Previous researchers have noted the problem of loyalty conflicts for children of divorce. We asked our adolescents about how often they felt caught between their parents, about specific instances of being used as a messenger or spy, and about how often they felt hesitant to talk to one parent about the other parent or household.

Analyses

We used a wide range of statistical analyses to address the questions of interest to us. Because of this variety, it is impossible to summarize our "analytic strategy" beyond what we have already described concerning how we handled the inclusion of more than one adolescent in our sample. Information about analyses appears in each chapter, as we address each specific question or set of questions.

3

The Adolescents

All the young people selected for our study were interviewed four to four and a half years after their parents filed for divorce. There was variation in the time it took for the legal divorce to become final, but in most cases, the divorce decree had been issued several years before we interviewed the adolescents. Our sample was therefore uniform with respect to the amount of time that had passed between the parental separation and divorce and our interview with the adolescent. In most other respects, however, the sample was heterogeneous.

In this chapter, we describe the adolescents who participated in our study: their age, sex, grade in school, and birth order within the family. Then we discuss some of the characteristics of their families: their parents' socioeconomic level, ethnic identity, and employment status, and the composition of each parental household. We outline the adolescents' residential history, noting which parent or parents they had lived with and whether they had changed their residence during the four and a half years since their parents' separation. In addition, the reasons for such changes are examined. We also briefly describe the level of visitation by our adolescents with their nonresidential parents. Finally, we consider some of the important and often stressful events that had recently taken place in the lives of the young people in our sample, as an aid to understanding something about the context of their behavior and adaptation.

The Sample

The sample of adolescents was equally split on gender; it was 50.8 percent male and 49.2 percent female. Our respondents were also fairly equally distributed across the eligible age range (see Appendix Table B.2). For the most part, their grade in school matched their ages, but a small group (about 2 percent) had dropped out of school before graduating from high school. The sample also includes a small group of older adolescents who had finished high school; about 2 percent were no longer in school, and about 6 percent were taking college courses. These young people were still within our ten-to-eighteen-year age range, and some were still living at home. Those who had gone away to college had lived at home until very recently, so that it was possible to get a picture from them of their living situation and their relationships with their parents prior to leaving home.

The majority of the young people in our sample had at least one natural sibling, although 15 percent were the only children of their parents' marriage. When there were siblings, the adolescents in our sample were more likely to be the eldest (41 percent), rather than either a middle child (12 percent) or the youngest of the children (30 percent). Two percent of the adolescents were members of twin pairs. Of course not all of our respondents' siblings were within the eligible age range for inclusion in our study, but in 37 percent of the sample families, more than one sibling was interviewed (see also Chapter 2).

Characteristics of the Adolescents' Parents

The diversity of the sample is apparent in the characteristics of the parents (see Appendix Table B.3). One-third of the mothers and almost as many fathers (30 percent) had only a high school education or less. At the upper end of the scale of educational attainment, fathers outnumbered mothers: 27 percent of the mothers and 42 percent of the fathers had graduated from college, and more than twice as many fathers (18 percent) as mothers had completed an advanced degree.

The employment status of the two parents also differed. Although most mothers and fathers were employed full time (defining full time as working forty or more hours per week), nearly three times as many mothers (17 percent) as fathers (6 percent) were not employed outside the home. Seventeen percent of mothers and only 3 percent of fathers were working less than full time, and twice as many fathers (55 percent) as mothers were working long hours—forty-five or more hours per week.

The employed fathers of the children in our sample had much higher annual earnings than the employed mothers. Although 50 percent of the employed fathers were earning $40,000 per year or more, only 7 percent of the employed mothers were earning that much. And although the majority of fathers paid child support when the children were living with the mothers, the amounts paid made up only a small fraction of the income differential (Maccoby and Mnookin, 1992). Because the large majority of the adolescents in our sample lived with their mothers, most were spending a great deal of time in poor or lower-middle-income households. It is important to note, however, that the sample covers a wide range of households, from the very poor to the wealthy.

We did not obtain information about ethnicity directly from the adolescents, but we did have information about the ethnicity of both parents. In 73 percent of the families, both parents were non-Hispanic White; in 7 percent both were Hispanic; in 4 percent both were Asian; and in 2 percent both were African-American. In 14 percent of the families, the two parents were from different ethnic groups.

Composition of the Parental Households

Adolescents were asked who lived in each parental household, and Appendix Table B.4 displays the information they gave us. A new spouse was sharing the parent's household in about a third of the cases, with 37 percent of the fathers remarried and 32 percent of the mothers. A substantial minority of the parents' households (15 percent of the mothers' and 19 percent of the fathers') included a new live-in partner to whom the parent was not (as yet) married. Thus about half the parental households either already formally contained a stepparent or were less formally using or testing such an arrangement, while approximately half were still single-parent households.

A father's new wife was more likely to have brought children from a previous marriage into the household than was a mother's new husband; there were thus stepsiblings present more often in fathers' homes. This discrepancy reflects the general tendency for children to live with their mothers following divorce. And a small proportion of the remarried couples (just under 10 percent) had had new children of their own by Time 4, adding half-siblings to the household. As already noted, the majority of the adolescents in our sample had full siblings as well. Father-resident adolescents were less likely to be sharing a household with natural siblings, in part because a higher percentage of father-residence adolescents had one or more siblings who were living with their mother (custody of multiple siblings having been "split" between mother and father).

In some cases (7 percent), the household was shared with an adult relative—a grandparent, aunt, or uncle of the adolescent. A few parents

(9 percent) shared households with unrelated "roommates" or "roomers," presumably to make housing costs more manageable. On the whole, however, the parental households contained only nuclear family members—either single parents with children, or repartnered parents with children.

Adolescents' Residential History

The parent interviews conducted during Study 1 provided information concerning the residence of each of our adolescents at three points in time after the parents separated. At Time 4, the adolescents themselves reported the amount of time they were spending with each parent. For all four time periods, we defined "dual" residence as meaning that a child usually spent at least four overnights per two-week period with each parent during the school year. If children usually spent eleven or more overnights with their mother, they were considered to be living primarily with her. Similarly, children who spent eleven or more overnights with their fathers during usual two-week periods in the school year were classified as father-resident.

Figure 3.1 shows that over two-thirds of the adolescents were living with their mothers at each of the four time periods, and the proportion changed very slightly over time—dropping off by 1.5 percentage points at Times 3 and 4. The proportion living primarily with their fathers increased somewhat, while the proportion living in dual residence dropped off slightly. In general, the adolescents who participated in Study 2 had been somewhat more likely to live with their fathers after the divorce than to live in dual residence. At Time 4, our sample consisted of 366 mother-resident adolescents, 100 father-resident adolescents, and 51 dual-resident adolescents. One percent of the adolescents were living primarily with someone other than their mother or father; these adolescents are excluded from the analyses about residence and visitation.

These proportions contrast with our earlier findings in Study 1 from the full sample of divorcing families (Maccoby and Mnookin, 1992). When families with children of all ages were included, more had adopted dual residence than father residence at Times 1, 2, and 3. The incidence of father residence was higher for older children than for younger children, and the authors suggested that this probably reflected an assumption on the part of many parents that father residence was more feasible for children who were no longer "of tender years." By contrast, the propor-

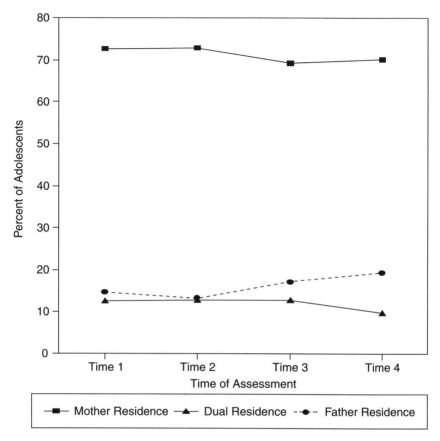

Figure 3.1 Percentage of adolescents in each residential arrangement at the four times of assessment following parents' separation.

tion living in dual residence was lower for older children than for younger. This fact may stem from older children having more "say" in where they will live, with a number of adolescents preferring to avoid the complexity and inconvenience of dual residence (Maccoby and Mnookin, 1992). Given these age trends documented in Study 1, it is not surprising to find that father residence is slightly more common than dual residence among the adolescents in Study 2.

Among our adolescents, more boys than girls lived with their fathers or in dual residence, and more girls than boys lived with their mothers (see Figure 3.2), indicating a same-sex-parent bias in children's de facto residence.

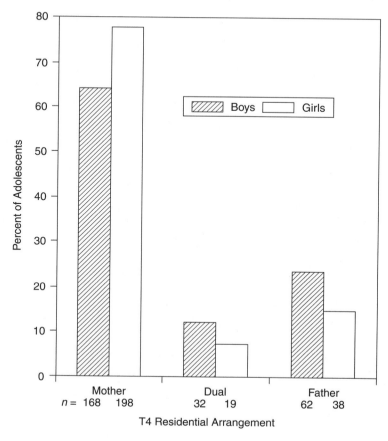

Figure 3.2 Percentage of adolescents in each residential arrangement at Time 4, by sex of adolescent. Excluded are five adolescents not living with either natural parent.

How many of our adolescents had been in the same residential arrangements over the four and a half years following their parents' separation? Figure 3.1 presents a misleading picture of great residential stability. In fact, these overall residence rates mask various compensating residential shifts. Nearly one-third of our adolescents had moved from one residential arrangement to another during the four-year period since their parents separated, and 13 percent had moved between households more than once.

When adolescents shifted residence, they were more likely to move out of dual residence than into it, and adolescents dropping out of dual residence most commonly moved into the mother's household rather than the father's (see Table 3.1). The number of adolescents who moved from the mother's household to the father's (10 percent of the total sample) was greater than the number who moved from the father's house to the mother's (6 percent). However, the *proportion* of adolescents initially in mother residence who moved in with their fathers (about one-sixth) was smaller than the proportion of adolescents who made the reverse move (over two-fifths of those initially living with fathers).

When adolescents had changed residences, they were asked the reasons for the change (see Table 3.2). The most common reason given was a move to a new location on the part of one or both parents, and this was mentioned more often by adolescents who had moved in with their mother than those who had moved into dual or father residence. Geographical moves on the part of parents brought a number of factors into play. For some adolescents the strongest motive was to remain near their friends. As one boy put it: "My mother moved from all my friends, so I wanted to live with Dad." An issue that was particularly important to older adolescents was the opportunity to finish school at the school they had been attending. A boy who had just finished high school said, "Mom moved . . . I decided for my senior year that I wanted to be at my old school. My dad lives closer to it." As is evident from these examples,

Table 3.1   The direction of residential moves[a]

Residential status	Percentage of entire sample	
Now living with mother		70.3
Have lived with her continuously	(57.0)	
Moved in from father residence	(5.5)	
Moved in from dual residence	(7.8)	
Now living in dual residence		9.9
Have lived in dual continuously	(5.9)	
Moved in from mother residence	(2.4)	
Moved in from father residence	(1.6)	
Now living in father residence		19.8
Have lived with him continuously	(6.9)	
Moved in from mother residence	(10.1)	
Moved in from dual residence	(2.8)	

a. This table excludes fifteen cases of adolescents who were living with someone other than their mother or father at one of the four interview periods. For those adolescents who had moved more than once, the most recent move is counted here.

Table 3.2 Reasons given for change in residence by adolescents whose residential arrangement changed between Time 1 and Time 4, by T4 residential arrangement, in percent[a]

	T4 residential arrangement		
Reason[b]	Mother (*n* = 62)	Dual (*n* = 13)	Father (*n* = 61)
A parent moved	45	23	21
Family conflict	15	0	30
Adolescent missed nonresidential parent	5	38	10
Other home provided better environment	10	0	16

a. For those adolescents who had moved more than once, the most recent move is counted here.

b. The reasons listed here are the four most frequently given. Percentages in each column do not sum to 100 because a variety of reasons were given less commonly and are not listed here. Also, more than one reason was coded for some adolescents.

when the residential parent moved and the adolescent switched to the other parent's residence, the switch usually represented the adolescent's own choice, reflecting the priority given by young people to stability in their out-of-home environments. In these cases, the parents appear to have gone along with the adolescent's choice, sometimes willingly, sometimes reluctantly.

The next most common reason for a change in an adolescent's residential arrangement was conflict among family members. This reason was given more often by adolescents who moved into either mother or father residence than by those who moved into dual residence; in addition, it was given more often as a reason for moving into father residence than into mother residence. Commonly, the conflict was between the adolescent and the residential parent:

(Adolescent who moved from mother's to father's household): "I got that role which you call 'teenager' and sometimes when I would sass back at my mother [her response] made me mad. So I didn't want to live with her anymore."

(Adolescent who moved from father to mother): "My dad wasn't treating me right. I didn't like living with him . . . I decided to move in with my mom."

(Adolescent who moved from mother to father): "I couldn't stand living with my mom . . . She said if I wanted to leave, leave. So I did."

In some cases, the familial conflict was between the adolescent and a parent's new partner:

(Adolescent who moved from dual residence to mother): "There was a lot of conflicts [*sic*] over the years. There was a big blow-up . . . and it sort of had to do with my stepmom. We didn't get along too well."

(Adolescent who had moved several times and was currently living alone): "I moved in with my dad 'cause I missed him. Then . . . I went back with my mother because I had disagreements with my father's partner. [Interviewer: How about getting your own place?] Well, I just had disagreements with my mother's boyfriend."

(Adolescent who had moved from father to mother): "Well, my stepmom moved in. I just didn't like her. That's when I moved in with my mom."

(Adolescent who moved from father to mother): "It was lack of communication between me and my dad . . . My stepmom and stepbrother are a problem . . . The rules are different . . . He didn't ask me about remarrying."

Although a variety of family conflicts were given as a reason for moving from one parental household to another, family conflicts were never given as the reason for moving into dual residence. Why did adolescents move into dual residence? Quite a few adolescents said that they had missed their nonresidential parent and wanted to spend more time with him or her. The parents responded by arranging a more equal division of the child's time between the two parents.

In contrast to the interpersonal conflict we have described, some adolescents moved because they felt that the parent with whom they resided was away too much or not attentive enough to their needs. As examples, adolescents cited moving in with parents who would have family meals, get home from work earlier, take the time to sign them up for special classes or sports teams, or simply have rules and discipline.

In some cases, moves were dictated by the desire (on the part of the adolescent, the parents, or both) to have the child live in the environment that would be most supportive for the child's schoolwork. A child who was doing poorly in school might be shifted to the other household in the hope that the other parent could provide better supervision of homework or school attendance:

(Adolescent who had moved in with her father): "I moved in with my father because of my school attendance record . . . He's more strict with me cutting."

(Adolescent who moved from mother to father): "I think one of the major reasons was basically I got a lot of educational support from my dad . . . And, he gets paid more, so I really didn't have to worry about financial support. I felt that perhaps my dad would be, uh, in a better position . . ."

Unfortunately the tape of this interview becomes inaudible at this point. Although we cannot be sure, we suspect this adolescent had future college expenses in mind.

Although these interview excerpts suggest a fairly high level of conflict between adolescents and their parents, we should remember that the remarks came from the minority of adolescents, about a third, who had moved from one parental household to the other, or in or out of dual residence. Adolescents who changed households reported higher levels of familial conflict than did the two-thirds who remained in their initial residential arrangement. In addition, those who moved for positive reasons usually gave few details about their situations, while those with negative reasons—like most of the cases cited above—tended to report at length. These negative cases are not typical of our sample as a whole, but they do represent an important subgroup of troubled families.

Siblings: Living Together or Apart?

So far, we have been describing the Time 4 residence situation—and residence history—for individual adolescents, without regard to where their siblings lived. For those adolescents who had siblings, most (65 percent) had the same residential arrangement as their siblings. In a substantial minority of families, however, the children did not have the same residential arrangement; one child might be sharing residential time fairly equally between the two parents (dual residence) while other children in the same family were living primarily with the mother or the father. More commonly, one or more of the children lived with the mother while one or more lived with the father. We have labeled families in which the children do not all share the same residential arrangement as having "split" residence. This pattern was relatively rare over the whole sample at the time of the third parent interview (10 percent of children aged three to eighteen had a sibling living in a different residential arrangement at that time), but in the present sample of children aged ten to eighteen it was more common (35 percent of adolescents with siblings). Young people living with their fathers were especially likely to have a sibling living in a different residential arrangement: 42 percent of these adolescents lived apart from a sibling, as opposed to 11 percent of mother-resident adolescents and 8 percent of dual-resident adolescents.

Visitation

Children who are in dual residence of course spend substantial amounts of time with each of their parents, but most children who live primarily with one parent are by no means cut off from the other parent. Among adolescents who lived primarily with their mother or their father, the amount of contact with the nonresidential parent varied from never seeing this parent to staying overnight at the other parent's household two or three times in a typical two-week period during the school year. When a divorce decree specifies that one parent shall have "reasonable visitation" with the children, a common arrangement is for the children to spend every other weekend with the nonresidential parent.

Visitation will be discussed in detail in Chapter 9. For the present, we simply note that levels of contact with the nonresidential parent were quite high. Only 7 percent of our adolescents had not seen a nonresidential parent (mother or father) within the past year. The numbers of adolescents who had very little or no contact with their nonresidential parent are similar to those derived from recent national studies. For example, Seltzer (1991) reported that for children under eighteen whose parents had been separated five years or less, 11 percent had not seen their nonresidential father in the past year. The rate of noncontact specifically for adolescents was not given, but visitation was generally higher the older the child,[1] so the rate of noncontact was likely quite similar to our own.

At the other extreme, 70 percent of our sole-resident adolescents reported having seen the nonresidential parent within the past month. And approximately half of sole-resident adolescents had regular visits with the nonresidential parent that involved an overnight stay during nonvacation portions of the school year. The number of adolescents that sustained high contact with nonresidential parents may be somewhat higher in our sample than in the country as a whole, although the comparison is harder to make than the comparison concerning no contact because the time units measured across studies are not identical. For example, Seltzer (1991) found that 58 percent of children under eighteen saw their nonresidential fathers at least once a month, and 33 percent saw him at least once a week, and as noted above, these rates would be somewhat higher if the sample were restricted to children in the adolescent age range. These numbers are lower than the ones we have cited, but the level of contact is also somewhat more restricted (for example, of the 70 percent of adolescents in our sample who had seen their nonresidential parent in the last month, at least some did not see that parent every month). On the whole, our assessment is that the levels of contact represented in our sample are fairly close to national norms; however, the possibility exists that visitation rates were somewhat higher in California at the end of the 1980s than was true for adolescents elsewhere in the country.

Life Stresses

In later chapters we will examine the adjustment of the adolescents in our sample. In doing so, it will be important to understand the situations to which they had to adapt. We asked our subjects a series of questions about events that had occurred in the past year—illnesses or deaths of people close to them, changes in schools or residence, changes in relationships with boyfriends or girlfriends, changes in parental jobs and family financial circumstances, and so forth. A complete list of life events about which we inquired appears in Table 3.3. Illness of close persons was a common occurrence. For a substantial minority, instability of the home and family situation also was reported: residential moves were common, sometimes accompanied by a change of schools, changes in parental jobs, or a new person (often the new partner of a parent) moving into the household. Changing relations with peers also figured strongly in our adolescents' reports of life events: a large number had had a fight with a close friend, and many had broken up with a boyfriend or girlfriend, or had begun to date or go steady—intensely important events in the eyes of teenagers.

Adolescent Adjustment

How well adjusted was this group of adolescents nearly five years after their parents' separation? There can be no general answer: young people differ enormously in how well they cope with any major life stress, including the divorce of their parents. Nevertheless, we would like to

Table 3.3 Life events occurring in the past year, from most to least common

Event	Percentage of adolescents reporting "yes"
A close person was seriously ill or hospitalized	49.8
Adolescent had serious fight with a close friend	47.9
Adolescent began to date or go steady with someone	40.8
Parent changed jobs	38.4
Adolescent changed schools	37.5
Adolescent broke up with boyfriend or girlfriend	32.6
Family moved to new house	30.7
New person joined the household	30.5
Favorite pet died or disappeared	29.7
Close person died	28.2
Family had serious financial troubles	23.1
Mother or father spent more time away from home (because of job change or for other reason)	21.3
A new baby was born in the family	20.7
Adolescent started wearing braces or glasses	19.2
Parent lost job	15.0
Someone in family was assaulted, or was victim of other violent crime	15.0
Adolescent was seriously ill or hospitalized	9.4

know whether most of our adolescents had managed to weather this enormous stress reasonably well, so that they were functioning within a "normal" range, or whether a substantial number carried deep and lasting scars.

Our study was not designed to answer this question. There are no national or regional norms on the measures we have used, so that we cannot say how a cross-section sample of all adolescents (including those with never-divorced parents) would have answered our questions. Furthermore, we did not interview a comparison group of adolescents from nondivorced families in our catchment area.[2] Our primary purpose was to compare the postdivorce adjustment of adolescents in different living situations. Furthermore, relying on the absolute level of self-reports is always risky, because people often see themselves in a rosier light than others see them. And identifying a cut-off point that separates "normal" from problematic functioning is, of course, an arbitrary decision. Keeping these caveats in mind, we still may learn something of value simply by taking the adolescents' answers at face value, to see how often these answers reflect what appears to be satisfactory functioning. We give only a rough sketch of these self-reports, however, because of the limitations on what can be gleaned from overall mean scores.[3]

Depression/Anxiety

The average score on this scale fell just at the midpoint of the range of possible scores (mean = 15.2, range 0–30), and approximately a quarter of the cases scored in the upper third of the range. This means that a sizable minority of our adolescents were reporting fairly frequent symptoms of depression or anxiety. Another quarter of the sample were in the lower third of the range, meaning that they reported that in the last month they had seldom or never experienced most of the fairly moderate symptoms (feeling tired, irritable, worried) included in the scale. We must remember that adolescence is a time when such symptoms usually increase among unselected groups of adolescents (Buchanan, Eccles, and Becker, 1992), so although we most likely have a higher proportion of depressed adolescents reporting substantial symptoms of depression than would be the case among adolescents overall,[4] the difference is probably not drastic.

Deviance

Our adolescents reported very low levels of all forms of deviant behavior. Nearly two-thirds reported not a single instance of using drugs or alcohol, stealing someone else's property, vandalizing property, or getting into any sort of trouble with the police during the past year. Only 15 percent reported more than one such event. Breaking school rules (cutting classes, arriving late, cheating on tests) was reported somewhat more often, but the mean score on these items was still only 7.2 out of a possible range of 4–16. Our measure of overall deviance, for which we combined breaking school rules, antisocial acts, and substance use, had a possible range of 15–60, and the median score was only 20, with no cases above 46. We recognize that even though we promised our subjects anonymity, they knew that we knew their identity. Delinquent activities were therefore undoubtedly somewhat underreported. Nevertheless, the reported levels are quite low.

School Performance and Effort

On the whole, the adolescents reported fairly good grades. The mean was 5.8 on a scale in which 5 means "about half B's and half C's" and 6 means "mostly B's." Only a little over 10 percent of the adolescents had grades at the low end of the scale ("mostly D's" or "about half C's and half D's"); over two-fifths said they were getting "mostly A's" or "about half A's and half B's." The meaning of these reports depends, of course, on the grading standards of the schools these adolescents attended, but it seems clear that many more adolescents were doing at least moderately well in school than were close to failure. With respect to the amount of effort put into schoolwork, scores clustered at the middle of the possible range.

Personal Resources

Our scores for adolescents' personal resources present a reasonably positive picture: most adolescents said they were more likely to try to resolve interpersonal conflicts through compromise and discussion than through aggressive tactics. But quite a few also said that they used avoidance (withdrawal). Most reported a variety of extracurricular activities that they enjoyed doing (such as sports, dancing, computer games, playing a musical instrument or singing, reading, collecting something), and very few presented a picture of aimless drifting in their use of out-of-school time. Most also reported having at least one close same-sex friend on whom they relied.

Relationships with Parents

Levels of conflict with parents were low. Adolescents were asked whether they had discussed with either parent during the past two weeks a variety of issues (for example, chores around the house, whether they could bring a friend to the house when no adult was home, how late they could stay out). If a discussion had occurred, they were asked how angry the discussion had become. Even for the issue that produced the most parent-child conflict, only two-fifths of the adolescents said that any significant amount of anger had been involved,[5] and most said that the discussion had not been heated. We suspect that this situation is comparable to that which prevails between most teenagers and their parents (see, for example, Montemayor, 1983).

Our adolescents were asked a series of questions concerning the closeness and openness of their relationship with each parent. For each item, the adolescent rated closeness on a five-point scale, for example, from "not at all open" to "very open." The mean scores (across items) fell at the level of 4 on the five-point scale for closeness to mothers, with a quarter of the sample answering "5" on a majority of the questions. Scores for fathers were somewhat lower. Most important, only a small proportion of adolescents described their relationships with 1's and 2's on the closeness items—5 percent did so for relationships with mothers, and 10 percent for relationships with fathers. On the whole, these adolescents described a close, trusting relationship with both parents.

Satisfaction with the Living Situation

The adolescents were asked to rate on a ten-point scale how satisfied they were with the way their time was divided between the two parental homes. The mean score of 6.9 indicates that the majority of adolescents rated themselves well above the midpoint of the satisfaction scale. One-third rated themselves at the upper end—at 8, 9, or 10—while only 13 percent rated themselves at the low end—at 1, 2, or 3. Although there was a considerable range in satisfaction, the majority of adolescents appeared to have adapted fairly well to the special conditions that arose when their parents formed two different households.

Summary

Although it is possible that there are somewhat more adolescents in our sample who are showing signs of significant depression than would be true of a sample of adolescents from nondivorced families, it is our judgment that the majority of our adolescents fall within a "normal" range of adjustment. This conclusion is consistent with other current assessments of adolescents whose families have experienced divorce (Amato and Keith, 1991; Barber and Lyons, 1994; Kelly, 1993). In terms of deviance, school performance, personal resources, relationships with parents, and adaptation to their residential and visitation arrangements, adolescent self-reports were typically positive. It is even more important to note, however, that variation was great on all our measures. There were many who were doing very well, living well-organized, goal-oriented, reasonably happy lives. A smaller group manifested problems of several kinds. The chapters that follow will attempt to uncover the conditions that affect whether an adolescent will adapt well or poorly to the circumstances following parental divorce.

Comparing Residential Arrangements

4

Adolescent Adjustment

Although most adolescents live with their mothers after their parents have divorced, some do not. Two alternative arrangements—father or joint physical custody—have become more common, and their benefits and drawbacks are actively debated. It has become important to learn as much as we can concerning these different custodial arrangements—how well they work as time passes, and what kind of conditions they provide for the young people living in them.

At the outset, we need to distinguish between the divorce decree's specifications for physical custody of the children and the children's actual residence. They are often not the same. As Maccoby and Mnookin (1992) reported for the sample of California families from which our adolescent sample was drawn, fewer than half of the families who had been awarded joint physical custody were actually maintaining a joint arrangement three years after filing for divorce. We saw in Chapter 3 that a substantial proportion of adolescents in these families had moved from one parental household to another since their parents had separated, although such moves usually meant that they would be living in an arrangement different from the one specified in the divorce decree. In this book, we are concerned with the actual residence of the adolescent, rather than with the physical custody specified in the legal divorce agreement.

Our goal in the next few chapters is to compare mother residence, father residence, and dual residence. We begin by examining how well the adolescents in each arrangement are adapting to their life situation—in other words, how they score on various measures of adjustment. We are aware, of course, that different residential arrangements can emerge under widely varying circumstances, so that a simple comparison of adolescent adjustment by type of arrangement can be misleading. Certain types of families or children may select certain arrangements, and these preexisting characteristics may, in turn, affect the way in which the arrangements work out for the adolescents. In order to clarify the source of any residence differences in adolescent adjustment, we have taken the following steps:

1. In this chapter, we first compare the different residential arrangements on their economic and "human capital" resources ("demographic factors"), and then statistically control for differences in resources related to residence in our comparisons of adolescent adjustment by type of residence.
2. In Chapter 5 we compare the different arrangements on a variety of aspects of home life, including residential stability over time, number of life stresses, past and present family relationships, and current parental styles of control and household management. By including indicators of earlier family functioning, in addition to information about the family's current status, we are able to gain insight into whether certain residential arrangements are associated with a more or less difficult history.
3. In Chapter 6, we examine the links between adolescent adjustment and multiple characteristics of the family or home, separately for each residential group. These analyses tell us which of the many indicators of family functioning—past or present—are most predictive of adolescents' adjustment four and a half years after their parents' divorce.

Residence Differences in Demographic Factors

Table 4.1 summarizes the residence differences in the demographic and "human capital" characteristics of families. Adolescents in dual residence were, on average, younger by about one year than adolescents in mother or father residence. Although others have found children in father residence to be older than children in mother residence (Maccoby and Mnookin, 1992; Sweet and Bumpass, 1987; Wallerstein and Blakeslee, 1989), within the limited age range of our sample, the adolescents in father and mother residence were almost identical in age.

There were proportionally more boys than girls in dual and father residence, and proportionally more girls in mother residence. These sex differences concur with those reported by Maccoby and Mnookin (1992) for the entire Stanford Custody Study sample, where it was found that boys were more likely to live initially in dual and father residence. Yet

Table 4.1 Demographic characteristics by residential arrangement

	Residence			
	Mother	Dual	Father	
Max. N (all cases)	366	51	100	
Max. N (random sample)	241	41	81	
Measure				Residence effect
Mean age of adolescent	14.2	13.2	14.3	$F(2,514) = 3.99*$ (D < M, F)
Percentage male	46	63	62	$\chi^2 (2, N = 517) = 11.44**$
Mother's education[a]	5.1	5.7	4.7	$F(2,358) = 10.26****$ (D > M > F)
Father's education[a]	5.4	6.0	5.2	$F(2,359) = 3.14*$ (D > M, F)
Mother's average earnings, T1–T3[a,b]	20.4	20.7	16.6	$F(2,350) = 3.11*$ (M > F)
Father's average earnings, T1–T3[a,b]	42.1	54.9	44.5	$F(2,340) = 3.28*$ (D > M)
Mother's household income[a,b]	36.1	34.3	25.7	$F(2,301) = 5.36**$ (M > F)
Father's household income[a,b]	45.8	54.4	49.8	$F(2,243) = 1.08$

a. Analyses done using a random sample.
b. In tens of thousands.
*$p < .05$.   **$p \leq .01$.   ****$p \leq .0001$.

for that larger sample, a child's sex was not related to whether a child would shift into or out of dual or father residence, which indicates that the residence differences in sex composition that were established during the initial custody decision largely remain four years later.

Because dual residence has the potential to be somewhat more complicated and require more resources than other arrangements (for example, places for children to sleep and keep belongings are needed in both homes), we anticipated that families who maintained this arrangement four and a half years after separation would be advantaged in some respects. Several previous studies have found higher socioeconomic levels among families with joint custody arrangements than among those with some form of sole custody (Kline et al., 1989; Pearson and Thoennes, 1990). And in the larger sample of parents from the Stanford Custody Study, families initially adopting dual residence had higher levels of education and income than did families adopting sole-residence arrangements (Maccoby and Mnookin, 1992). Table 4.1 shows that, in families with adolescent children, the educational advantage of dual-resident families remains. Both mothers and fathers in families that were maintaining dual residence at Time 4 had higher levels of education than did their sole-resident counterparts. Mothers' education was higher in dual-resident families than in mother-resident ones, and lowest of all among families in which the children lived with their fathers. The education of fathers in dual residence was higher than that of fathers in either sole-resident arrangement. The education of sole-resident mothers did not differ from that of sole-resident fathers.

In terms of economic resources, however, dual-resident families did not have so clear an advantage. Whether we consider personal average earnings over the postseparation period or total household income at Time 3 (which includes support payments from nonresident parents and contributions from remarried new partners), mothers' income was similar in dual and mother residence. As was true for education, mothers in families in which the adolescent was living with the father had the lowest incomes. Fathers in dual residence had higher personal earnings, but not significantly higher household income, than did fathers in other residential arrangements.[1]

More striking than the differences in resources between dual-resident families and sole-resident families was the difference between the earnings of mothers and fathers. Over all residential arrangements, fathers' earnings were more than twice as high as mothers', and fathers' household incomes were substantially higher even after the effects of new spouses' incomes and child-support payments were taken into account. In terms of the income in the residential household, adolescents living primarily with their fathers were economically better off in comparison with mother-resident adolescents.

As we considered which statistical controls to employ for comparisons of adolescent adjustment in the three types of residences, it was clear that we needed to control for age and sex of the adolescent. (In addition, in all of our analyses we look at whether residence differences vary for boys and girls.) We wondered, however, whether it was necessary to control for both parental education and parental income. The two were, of course, correlated ($r = .42$ for mothers, .41 for fathers). Somewhat surprisingly, associations between parental education or income and our adjustment measures were quite weak, with most close to zero. One exception was the link between higher parental education and higher school grades, higher school effort, and a lower likelihood of problems as measured by our "worst problem" scale. In another exception, higher income of the residential parent was associated with *higher* levels of overall deviance and substance use ($r = .11, p < .05$ and $r = .12, p < .01$, respectively). Thus parental education appeared to have a stronger positive relation to adjustment than did parental income, although neither set of relations was impressive.

When parental education and income were considered jointly in their relation to residence, parental education was more strongly related. Not surprisingly, given the similarities in income between parents in dual residence and other parents, education had considerably more weight than the income of either parent in determining whether an adolescent would be in dual residence. A mother's earnings were also unrelated to her adolescents' residence type once education was controlled, but a low level of education remained significantly associated with the adolescent's being in father residence. For fathers, a high level of education meant that a father was less likely to have primary custody of his adolescent children, but as with mothers, fathers' incomes bore no relation to the probability of their children living with them after education was controlled. Given these findings, we controlled for parental education, not income, in the comparisons that follow. In order to simplify the analyses, we controlled for average parental education, which was at least as highly correlated with adjustment as was the education of the residential parent.[2]

Residence and Psychosocial Adjustment

Several previous studies have provided information on children's adjustment in different custodial arrangements. Most of these studies, however, have methodological limitations that constrain our ability to generalize from them. Some investigators have stated that children benefit from joint custody, but base these claims on small, primarily clinical, samples (Abarbanel, 1979; Glover and Steele, 1989; Neugebauer, 1989; Steinman, 1981), often lacking a sole-residence control group (Abarbanel, 1979; Irving, Benjamin, and Trocme, 1984; Steinman, 1981). Others assume that because fathers are happier and feel more involved in joint custody arrangements than in other arrangements, this must mean that children do better in joint custody; outcomes for the children, however, are not examined (Grief, 1979; Simring, 1984). Larger studies that have used comparison groups and have controlled for confounding background factors suggest that when families are relatively cooperative and low in conflict, joint-residential arrangements are, indeed, associated with positive child outcomes (Luepnitz, 1986; Shiller, 1986a, 1986b), but that when families remain in conflict, joint custody leads to poor child outcomes (Johnston, Kline, and Tschann, 1989; Nelson, 1989).

The rare studies that have included a group of families in which the children live with their fathers after divorce have, for the most part, focused on the question of whether children fare better when living with a same-sex parent. It has been argued that each parent is more effective when dealing with a same-sex child, and that the loss of a same-sex parent after divorce is more damaging for children than the loss of an opposite-sex parent—presumably because children need an adult same-sex role model. Several small-sample studies of elementary school–aged children support this view. Among their conclusions, they find that children living with a same-sex parent have greater social competence, more appropriate sex-role development, higher self-esteem, lower levels of behavioral problems, better understanding of the divorce, and greater satisfaction with visitation and living arrangements than do children living with an opposite-sex parent (Camara and Resnick, 1988; Santrock, 1970; Santrock and Warshak, 1979; Santrock, Warshak, and Elliott, 1982; Warshak and Santrock, 1983). One study also reported on adolescents, again finding better outcomes among those living with their same-sex parents (Peterson and Zill, 1986). In a review of the literature, Zaslow (1988, 1989) concluded that sex differences in children's response to divorce—with boys adjusting more poorly—arise primarily from this phenomenon. Not all studies, however, have found adjustment to be related to residence with a same-sex parent (Kurdek, Blisk, and Siesky, 1981), and therefore we examine this issue with our data.

As noted in Chapter 2, our investigation of the links between residential arrangement and adolescent adaptive characteristics and adjustment focused on the following aspects of adjustment: personal resources (conflict resolution styles, breadth of activities enjoyed, closeness of peer relationships), internalizing problems (depression/anxiety), externalizing problems (overall deviance and subtypes of deviant behavior), and school adjustment (grades, school effort).

Personal Resources

Means, by residence, for the "personal resources" scales are in Appendix Table B.5.

Conflict resolution styles. Among children of divorce aged six to seventeen years, Kurdek (1987) found that the best-adjusted children were good at conflict resolution. The ability to resolve conflict in constructive ways may be an indicator of psychosocial maturity; it may also be an asset that leads to positive adjustment through optimal resolution of difficult situations. We asked adolescents how they ordinarily dealt with interpersonal conflict, specifically when they had a disagreement with a friend. As noted in Chapter 2, three major modes of resolution emerged: compromise, avoidance or withdrawal, and confrontation or attack. Considerable variation among adolescents in self-reported styles of conflict resolution was evident, and adolescents—especially girls—in all three residential groups were more likely to say that they used a compromising approach than an attacking or avoidant one. There were no residence differences, however, in the mode of resolution used.

Enjoyment of activities. The importance of academic and social competence has been cited as a factor in children's resilience to stress (see, for example, Garmezy, Masten, and Tellegen, 1984; Rutter, 1979). In a broader sense, involvement in a variety of activities that one finds enjoyable may be considered a sign of positive adaptation. Furthermore, having enjoyable activities to absorb one's time and attention under stressful circumstances may buffer the stressors and promote positive adjustment more generally. Thus we asked the adolescents about activities—including, for example, sports, using a computer, playing a musical instrument, or singing—that they engaged in *and* enjoyed. Although some adolescents had many activities they enjoyed and others had few, variation in enjoyable activities was not related to residential arrangements.

Friendships. A close relationship with a same-sex friend provides an important source of social support for adolescents (Kurdek, 1987; Werner and Smith, 1982), so we examined adolescents' ability to have and keep a close friend. We found, as have other studies, that girls reported greater closeness in their same-sex friendships than did boys, but for neither sex was there any difference in this closeness by residential arrangement. In a similar vein, we asked our respondents how they usually spent their after-school time, and the girls were more likely than the boys to mention talking on the phone, hanging out with friends, or partying—forms of time use that imply involvement in a social network. Once again, however, these kinds of after-school activities did not differ by residence.

Internalizing and Externalizing Problems

Means, by residence, for internalizing problems, externalizing problems, and school adjustment are in Appendix Table B.6.

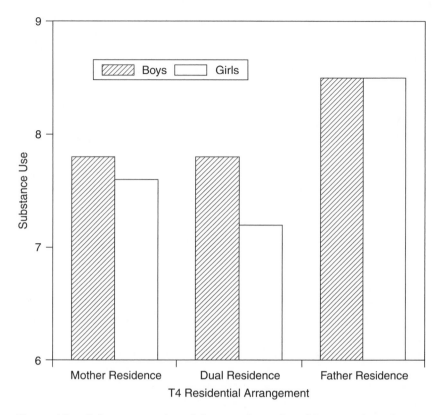

Figure 4.1a Substance use by adolescents in each residence and gender group. Means are adjusted for age of adolescent and the average education of the two parents.

Depression/anxiety. Adolescence is a time when sex differences in depression become substantial (Buchanan, Eccles, and Becker, 1992; Nolen-Hoeksema and Girgus, 1994). Our findings are consistent with the existing literature in showing higher levels of depression/anxiety among girls than among boys. However, levels of depression/anxiety did not depend on the adolescent's residential arrangement.

Deviance. As noted in Chapter 2, we approached the question of "externalizing" (deviant) behavior with questions about three subareas: substance use, school deviance, and antisocial behavior. Our measure of overall deviance was the sum of the items from these three subscales. The boys in our sample were somewhat more likely to report deviant behavior in general than were the girls; in particular, they were more likely to report

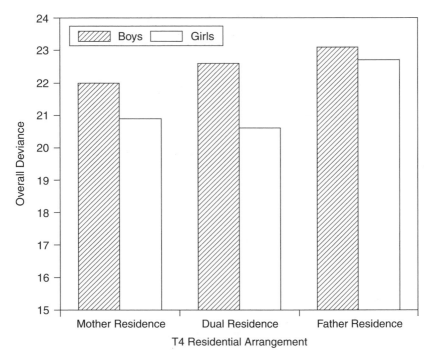

Figure 4.1b Overall deviance of adolescents in each residence and gender group. Means are adjusted for age of adolescent and the average education of the two parents.

antisocial forms of deviant behavior (for example, damaging property or carrying a weapon). This sex difference is consistent with a considerable body of evidence that boys are more likely than girls to display a variety of antisocial behaviors during adolescence as well as at younger and older ages (Eagly and Steffen, 1986; Hyde, 1984; Maccoby and Jacklin, 1974).

There were also small differences in the level of deviance by residence. Adolescents who were living with their fathers reported more substance use (use of tobacco, alcohol, and other illicit substances) than did other adolescents, and in this residential group, girls' scores were as high as boys' (see Figure 4.1a). The incidence of school deviance and other forms of antisocial behavior did not differ among the residential groups, but when the three subscales were combined into the overall deviance scale, the level of deviance was somewhat (and significantly) higher among adolescents living with their fathers than among adolescents living with their mothers (see Figure 4.1b). Deviance was as low among adolescents in dual residence as it was among adolescents in mother residence, but lower among dual-resident adolescents than among those in father residence. Given the lower number of cases in dual residence, the difference between dual and father residence was statistically significant only for substance use, but the order of magnitude of the difference on overall deviance was as great as for the mother-father comparison.

Because of the relation between higher parental income and higher deviance reported earlier, we repeated these analyses controlling for residential parent's income instead of average parental education. Using income as a control eliminated the differences in deviance between residential groups. Thus the father's higher income appears to be a *disadvantage* with regard to involvement in deviant activities among the adolescents in his care. In Chapters 5 and 6 we investigate whether this is because fathers, in working at more lucrative jobs, work longer hours and consequently have less time to supervise or monitor the activities of their adolescents.

School Adjustment

Grades. We have only the reports of the adolescents themselves concerning their school grades, but self-reports are reasonably good indicators of actual grade levels (Dornbusch et al., 1987). A score of 6 reflects grades of "mostly B's," and this is the average level for the girls in our sample. The boys' average was at the "about half B's and half C's" level, although the sex difference was not significant. The adolescents in dual residence reported the highest grades, but this residence difference was of borderline significance.[3]

School effort. The degree of effort adolescents put forth in school was not related to residence for boys, but was lower for father-resident girls than for mother-resident girls. Even so, the sex difference in the impact of residence was weak, and dropped out when analyses were conducted on subsamples using one adolescent per family rather than the entire adolescent sample. If dual-resident adolescents were dropped from the analysis, and the comparison was done only with mother- and father-resident adolescents, the difference for girls was stronger, although it was still only of borderline ($p \leq .10$) significance in random samples.

Worst Problem

When an adolescent is troubled, this may express itself in different ways: some individuals may become depressed or anxious, some may "act out"

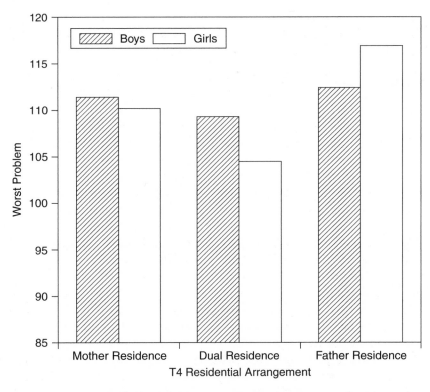

Figure 4.2 "Worst problem" score of adolescents in each residence and gender group. Means are adjusted for age of adolescent and the average education of the two parents.

in deviant ways, and some may lose motivation to do well in school. As noted in Chapter 2, we created a "worst problem" score to account for this diversity of ways to express maladjustment. The "worst problem" score reflects the worst score an adolescent received in any of three domains—depression/anxiety, overall deviance, or school effort.[4] Thus this score indicates how troubled adolescents were in the domain for which they showed the most problematic behavior. Using the "worst problem" score, we find that adolescents living with their fathers ($M =$ 114.6) had a higher incidence of troubled behaviors than those in either maternal ($M = 110.8$) or dual ($M = 106.9$) residence (see Figure 4.2). Although, statistically speaking, the difference applied equally to both sexes, examination of Figure 4.2 suggests that the difference between father residence and the other residence groups is larger for girls than it is for boys. For both boys and girls, dual-resident adolescents were slightly better off than those in mother residence on this measure.[5]

Summary

As noted in Chapter 3, our adolescents' reports about their behavior and feelings indicated that their adjustment was, on average, satisfactory. Still, we have identified considerable variation within our sample, and some of our adolescents were considerably better adjusted than others. How much of this variation was associated with residential arrangements? Our answer is: not a great deal. Variation within each of the groups was large, and the three groups had similar group averages on both personal resources and adjustment. Nevertheless, some small group differences did emerge, especially when we considered each adolescent's most severe problem. On our "worst problem" measure, an adolescent was considered to be functioning suboptimally if she or he was "acting out," depressed, or doing poorly in school. Young people in father residence were, on average, functioning less well in at least one area than were young people in the other residential groups. The group who appeared to be functioning best were those in dual residence, and the mother-resident group was intermediate. These findings are made more striking by the fact that father residence might be considered advantaged in that residential fathers typically had considerably higher incomes than residential mothers. Yet, in our sample, household income did not appear to have an important direct link with adjustment, and where it did, it was linked to worse adjustment (a higher level of deviance).

It is, of course, possible that the advantages of father residence with regard to household income are offset by other disadvantages that co-occur with father residence. Despite recent increases in the incidence of father residence, it is still a relatively uncommon arrangement. Fathers get custody more often when the mother has been relatively uninvolved with the children before the separation (see Maccoby and Mnookin, 1992). They may also be more likely to get custody when the mother has personal problems or when the children are difficult to handle. In Chapters 5 and 6, we further examine the question of whether father residence at Time 4 is associated with a more difficult family history, to investigate whether the slightly higher level of difficulties among adolescents living with their fathers is a result of fathers' having gained custody in particularly disadvantageous situations.

As we saw earlier, a number of researchers have claimed that children of divorce fare better when in the custody of the same-sex parent. In general, we did not find support for this hypothesis. The boys in our sample were generally doing as well when living with their mothers as when living with their fathers, and sometimes slightly better. When we found significant differences among residential groups, they generally applied to adolescents of both sexes. That is, statistically speaking, there were no grounds for concluding that residence differences applied only to girls or only to boys. A more informal inspection of the means for the two sexes, however, indicates that difficulties in father residence are sometimes limited to, or more pronounced for, girls. So it may be true that, on average, girls are better off when living with their mothers. But it may also be the case that boys are better off in their mothers' care—they certainly are no worse off.

In attempting to understand what might underlie these small residence differences in adjustment, we need to consider the environments of different residences in more detail. In the next chapter, we turn to an exploration of life in each residential arrangement: Who lives in the home? How much do parents work? How many major life stresses have been experienced? What are family relationships like? What styles of parental control and management are used? We look at whether and how these aspects of life in one's home differ by residential arrangement. After considering such factors in Chapter 5, in Chapter 6 we examine the links between the characteristics of these environments and the adaptation of the adolescents in them.

5

Life in the
Residential Home

In this chapter we examine what life is like for adolescents in the different residential arrangements. First, we compare the arrangements with respect to several past and current contextual factors likely to influence the kind of life an adolescent experiences in the home: (a) How stable has the residential arrangement been over the time since the parental separation? In other words, how likely is it that an adolescent has been in his or her current arrangement ever since the separation, and how likely is it that he or she has changed residences at least once? (b) How stressful has life been for the adolescent in the past year? Are some arrangements linked with more life stress than others? (c) How many children are in the original family? Do parents' decisions about where their children are to live depend on how many children they have? (d) How many people are currently living in the residential home, and who are they? For example, what is the likelihood that stepparents, stepsiblings, or half-siblings are present in each arrangement? and (e) How many hours does the residential parent work per week?

Second, we examine the quality of relationships within the family, including the nature of the ongoing relationship between the parents as well as the nature of the relationship between the residential parent and the adolescent. Third, we compare the extent to which parents exert control in the household, and the ways in which households are managed.[1] The quality of family relationships and the styles of parental control and management have been consistently linked to psychosocial adjustment among children and adolescents in both divorced and nondivorced families.

58

Contextual Factors

Stability of the Residential Arrangement

There were large residential differences in the stability of residence over time (see Figure 5.1).[2] Adolescents in mother residence at Time 4 were much more likely than adolescents in father or dual residence to have remained in their initial residential arrangement since the separation. Adolescents in father residence were the most likely to have shifted residence at some point since the separation. There was a trend for these differences in stability of residence to be somewhat stronger for girls than for boys; in other words, girls in mother residence were especially likely to have been there ever since the parental separation, and girls in father residence were especially likely to have moved in with their fathers after initially living elsewhere (for most, with mothers).

The differences in stability of residence most likely have to do with the reasons different residential arrangements are adopted. As we have noted

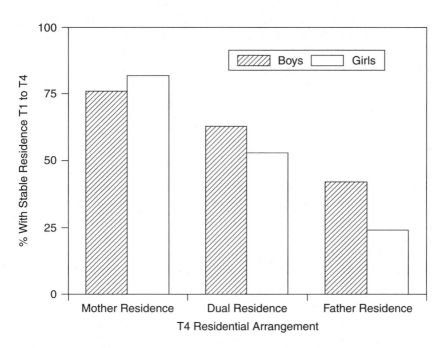

Figure 5.1 Stability of residence for adolescents in each residence and gender group.

in previous chapters, despite recent shifts toward gender-neutrality in divorce law, a strong preference for maternal custody remains in both legal decrees and actual practice (Maccoby and Mnookin, 1992). When parents arrive at their own decision about custodial arrangements with little disagreement—as most do—they usually opt for maternal physical custody. Furthermore, legal processes probably embody some de facto presumption for mother custody, and most mothers are strongly determined to retain custody of their children after divorce. Those mothers who might not otherwise insist on mother custody often feel social pressure to do so. Among families who do elect sole-father residence, therefore, there may often be special family circumstances that make it difficult for the mother to retain some form of custody. Alternatively, the children themselves may have chosen to live with their fathers, often after spending some time living with their mothers. Adolescents who switch to father residence at some point after the separation do so because of complications in the mother's ability to maintain a household, conflict between the mother and child, the inability of the mother to "control" a difficult child, or simply because of the adolescent's desire to live with her or his father after a time away from him (see Chapter 3). The fact that father residence is more likely to be chosen in situations of maternal or familial difficulties, or at the adolescents' initiative, may help to explain why this residential arrangement is more unstable than other arrangements and also why it carries a higher likelihood of life stress, as we see next.

Life Stresses

As Figure 5.2 shows, adolescents living with their fathers reported more total stresses within the past year than did adolescents in other arrangements. We examined each individual stress in order to see which specific life stresses were experienced more often by father-resident adolescents. We found that a new baby was more likely to be born into the father's household than the mother's, and that father-resident adolescents were slightly more likely to say that they had moved in the past year than were mother-resident adolescents. Boys in father residence were more likely than boys in mother residence to report that someone close to them had died. Adolescents who lived primarily with their fathers were also more likely than other adolescents to have broken up with a boyfriend or girlfriend. This difference remained even if we took into account the differences in age between the groups. Adolescents in dual

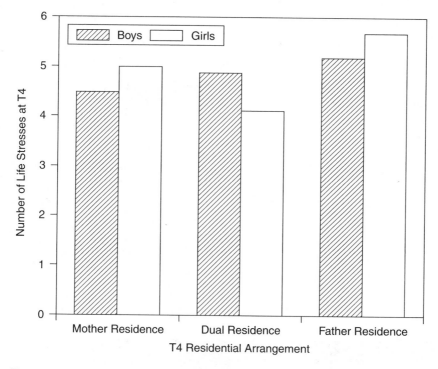

Figure 5.2 Number of life stresses in the last twelve months for adolescents in each residence and gender group.

residence were least likely to say that their families had experienced serious financial difficulties.

Family Size and Household Composition

Dual-resident families had slightly fewer natural children than those using father residence. Given the complexities of dual residence, it is not surprising to find evidence that such an arrangement is somewhat more likely to be maintained when fewer children are involved; even so, the difference is very small. Residential fathers and residential mothers had similar numbers of children living in their homes, but there *was* a difference in who those children were: girls living primarily with fathers were more likely to live with stepsiblings than girls living primarily with mothers, and both boys and girls were more likely to live with half-siblings in father residence than in mother residence (see Figure 5.3). The greater

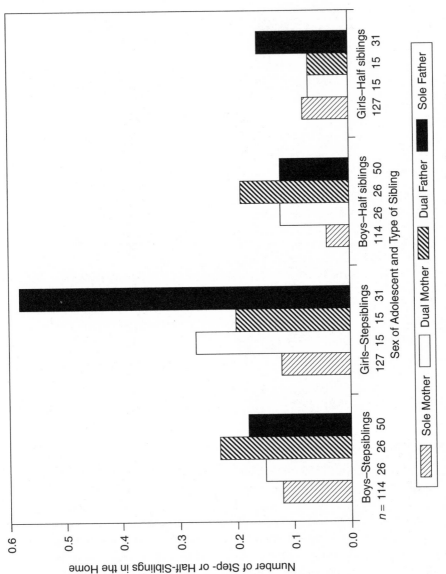

Figure 5.3   Average number of stepsiblings and half-siblings in the home for adolescents in each residence and gender group. Numbers are based on a random sample of adolescents using only one adolescent per family.

number of half-siblings in father residence than mother residence is consistent with adolescents' reports that father-resident households were more likely to have experienced a new birth within the past twelve months. There were no differences by residential arrangement in the likelihood that the mother or father was remarried, or had a new unmarried partner living in the home. Although fathers were no more likely to be remarried than mothers, the greater number of new births in the fathers' households is most likely due to the fact that fathers' new wives were often younger than their former spouses (Maccoby and Mnookin, 1992).

Parents' Working Hours

Fathers worked more hours per week, on average, than mothers (see Figure 5.4). In addition, girls in mother residence had mothers who worked more hours per week, on average, than did girls in dual residence.

Interparental Relationships

Joint physical custody is sometimes awarded by the courts to parents who cannot agree on a residential arrangement. Not surprisingly, some researchers have found higher levels of conflict and hostility between parents implementing joint physical custody than among other parents (Nelson, 1989). Among the full sample of parents in the Stanford Custody Study, parents who had been awarded joint physical custody were more likely to have experienced high legal conflict during the settlement process. Nonetheless, we expected that parents still maintaining dual-residence arrangements four and a half years after their separation would be less conflictual and more cooperative than other parents, in part because a number of the more highly conflictual families who had been awarded joint custody had shifted to a sole-residence arrangement (Maccoby and Mnookin, 1992). In addition, there are some parents who voluntarily implement joint physical custody—either initially or at some point after the initial separation—because they are more cooperative and agreeable than other parents (Pearson and Thoennes, 1990). Because of these trends, we expected that parents using dual residence several years after separation would be those who had been able to cooperate well over time. We also expected that interparental conflict might be higher in father residence than in other arrangements, because a higher proportion of father-residence arrangements come about because of family difficulties.

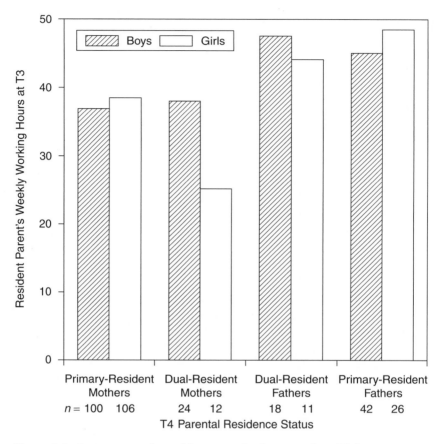

Figure 5.4 Average number of hours worked per week at T3 by parents of adolescents in each residence and gender group. Numbers are based on a random sample of adolescents using only one adolescent per family.

To our surprise, we found that Time 4 residence was generally unrelated to past or present conflict or cooperation in co-parenting as reported by parents or adolescents. Adolescents in dual residence did report parents as more cooperative at Time 4 than did adolescents in other residential arrangements, and at Time 2, a similar finding emerged for boys only. These differences indicate some tendency for the relatively small group of families who were maintaining a dual-resident arrangement at T4 to be more cooperative than other divorced parents, although the differences are generally small and not pervasive across all measures or subgroups.

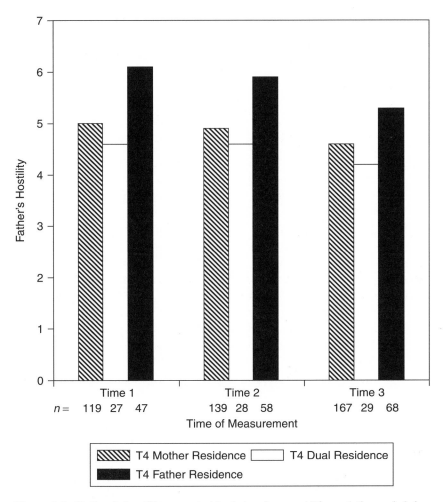

Figure 5.5   Father's hostility as rated by interviewer at Times 1 through 3, by adolescent's residential arrangement. Numbers are based on a random sample of adolescents using only one adolescent per family, and means are adjusted for age of adolescent and the average education of the two parents.

More consistent differences emerged on interviewers' ratings of parental hostility made during the interviews with the parents (Times 1–3). With only one exception (ratings of mother's hostility at T1), the hostility of parents toward each other was rated as having been higher in families that were maintaining father residence at T4 than in other families.[3] Figure 5.5 illustrates these differences using ratings of fathers' hostility.

The level of hostility between parents in mother residence as compared with dual residence was not significantly different. Similar residence differences, showing higher levels of hostility in the homes of adolescents in father residence, emerged if we compared measures of "residential parent's hostility" and "maximum parental hostility."

Parent-Adolescent Relationships

We anticipated possible differences between adolescents in the primary care of their mothers and those in the care of their fathers in terms of the quality of their relationships with the residential parent. Youniss and Smollar (1983) documented rather extensively the ways in which relationships between adolescents and mothers differ from relationships between adolescents and fathers in two-parent families. In families in which parents remain married, adolescents tend to have multidimensional relationships with their mothers. Mother-adolescent relationships are usually close and intimate, with the mother playing the role of confidante and friend at the same time that she functions as an authority figure and disciplinarian. Relationships between children and mothers also tend to have higher levels of conflict, however. Fathers usually have a less intimate or expressive relationship with their children, serving primarily as authority figures, advisors, and models. Relationships tend to be respectful but more distant than those between an adolescent and mother. Collins and Russell (1991) have noted that fathers may withdraw, especially from daughters, after the start of puberty.

With younger children, fathers also tend to have a more playful relationship than do mothers (Maccoby, 1995; Parke and Tinsley, 1981; Russell and Russell, 1987). The playful aspect of father-child relationships likely extends into adolescence, although this has been less well documented. In one relevant study, Montemayor and Brownlee (1987) did find that although adolescents spent less time with their fathers than with their mothers, their time with their fathers was more playful and more likely to center around leisure activities than time with their mothers. In fact, in these researchers' sample, 69 percent of the time adolescents spent with their fathers was spent in leisure activities.

If these qualitative differences between parents hold up in single-parent families, one might expect adolescents in our sample to feel closer to residential mothers than to residential fathers. It is possible, however, that such differences are reduced or eliminated in situations of divorce for several reasons. For example, single mothers may not have the same time to be emotionally available that mothers in two-parent families have (Stolberg and Cullen, 1983). In one study, relationships with both parents were more subdued and guarded among adolescents in divorced families than among adolescents in two-parent families (Smollar and Youniss, 1985). Furthermore, fathers who obtain sole custody of their children may be the very fathers who have developed or are able to develop warm relationships with their children.[4] Or fathers may develop more intimate relationships with their children over time in a situation where the mother is not present (see Gjerde, 1986).

It is also possible that adolescents maintain closer relationships with the residential parent of the same sex. In other words, we might expect girls to be closer to residential mothers than residential fathers, while expecting the reverse to be true for boys. Santrock and Warshak (1979, p. 115) hypothesized that parents may "know how to interact more effectively and feel more comfortable" with a child of the same sex. If this is true, closer relationships between same-sex parents and children than between opposite-sex parents and children would be expected.

How might relationships between adolescents and their parents in dual residence compare with parent-adolescent relationships in sole residence? Because adolescents in dual residence continue to see both parents on a regular basis, we might expect that these adolescents would maintain relationships with both parents that are at least as close as relationships between adolescents and their sole-resident parents. It may even be the case that relationships between dual-resident parents and adolescents are closer than those between sole-resident parents and adolescents if, by giving parents a regular "break" from parenting, dual-resident arrangements allow parents to focus more fully on parenting during times when their children are with them. Some have argued, however, that children who have high levels of contact with parents who are or have been in conflict may have trouble maintaining attachments to both parents, owing to a higher likelihood of divided loyalties (Goldstein, Freud, and Solnit, 1979). If this latter speculation is correct, adolescents in dual residence may in fact report lower levels of closeness to both parents than adolescents in sole-resident arrangements report for their sole-resident parent.

As Table 5.1 shows and as we noted in Chapter 3, our adolescents generally reported feeling close to their parents. The range of possible scores on our closeness scale was from 9 to 45, and the average of each residential group was well above the midpoint on this scale. This indicates that most of our adolescents felt "quite" or "very" close to each par-

Table 5.1 Parent-adolescent relationships in three residential arrangements, by sex of adolescent[a]

Measure of parent-adolescent relationship	Mother-resident mothers		Dual-resident mothers		Dual-resident fathers		Father-resident fathers		Significant differences[b]
	M	(n)	M	(n)	M	(n)	M	(n)	
Closeness to (range: 9–45)[c]									
Boys	37.3	(168)	37.3	(31)	35.9	(32)	35.7	(62)	PM > PF
Girls	35.9	(197)	39.3	(18)	37.8	(19)	32.7	(38)	Girls: DF > PF
Trust of (range: 2–12)									
Boys	9.8	(168)	10.0	(31)	9.8	(32)	9.9	(61)	
Girls	9.4	(197)	10.1	(18)	9.5	(19)	9.5	(38)	
Identification with (range: 2–10)									
Boys	7.6	(168)	8.3	(31)	7.8	(32)	7.1	(62)	PM > PF
Girls	7.0	(196)	7.8	(18)	7.5	(19)	6.8	(38)	*DF > PF*
Activities with (range: 0–11)									
Boys	4.1	(162)	4.9	(31)	5.3	(32)	5.0	(62)	Boys: PF > PM, DM > PM
Girls	4.3	(184)	3.9	(16)	4.6	(17)	4.0	(36)	
Average conflict with (range: 0–5)									
Boys	1.9	(162)	1.6	(31)	1.7	(32)	1.8	(62)	
Girls	1.9	(184)	1.8	(16)	1.8	(17)	1.8	(36)	
Maximum conflict with (range: 0–5)									
Boys	2.5	(162)	2.1	(31)	2.1	(32)	2.3	(62)	
Girls	2.6	(184)	2.4	(16)	2.4	(17)	2.5	(36)	

Disengagement from household (range: 3–14)									
Boys	7.2	(168)	6.9	(31)	7.2	(32)	7.2	(62)	PM > DM
Girls	7.4	(197)	5.9	(18)	6.1	(19)	7.7	(38)	*PF > DF*
Remembers special days (range: 1–3)									
Boys	2.93	(168)	2.92	(31)	2.82	(32)	2.85	(61)	PM > PF
Girls	2.91	(195)	2.99	(18)	2.98	(19)	2.81	(38)	
Eagerness to see (range: 1–5)									
Boys	3.5	(146)	3.7	(31)	3.3	(32)	3.4	(58)	
Girls	3.7	(173)	3.5	(16)	3.3	(17)	3.6	(36)	
Parent confides in adolescent (standardized; actual range: 0–7)									
Boys	3.7	(168)	4.0	(31)	3.3	(32)	2.9	(62)	PM > PF (esp. for girls)
Girls	3.8	(197)	3.8	(18)	3.2	(19)	2.1	(38)	DF > PF
Adolescent nurtures parent (standardized; actual range: 0–6)									
Boys	3.4	(168)	2.7	(31)	2.4	(32)	2.8	(62)	PM > PF
Girls	3.3	(197)	3.2	(18)	2.9	(19)	2.7	(38)	PM > DM

a. Means and standard deviations are adjusted for age of adolescent and the appropriate form of parental education (that is, mother's education when comparing relationships with mothers; father's education when comparing relationships with fathers) by entering these variables as covariates in the analysis. Means presented for sole-mother and sole-father residence are from analyses comparing each with their counterparts in dual residence; these means differ only slightly from the adjusted means that emerge from analyses comparing sole-residence mothers to sole-residence fathers. Significant differences in italics indicate borderline (weak) effects.

b. PM = primary-mother residence; PF = primary-father residence; DM = dual-mother residence; DF = dual-father residence.

c. Unless otherwise noted, ranges are possible, not actual, ranges.

ent—they felt, for example, that they could talk openly with the parent, that the parent was genuinely interested in the adolescent's problems, could be relied on for needed help, often expressed affection, and so forth. In a similar vein, the majority of adolescents said they would like to resemble their parents, and reported low levels of conflict with them. Variation existed within each residential group, of course, and some adolescents reported feeling very close to both parents, some to only one, and a few to neither (in Chapter 10, we look more specifically at these different patterns of closeness). Similarly, some adolescents reported frequent conflict with their parents, although most did not.

Within the general pattern of close relationships, there were some differences in the quality of the parent-adolescent relationship depending on the adolescent's residential situation.

Primary Mother versus Primary Father Residence

Did the quality of the relationship adolescents had with their primary residential parent depend on whether the adolescent was living with the mother or the father? The answer to this question can be found by comparing the means for relationships with "mother-resident mothers" with the means for relationships with "father-resident fathers" in Table 5.1. For both boys and girls, relationships with the residential parent were closer if that parent was the mother, rather than the father. Identification with the residential parent was also somewhat greater for mother-resident than for father-resident adolescents, and residential mothers were more likely to remember special days than residential fathers. It is important to note that there were no differences between sole-resident mothers and sole-resident fathers on several other indices of the affective relationship, including trust, conflict, and disengagement from the home. The findings provide some general evidence, however, for closer emotional and affective relationships with mothers than with fathers. We did not find that adolescents were closer to the same-sex parent, because boys as well as girls showed the tendency toward greater closeness to their mothers.

Fathers' tendency to "play" more with children (at least with their sons) was also noted: boys in the custody of their father had more joint activities with him over a month's time than boys in the custody of their mother had with her.

Given a tendency for adolescents to report greater emotional closeness to mothers than to fathers, it was not surprising to find that residential mothers were much more likely to confide in and lean on their children than were residential fathers. This was especially true if the adolescent was a girl, but it was true for boys as well. Adolescents also felt more need to take care of, and worried more about, residential mothers than residential fathers.

Dual versus Sole Residence

In several respects the relationships between an adolescent and a given dual-resident parent resembled the relationship an adolescent would have with that parent were he or she in the primary care of that parent (see Table 5.1: compare mother-resident mothers with dual-resident mothers and father-resident fathers with dual-resident fathers). In this sense, dual-resident adolescents appear to spend enough time with each parent to sustain relationships at the level that one could expect from a sole-residence arrangement with each parent. In fact, in some cases, the parent-child relationship was even better for adolescents in dual residence than for adolescents in sole residence. Boys in dual residence had more activities with their mothers than boys in sole-mother residence, and both boys and girls felt less disengaged from the mother's home when they were in dual residence than when in sole-mother residence. This difference in disengagement may reflect the fact that there are more opportunities to disengage the more total time one spends in a home. The fact that adolescents spent less time with their mothers when in dual residence than when in primary maternal residence, however, did not impair their ability to remain close to their mothers, as already noted. In addition, adolescents in dual residence were slightly less likely to find themselves in a "nurturing" role for their mothers (that is, to worry about their mothers and to feel that mothers needed to be taken care of) than were adolescents in primary mother residence.

Adolescents also had somewhat better relationships with their father when they lived with him only part of the time (in dual residence) than when they lived in his primary care. Girls felt closer to fathers in dual residence than to fathers in sole residence, and identification with their father was slightly higher among dual-resident adolescents (both boys and girls) than among father-resident adolescents. Dual-resident fathers also confided in their adolescents slightly more than did primary-resident fathers.

All of the evidence presented thus far indicates that relationships with each parent individually are at least as good for adolescents in dual residence as they are for adolescents in the primary care of a particular parent. As such, these results discount the hypothesis that adolescent children of divorce are not able to maintain positive relationships with both parents after divorce. In confirmation of this, when we examined residence differences on measures that captured closeness to *both* parents, or comfort in *both* homes, dual-resident adolescents were equally happy, if not happier, with their relationships than were adolescents in sole residence (see Chapter 8). In addition, as we will show in Chapter 11, dual-resident adolescents were not more likely, in general, to feel caught between their parents than other adolescents.

Parental Control and Management

Goldstein and colleagues (1979) argued that splitting time between parents—and thereby splitting authority for a child between the parents—would be dangerous. Presumably, it was thought to be difficult under such circumstances for either parent to exert authority and maintain control. For example, the mere fact that one's child is not present in the household for a significant part of every week, month, or year may make it difficult for dual-resident parents to monitor their children's activities and behavior adequately. The frequent transitions usually involved in dual-residence arrangements may also make it more difficult to maintain established patterns such as a consistent dinner time or a routine for cleaning the house. Thus, on the one hand, families in dual residence may exhibit lower levels of parental control and household organization than other families. On the other hand, if parents in dual residence can cooperate (back each other up, keep each other informed), monitoring and control might be better than in families where only one parent is integrally involved and vigilant. In this case, dual residence may be the closest one can come to the two-parent, nondivorced situation.

Parental control and organization may also differ in households run by fathers and those run by mothers. There is some evidence that adolescents have less parental supervision in single-mother homes than they do in non-divorced families or reconstituted families (Dornbusch et al., 1985). Yet in two-parent families, mothers are as likely to be disciplinarians and authority figures as fathers (Youniss and Smollar, 1983). Perhaps single mothers do no worse than single fathers. Fathers often have had less experience in household management than mothers (Lamb et al., 1987) and may, therefore, be less effective at establishing and maintaining organization and routines. No study to date has examined these aspects of parenting among single-parent fathers in comparison with single-parent mothers.

We turn to this comparison now, utilizing the reports of adolescents concerning the nature of control and management experienced in mothers' and fathers' households. As noted in Chapter 2, we assessed several aspects of control and management. We asked adolescents how much they thought each parent really knew about a variety of things: their whereabouts and activities during their free time, how they spent their money, and who their friends were. We also asked what rules there were (if any) about how late they could stay out on weeknights and weekend nights. Building on previous work by Dornbusch and colleagues (for example, Dornbusch et al., 1985), we asked about the locus of decision making concerning issues affecting the adolescent's daily life (for example, who decides how late he or she may stay out, what classes to take in school, what clothes to buy or wear, or how to spend money). A "Household Organization" scale reflected the regularity and predictability of household routines. Adolescents were also questioned about their perception of the fairness and consistency of household rules, about how frequently they did a number of household chores in each home, and about whether an adult was present when they came home after school.

Primary Mother versus Primary Father Residence

As can be seen in Table 5.2, styles of parental control and management were remarkably similar in maternal and paternal households. We found no notable differences in decision-making practices, school night or weekend curfews, how well household routines were organized and maintained, chores, or whether an adult was home after school. The single consistent difference had to do with monitoring, and this was found only for girls, not boys: father-resident girls were more likely to say that their fathers did not "really know" as much about their activities, in comparison with the level of parental knowledge attributed to mothers by mother-resident girls. Adolescents living primarily with their mothers were also somewhat more likely to think that rules were fair and to accept those rules than were adolescents living primarily with their fathers.

Dual versus Sole Residence

To our surprise, we found that dual-resident households appeared to function somewhat differently for adolescents of the two sexes. Boys in

Table 5.2　Parental control and management in three residential arrangements, by sex of adolescent[a]

Measure of parental control/management	Mother-resident mothers		Dual-resident mothers		Dual-resident fathers		Father-resident fathers		Significant differences[b]
	M	(n)	M	(n)	M	(n)	M	(n)	
Monitoring (range: 5–15)[c]									
Boys	11.7	(162)	11.6	(31)	11.4	(32)	11.8	(61)	Girls: PM > PF
Girls	12.1	(184)	12.6	(16)	12.1	(17)	10.9	(36)	Girls: DF > PF
Youth-alone decision making (range: 0–1)									
Boys	.46	(162)	.51	(31)	.51	(32)	.44	(62)	
Girls	.41	(184)	.37	(16)	.39	(17)	.42	(36)	
Youth-decides decision making (range: 0–1)									
Boys	.62	(162)	.70	(31)	.71	(32)	.62	(62)	Boys: DM > PM
Girls	.59	(184)	.52	(16)	.51	(17)	.57	(36)	
Joint decision making (range: 0–1)									
Boys	.68	(162)	.58	(31)	.58	(32)	.69	(62)	
Girls	.76	(184)	.79	(16)	.82	(17)	.72	(36)	
School night curfew (range: 0–6)									
Boys	2.1	(162)	2.4	(30)	2.6	(28)	1.9	(62)	
Girls	2.2	(184)	2.2	(16)	1.9	(12)	2.0	(35)	
Weekend night curfew (range: 0–8)									
Boys	3.5	(162)	3.8	(28)	4.5	(31)	3.3	(62)	Girls: PM > DM
Girls	3.6	(184)	2.8	(15)	3.1	(17)	3.4	(35)	Boys: DF > PF

Household organization (range: 9–63)								
Boys	38.6	(168)	40.2	(31)	40.1	(32)	39.3	(62)	PM > PF
Girls	36.9	(197)	40.7	(18)	40.0	(19)	37.4	(38)
Acceptance of rules (range: 5–25)								
Boys	19.2	(168)	19.0	(31)	19.0	(32)	18.8	(62)
Girls	18.9	(197)	19.6	(18)	19.1	(19)	17.7	(38)
Chores (range: 11–44)								
Boys	27.6	(168)	25.6	(31)	25.4	(32)	27.3	(62)
Girls	26.5	(197)	25.8	(18)	23.9	(19)	25.8	(38)
Adult home after school (range: 0–1)								
Boys	.46	(145)	.41	(30)	.53	(27)	.42	(57)
Girls	.50	(168)	.46	(14)	.44	(11)	.35	(31)

a. Means and standard deviations are adjusted for age of adolescent and the appropriate form of parental education (that is, mother's education when comparing control by mothers; father's education when comparing control by fathers) by entering these variables as covariates in the analysis. Means presented for sole-mother and sole-father residence are from analyses comparing each with their counterparts in dual residence; these means differ only slightly from the adjusted means that emerge from analyses comparing sole-residence mothers with sole-residence fathers. Significant differences in italics indicate borderline (weak) effects.

b. PM = primary-mother residence; PF = primary-father residence; DM = dual-mother residence; DF = dual-father residence.

c. Ranges are possible, not actual, ranges.

dual residence reported making more decisions on their own—with or without discussion with parents—than did boys living with either their mothers or their fathers.[5] Weekend curfews set in fathers' homes were also later for dual-resident than for single-resident boys. These findings suggest that controls are relaxed or attenuated somewhat for boys if they are living in dual residence. The opposite appears to be the case, however, for dual-resident girls. Dual-resident fathers knew more about what their adolescent daughters were doing than did sole-resident fathers, and dual-resident girls had earlier weekend curfews than girls living with their mothers.

Putting our findings another way, we found evidence of a slight double standard in parental dealings with adolescents of the two sexes when they were in dual residence. With regard to decision making and weekend curfews, boys in dual residence were granted more freedom than were girls, and these sex differences did not exist or were not as large for adolescents living with either their mothers or their fathers.

Summary

The expectation that adolescents might adjust differently when living in mother, father, or dual residence is based on the assumption that these arrangements might differ with respect to processes we know to influence developmental outcomes. Of primary interest is the question of whether these arrangements differ with respect to the interpersonal dynamics prevailing among family members and whether there are differences in the degree to which parents maintain optimal levels of control and organization in the home. Therefore, in this chapter, we have compared the three groups with respect to (a) contextual factors, including who lives in the home and whether the adolescent has lived in this home ever since the divorce; (b) the quality of the relationship between the two parents; (c) the quality of the relationship between the adolescents and their residential parent(s); and (d) the degree of parental control and management in the household.

Having compared our three residential groups with respect to this variety of contextual and interpersonal factors, we can now identify the factors that have the potential to explain the modest differences in adjustment among adolescents living in the different residential arrangements. Identifying differences among residential groups in such areas as the amount of interparental hostility or the stability of residence over time is only the first step, of course, in discovering whether such differences are indeed related to the fact that adolescents in one residential group are doing better or worse than adolescents in another residential group. The complex interrelationships among multiple potential causal factors, and between the potential causal factors and adolescent adjustment, will be taken up in the next chapter. For the present, we simply summarize what we have found about the differences among our residential groups, and discuss briefly how these *might* be related to the differences in adolescent adjustment.

In Chapter 4, we reported that there were somewhat more well-functioning adolescents among our dual-resident adolescents, and somewhat fewer among those living with their fathers. Why might this be? Let us first consider why there might be a higher incidence of problems among adolescents living with their fathers. An obvious possibility is the residential instability of this group. Only about one-third of the adolescents who were living with their father at the time we interviewed them had been living with him all along. This proportion stands in contrast to the other two groups: 79 percent of the adolescents in mother residence and 60 percent of those in dual residence had lived in these arrangements continuously over the four and a half years since their parents separated. The simple fact that most of the adolescents in father residence had moved in after initially living with their mothers (or in dual residence) presents the following question: to what extent is the higher incidence of poor functioning among adolescents living with their fathers explained by a drift of especially troubled children into father residence, and to what extent is it the case that father residence is in some way more difficult to adjust to, at least for a subgroup of the adolescents in this arrangement?

Apart from residential instability, there are other aspects of the father-residence situation that might help to account for difficulties experienced by the adolescents living there. Adolescents in this group had experienced certain life stresses somewhat more often in the past year than other adolescents, and they were more likely to have had to adapt to living with stepsiblings (if the adolescent was a girl) and half-siblings. In addition, as already noted, the father-residence group was the one with the highest average level of prior hostility between the parents. To the extent that ongoing conflict is a central factor in children's adjustment to divorce, this may explain the higher number of problems among father-resident adolescents.

Adolescents (especially the girls) living with their father also reported feeling somewhat less close to him than young people living in other arrangements felt toward their residential parents. In fact, girls felt closer to their father when they were in dual residence than they did when they were living with him most of the time. We asked the adolescents how much they would like to be like each parent, and for children of both sexes, the wish to emulate the father was greater in the dual-resident group than it was among those who lived primarily with their fathers. We see, then, that at least in a subgroup of father-resident cases, there is tension or emotional distance in the father-child relationship when the two live together most of the time.

Finally, fathers also appeared to have some difficulty monitoring the whereabouts and activities of adolescent daughters who lived primarily with them. This finding is consistent with what the parents themselves reported at earlier times: although most residential fathers did not report great difficulty in monitoring their children, their average level of self-reported difficulty in this respect was significantly greater than that of residential mothers (Maccoby and Mnookin, 1992).

We also need to consider the somewhat better functioning of the dual-resident adolescents. The favorable status of dual-resident youth is somewhat surprising, in view of the stresses that surely must be involved in going back and forth between parental households and trying to maintain school-related activities, friendships with peers, extracurricular activities, and family relationships while living in two different places. Such stresses must be outweighed by advantages inherent in the arrangement. In Chapter 4 we saw that the dual-resident families included more parents from the upper end of the socioeconomic spectrum. The adolescents were also younger, on the average, than those in the other groups, and our younger adolescents had lower scores on deviance and depression. Yet these factors cannot account for the differences that emerged on our measures of adolescent functioning, because we controlled for age of adolescents and education of parents in our analyses.

Our dual-resident children had other advantages, however. To begin with, their parents had somewhat more harmonious relationships with each other. According to ratings of each parent's hostility toward the former spouse made by interviewers at Times 1, 2, and 3, levels of hostility were lower between parents whose adolescents were in dual residence than between parents whose adolescents were in father residence. And according to the reports of the adolescents, there was somewhat more active cooperation between parents in dual residence than between parents in either mother or father residence. A further possible advantage for dual-resident adolescents is the fact that they maintained close positive bonds (of trust, affection, and identification) with both their mother and their father, remaining as close or closer to each parent as adolescents in sole-resident arrangements were with their residential parent. As we shall see in Chapter 10, adolescents in sole-resident arrangements (especially mother-resident arrangements) were not as close to their nonresidential parent as they were to their residential parent, meaning that close relationships with both parents were in fact more common among dual-resident adolescents.

Finally, we must consider the possibility that the relatively favorable status of dual-resident adolescents is due, at least in part, to self-selection. A substantial portion (40 percent) of our small group of dual-resident adolescents had moved into this arrangement after initially living primarily with either their mother (in the typical case) or their father. Generally speaking, the reasons children move into dual residence were more child-centered than those underlying other residential moves (see Chapter 3; Maccoby and Mnookin, 1992). Furthermore, families who try dual residence and find it unworkable for some reason select themselves out, leaving in our dual-residence group those who were willing to expend the extra effort entailed in the dual arrangement.

When legal policymakers pressed for changes in divorce statutes in the late 1970s and early 1980s—changes that would permit wider adoption of joint physical custody and liberal visitation—they believed that children would benefit from frequent and continuing contact with both parents. Our results so far are consistent with the view that de facto joint physical custody (in other words, dual residence) can indeed be supportive to adolescent children of divorced parents: these children do stay emotionally close to both parents, and in terms of adjustment we certainly have not found dual residence to be harmful, in comparison with the alternatives. Clearly, however, considering the variation in functioning among the adolescents in dual residence, it is important to examine further the conditions under which a dual arrangement does and does not work well for the children involved (see Chapters 6 and 11).

In the next chapter, we will address the question of whether residence differences in adjustment can be explained by residence differences in any of the household characteristics we have examined here. Given the rather small differences in adjustment between residences, however, we first take up the additional question of how the aspects of the residential household that we have considered in this chapter are related to various aspects of adolescent functioning *within* each residence and gender group, regardless of whether absolute levels of a characteristic differed among the residential groups.

6

Linking Home Life and Adjustment

Our goal in this chapter is to examine the connections between the quality of adolescents' adjustment and the characteristics of the environment in their residential homes (also referred to as "family processes" or "household processes"). In Chapter 4, we compared adolescents in the three major residential arrangements with respect to their adjustment and found small differences, with adolescents in father residence functioning somewhat less well than other adolescents. In Chapter 5, we documented various differences in the family relationships and in parental control and management that existed in each arrangement, but as with adjustment, most differences were small, and the similarities between residential arrangements outnumbered the differences. Given such findings, our major interest became determining which processes were linked to adjustment within each residential group.

In particular, we wanted to see whether family environments in each kind of household were linked in similar ways to adjustment. Although certain basic processes (for example, parent-child closeness, parental supervision) are important in all homes, adolescents living with their mothers may benefit from somewhat different aspects of parenting than do adolescents whose primary parent is the father. As we have noted, the parenting styles of mothers and fathers tend to differ on the average, leading some experts to speculate that each parent contributes something unique to children's development. In a similar vein, boys and girls may need different things from mothers and from fathers; thus there may be differences in the relations between family environments and adjustment depending on the sex of the adolescent. Finally, differences in the temperament or background of those youngsters who end up living in different residence arrangements may cause them to benefit from different aspects of parenting.

There are several reasons, then, to expect that the conditions that promote positive adjustment after divorce may differ by residence, by sex, or both. Consequently, we explored extensively which processes were most important for the adjustment for boys and girls in each residential arrangement. In what follows, we first report predictors of adjustment for adolescents in the two sole-resident arrangements (in other words, father residence versus mother residence); at the end of the chapter we look at predictors of adjustment for dual-resident adolescents.

Simplification of Measures and Method of Analysis

Even with our relatively large sample, we could not simultaneously include in our analyses all the detailed measures of the family and household environment that we considered in Chapter 5. In that chapter, the processes we considered were grouped into four sets of characteristics that we believed were potentially important:

1. The family context (for example, the number and kind of individuals living in the home, the stability of the residential arrangement, the number of life stresses);
2. The quality of the interparental relationship;
3. The quality of the parent-adolescent relationship; and
4. The degree and kinds of parental control and management in the home.

We thus approached the question of "What best predicts adjustment?" with these sets of processes in mind. For ease of reference, we will call them "context" (set 1), "interparental relationship" (set 2), "parent-child relationship" (set 3), and "parental control and management" (set 4).

For each of these sets except the first, we combined several of the more detailed measures into an overall score representing that set.[1] To measure the closeness and warmth of the adolescent's relationship with the residential parent, we combined our earlier measures of closeness, trust, identification, and amount of joint activity (henceforth called "overall closeness"). We also combined our measures of parental monitoring, school night curfew, weekend night curfew, youth-alone decision making, household organization, and acceptance of rules into a composite we call

Table 6.1 Variables entered into analyses predicting adolescent adjustment for each residence and gender group

Context
  Age of adolescent
  Residential parent's education
  Stability of residence (T1–T4)
  Life stress (T4)
  Original family size
  Stepparent in home (T4)
  Nonremarried new partner in home (T4)
  Number of stepsiblings in home (T4)
  Number of half-siblings in home (T4)
  Residential parent's working hours (T3)

Interparental Relationship
  Maximum parental hostility or parental conflict composite (T3)
  Frequency of parental arguing (T4)
  Parental agreement (T4)

Parent-Child Relationship
  Parent-child "overall closeness" (T4)
  Disengagement from home (T4)
  Parent-child conflict (T4)
  Parent confides in child (T4)
  Child nurtures parent (T4)

Parental Control and Management
  Household management (T4)
  Chores (T4)

"household management." Other aspects of the parent-child relationship and of parental control and management that were not highly related to "overall closeness" or "household management" were kept separate in the analyses.

To measure the interparental relationship, we considered using a composite score based on parental discord at T2 and T3, lack of parental cooperative communication at T2 and T3, and both mother's and father's hostility at T1 and T3. Exploratory work with this composite, however, revealed that maximum parental hostility at T3 (a score taking either the mother's or father's hostility score, whichever was higher) was at least as powerful as the composite, and sometimes more so, in predicting adjustment. The information we provide below concerning the relations be-

Table 6.2 Correlations of selected measures of context, family relationships, and household processes with "worst problem," by sex and residence, for sole-resident adolescents[a]

	Mother residence		Father residence	
Maximum n	Boys (167)	Girls (196)	Boys (61)	Girls (37)
Set 1: Context				
Stability of residence	−.01	−.01	−.29*	−.32+
Life stress	.27***	.23**	.34**	.16
Residential parent remarried[b]	−.10	−.12	−.10	−.19
Residential parent has cohabiting new partner[b]	.06	−.02	.25+	.08
Set 2: Interparental Relations				
Maximum hostility (T3)[b]	.15	−.16+	.16	.24
Parents agree (T4)	−.17*	−.13+	−.09	−.03
Parents often argue (T4)	.26***	.07	.41**	.22
Set 3: Parent-Child Relationship (Residential Parent)				
Overall closeness	−.31****	−.34****	−.06	.09
Child disengaged from res. parent's household	.20*	.40****	.43***	.14
Parent-child conflict	.23**	.17*	.27*	.12
Parent confides in child	−.15+	−.14+	−.18	.26
Child nurtures parent	−.00	.12+	.10	.23
Set 4: Parental Control and Management (Residential Parent)				
Household management	−.41****	−.40****	−.34**	.18

a. Correlations are controlled for adolescent's age and residential parent's education.
b. Based on a sample of only one adolescent per family, selected randomly.
+$p \le .10$.   *$p \le .05$.   **$p \le .01$.   ***$p \le .001$.   ****$p \le .0001$.

tween interparental conflict on adolescent adjustment will therefore be based primarily on our score for maximum parental hostility at T3.

Table 6.1 lists the variables in each set that were used to predict adjustment.

Table 6.2 shows the correlations of our major predictor variables with the "worst problem" score (as an illustrative index of adjustment) by sex and residence group, for adolescents living primarily with either their mother or their father. Although these correlations give basic information about the relation between family processes and adolescent adjustment in each group, and in most cases will serve to demonstrate the points we want to make, they represented only a starting point for our purposes. Because the predictor variables were related to one another in complex ways—sometimes in ways that differed by residence or sex—we needed to consider the sets of variables jointly and successively, to try to identify the factors that had the strongest impact, overall, on adjustment. For three of the four residence-by-sex groups (all except father-resident girls), we used multiple regression to do this.[2] Our procedure for exploring process-adjustment links for father-resident girls and for dual-resident adolescents of the two sexes was necessarily more limited, because there were not enough cases in these three smaller groups to carry out analyses with more than four or five predictors at a time. Thus our analysis for father-resident girls and dual-resident boys and girls is more qualitative in nature, based on examination of correlations and simple regressions using each individual predictor (controlling for age) and comparing the relations with those that emerged for the other three groups.

Although we rely, in the discussion that follows, on the correlations in Table 6.2 to demonstrate many of our findings, we will note instances where results of our more complex analyses differed from those indicated by the correlations in Table 6.2. We turn now to a consideration of the specific aspects of context and family process that proved to be important in predicting adolescents' adjustment in sole-resident families.

Predictors of Adjustment for Sole-Resident Adolescents

Stability of Residence

We reported in Chapter 3 that approximately one-third of the young people in our sample had moved between parental households—or into or out of dual residence—at least once during the four and a half years since their parents had separated. The rate of residential instability was particularly high among adolescents who ended up living with their fathers. Although the *proportion* of adolescents living with their mother at Time 4 who had not lived with her continuously was low, the *number* of adolescents who moved in with their mothers at some time after parental separation was comparable to the number who moved in with their fathers.

Moving from one parental household to another can be a stressful event in itself, especially if accompanied by parental disputes. At the same time, it can be a symptom of other problems if it occurs because of conflict between the child and the parent whose house the child is leaving. In such situations, adolescents who move from one parental household to another might include a substantial group of difficult children. We expected, therefore, that children who moved would have higher levels of adjustment problems than children who were residentially stable, and this turned out to be true—but only (to our surprise) for the adolescents currently in father residence. Adolescents in father residence who had moved one or more times since their initial residential arrangement were doing worse in several respects than adolescents who had been with their father all along. Instability of residence was linked to lower levels of school effort and to poorer adjustment on the "worst problem" scale for both boys and girls in father residence, and to higher levels of substance use for boys in father residence. None of these negative findings was present for the adolescents who had moved in with their mothers at some point after the initial residential arrangements were established.

Why was instability linked with the expected negative outcomes only among father-resident adolescents? Is it because the adolescents who chose to move in with their fathers over time were more troubled to begin with? Data reported in Chapter 3 indicated that negative family circumstances were more likely to precipitate moves into father residence than mother residence. For example, our adolescents cited family conflict more often as a reason for moving in with their father than for moving in with their mother, whereas a parent's relocation was more often given as a reason for moving in with their mother. This provides some evidence that problems in family relationships—and possibly problems in children's adjustment as well—are more likely to predate moves into father residence than moves into mother residence.

Unfortunately, data on children's adjustment prior to shifts in residence that would be comparable to the data we obtained at T4 did not exist. In the earlier parent interviews, however, parents reported briefly on their children's unhappiness, irritability, and problems in school, and the adolescents who had moved in with their fathers by T4 were not different on these measures than the adolescents who had shifted to mother residence. Thus the meager evidence we have on adjustment over time does not indicate that fathers' households were accumulating more troubled adolescents. We recognize, however, that these earlier measures of adjustment are limited and may not be sensitive enough to capture early problems among these children.

Our data also do not indicate that the relation between residential stability and poor adjustment among father-resident adolescents is completely attributable to poor family relationships that might predict both instability and poor adjustment. Although the relation between stability and adjustment weakened somewhat when interparental hostility and current household processes were controlled, it never dropped out entirely. Thus the fact that father-resident adolescents who have not lived with their father continuously since the divorce were less well adjusted is not completely explained by a drift of children from homes with poorer family relationships or other household conditions. It is possible again, however, that we have not captured the essential components of those relational or personal problems that might contribute to less optimal outcomes among those adolescents who later move in with their fathers.

One further possible explanation for the link between residential instability and poor adjustment only in father residence may have to do with the ability of this particular group of adolescents to adapt to stressful circumstances. A change in residence can be stressful, no matter what the reason for the change. Perhaps the adolescents in father residence were less able to cope with this particular stress, either because they were more likely to be experiencing other simultaneous stresses (see Chapter 5) or because they had fewer personal or family resources available to rely on.

Life Stress

The amount of life stress that an adolescent reported experiencing in the preceding twelve months turned out to be a strong and pervasive predictor of a number of problems in adjustment. Higher life stress was linked to a greater tendency to use attacking conflict-resolution strategies in conflict with peers, especially among father-resident adolescents. It was also predictive of higher depression, higher substance use, higher school deviance, higher antisocial behavior, and—not surprisingly given these links—was associated with higher overall deviance and more extreme "worst problem" scores. For almost every aspect of adjustment, the association between life stress and negative adjustment was present for both boys and girls, and mother- and father-resident adolescents alike.

Furthermore, life stress had a direct association with poor adjustment. We considered the possibility that stress might have negative consequences mainly by undermining the quality of parent-child relationships or by weakening parental management and control. We found, however, that even after taking these factors into account, life stress retained its predictive power.

Parents' New Partners

With few exceptions, previous research on parental repartnering after divorce, and its effects on children, focuses on situations where a remarriage has taken place. We know a fair amount about the relationships between children and their stepparents, and about the challenges stepparents face with stepchildren (see, for example, Bray and Berger, 1993a; Hetherington and Clingempeel, 1992; Lutz, 1983; Pasley and Ihinger-Tallman, 1987). In our study, we looked not only at whether a parent had remarried but also at whether a parent had a new partner living in the home to whom he or she was not married. We examined each of these repartnering conditions separately. We consistently found that having a stepparent was associated with positive adjustment. For both boys and girls, having a stepparent in the home was linked with higher levels of compromise as a conflict-resolution strategy used with peers, and father-resident boys with a stepmother also reported less use of attack as a strategy during peer conflicts. For all adolescents, having a stepparent in the home was also linked with lower levels of school deviance and with better adjustment on the "worst problem" scale.[3] Boys with stepparents also had lower levels of substance use, antisocial behavior, and overall deviance, and higher grades in school.

The presence of an unmarried new partner in the home, by contrast, was associated for boys with higher levels of almost every problem we measured: higher use of attack and lower use of compromise in peer conflict-resolution, higher substance use, higher school deviance, higher antisocial behavior, higher overall deviance (see Figure 6.1), lower grades, lower school effort, and poorer adjustment on the "worst problem" scale.[4] Father-resident girls were also less likely to use compromise in resolving peer conflicts and more likely to use substances when there was an unmarried new partner living in the father's home.

Why is the presence of a parent's new partner in the home more problematic if remarriage has not occurred? We will consider this question further in Chapter 7, but here we simply note some possibilities. First, unmarried new partners may not have legitimated their presence in the eyes of an adolescent, and adolescents may respond to that presence

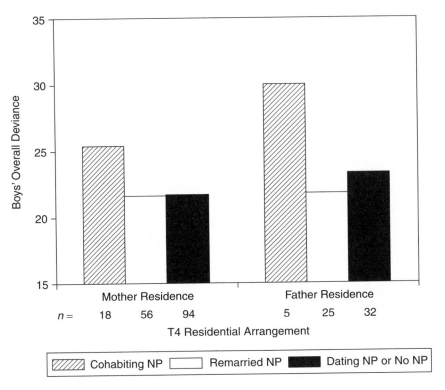

Figure 6.1 Overall deviance by residential parent's new-partner (NP) status for boys in mother and father residence. Means are adjusted for age of adolescent and residential parent's education.

with a lack of acceptance and respect that has subsequent repercussions in terms of adolescent "rebellion" or acting out. Adolescents may interpret a parent's relationship with an unmarried partner as primarily sexual; marriage, on the other hand, may be seen as a commitment by the new partner to care for the family.

It is also possible that relationships and processes in the home are less optimal for child rearing when an unmarried new partner is present in the home. For example, the presence of an unmarried new partner in the home may absorb the attention of the residential parent in an exclusive way, thus disrupting the relationship between the resident parent and the adolescent or weakening the residential parent's control. Our results suggest that these hypotheses may partly explain the association between the presence of an unmarried new partner and adolescent adjustment.

When the quality of the parent-child relationship and the level of parental management are considered, the association between having an unmarried new partner present and adolescent adjustment is reduced in magnitude.[5] The positive effects of parental remarriage are also attenuated (although they do not disappear) when the affective quality of the parent-child relationship and household management are considered. Thus it would appear that the presence of a new spouse tends to strengthen a resident parent's parenting, while the presence of an unmarried new partner tends to weaken it.

These are not the only possible routes by which parents' new partners could be related to adolescent adjustment. An alternative possibility is that new partners may be more reluctant to marry into a family with children when those children are less well adjusted. The number of adolescents in our sample whose parents had a cohabiting partner was small relative to the other new-partner groups, but the association between having an unmarried new partner in the home and poor adjustment was surprisingly strong and consistent, especially for boys. Future research clearly needs to pay attention to the role of unmarried new partners and to household processes associated with the presence of unmarried new partners in the home.

Interparental Relationships

When interparental relationships were assessed from the reports of the adolescents at T4, we found that, in general, the more conflictual the interparental relationship, the more problems the adolescent exhibited. Adolescent-reported parental arguing was associated with higher levels of depression and lower school effort among adolescents, particularly boys. Similarly, every group except mother-resident girls reported higher levels of overall deviance and a more severe "worst problem" in situations when parents argued frequently. And in all groups of sole-resident adolescents, school deviance was higher under conditions of frequent parental arguing. Consistent with these findings, adolescent-reported parental agreement on issues concerning the child was generally modestly associated with positive adjustment.

Although these findings fit with our hypotheses and the reports from many other studies that interparental conflict is injurious to children, it is possible that when we use adolescents' reports of their parents' relationship, we get a reporting bias: unhappy or poorly functioning adolescents may also tend to see their parents negatively. When we use our independent measures of the interparental relationship, derived from the parents themselves at earlier points in time, we get a mixed picture, with negative associations sometimes emerging for boys only, or for father-resident adolescents only. Specifically, the higher the maximum level of hostility between parents at T3, the more substance use among father-resident adolescents and the more overall deviance among father-resident adolescents and mother-resident boys (in other words, only for mother-resident girls was overall deviance *not* linked to higher levels of hostility). Higher levels of hostility were also linked with more use of attacking conflict-resolution strategies among father-resident boys. Counterintuitively, hostility was associated with better adjustment on the "worst problem" scale for girls in mother residence. Given that we have no theoretical backing for this result, and that it does not fit with the general pattern of results concerning interparental conflict, we believe that it is a chance occurrence.

This package of results indicates that ongoing parental conflict is associated with minor negative outcomes, such as school deviance, for all adolescents. In addition, parental conflict is associated with more extreme negative outcomes for boys in particular, and sometimes for father-resident girls as well. In general, these associations do not change when we add measures of parent-child closeness and/or parental management to the prediction of adjustment, so the link between parental conflict and adolescent adjustment does not appear to be accounted for by these factors.

Parent-Child Relationships

The overall closeness of the relationship between residential parent and child was positively associated with adjustment, but primarily for adolescents living with their mothers. For example, higher levels of overall closeness predicted less depression and less school deviance only for adolescents in mother residence. There were, however, a couple of positive associations for father-resident girls as well: among these girls, a warm father-daughter relationship was associated with more compromise in conflicts with peers, as well as with lower levels of substance use. Although Table 6.2 indicates that parent-child closeness also predicted an adolescent's "worst problem" for adolescents in mother residence, this association disappeared in analyses in which parental management was included. The link between parent-child closeness and parental management, and their combined impact on adjustment, is considered separately below.

What did we find with regard to negative aspects of the parent-adolescent relationship? For all sole-resident adolescents, disengagement from the residential home was strongly related to depression. Clearly, disengagement from the home might be a symptom of depression as much as a cause. We cannot pin down the causal direction with our data. Even if disengagement were primarily a symptom of depression, however, it is a symptom with worrisome implications. When adolescents stay away from home and avoid contact with the adults in the household when they are at home, it implies that there are a number of difficulties in the home environment, at least from the adolescent's point of view. Emotional withdrawal from the home may also make a child more prone to act out and more vulnerable to negative peer influences. Our data suggest that this occurs mainly among boys, who are, in general, more likely than girls to engage in deviant or antisocial activities: for boys in our sample, disengagement from the residential home was linked to several aspects of problematic behavior, including antisocial behavior, low grades, and weak school effort. Disengagement from the residential home also presumably means that there are more out-of-school hours in which an adolescent not only has no place to study but has fewer opportunities to receive adult encouragement, support, or supervision for homework, which may contribute to a weaker school performance.

A small number of negative outcomes were also more likely when there were higher levels of parent-child conflict.[6] Adolescents reporting higher levels of conflict with their parents were more likely to use attack strategies and less likely to use compromise in conflictual interactions with their peers. Conflict with father for adolescents in father residence was also associated with higher levels of substance use and higher levels of overall deviance, although the relations were weaker (and insignificant) for girls than they were for boys. Girls in father residence were especially likely to report lower school effort when they had higher levels of conflict with their fathers. In all of these cases it is possible that conflict not only provokes these kinds of behaviors, but that the reverse process may be at work: conflict may occur as a result of the problematic behavior on the part of the adolescents. In all likelihood, the process is a circular one.

A parent's tendency to confide in an adolescent, reflecting some degree of role reversal, may be seen as a danger sign. With only one exception, however, we did not identify any negative outcomes of such confiding.

For girls living with their fathers, the more a father confided in that daughter, the more school deviance she reported. With regard to an adolescent's "worst problem," there was, initially, a modest association between parental confiding and *positive* adjustment. When other aspects of context and family relationships were accounted for, however, this relationship disappeared. Confiding by the parent was most likely part of a pattern of parent-child closeness, and had little independent importance.

Feelings of having to nurture, or take care of, a parent had more consistent and pervasive negative consequences. (These associations emerged only after taking into account other aspects of family context, interparental relationships, and the parent-child relationship, and are not apparent in the correlations presented in Table 6.2.) More feelings of care-taking responsibilities toward the residential parent were linked with higher levels of depression and a more severe "worst problem" score for girls in both mother and father residence.[7] Boys who felt the need to care for a residential parent showed the effects in their school effort and performance: they had lower grades and lower school effort.

Parental Control and Management

The extent to which the residential parent was aware of the adolescent's activities, and maintained an organized home where there were consistent and predictable rules and expectations, was a strong predictor of adjustment. For all groups except father-resident girls, higher levels of household management were linked to lower substance use, lower school deviance, less antisocial behavior, less overall deviance, higher school effort,[8] and lower "worst problem" scores.

The relation between household management and positive adolescent adjustment remained strong and significant even after the context (set 1), the interparental relationship (set 2), and the parent-child relationship (set 3) were controlled. Thus the importance of management and control does not simply reflect other aspects of an adolescent's home environment, but stands independently as a powerful element in adolescent well-being.

Why were father-resident girls an exception? Why, for them, did correlations indicate that higher levels of management might be linked to poorer overall adjustment, as indexed by "worst problem"? Although the correlation was not significant, it went counter in direction to our hypotheses and to the results for other sole-residence adolescents. To investigate this anomaly, we looked at the relations between "worst problem" and each component of "household management" individually, and separately for younger (fourteen years old or younger) and older adolescent girls.[9] We found, first of all, that for the younger daughters, the more the father knew about their activities, the more organized the household was, and the more consistent and fair the rules were, the less severe the worst problem score was.[10] For these young girls in the care of their fathers, however, adjustment was better the more these girls made their own decisions (apart from the father) and the later their curfews. The correlation between youth-alone decision making and "worst problem" for father-resident girls fourteen years and under was particularly strong ($r = -.52$, $p \leq .05$). We hesitate to attach too much importance to these counterintuitive findings, given the small number of girls on which they are based. On the one hand, it is possible that if girls who live with their fathers following divorce are more independent, or have "grown up" especially fast, they can handle higher levels of autonomy at earlier ages. If fathers attempt to impose too much control on these girls, already experienced in making their own decisions, the girls may in fact react negatively. On the other hand, the results suggest that it is still beneficial for these fathers to monitor their daughters' activities, run an organized and predictable home, and set rules that are consistently enforced and well explained.

Parent-Child Closeness and Parental Management Considered Jointly

Parent-child closeness and parental control and management are not independent of each other; in our sample, overall closeness and household management were correlated at .62. And as we reported above, the overall closeness of the parent-child relationship was more frequently and more strongly related to adjustment (particularly for mother-resident adolescents) when parental management was not simultaneously considered. When "overall closeness" and "household management" were considered jointly, however, management was a more important direct predictor of most aspects of adjustment, especially of what we might consider "externalizing" behaviors (for example, deviance). In an earlier publication, we reported the same finding with regard to parent-child closeness and parental monitoring (a major component of "household management") (Buchanan, Maccoby, and Dornbusch, 1991). Our conclusion in that earlier report was that parent-child closeness enabled parents to monitor their adolescents more effectively, which in turn promoted better adjustment. Our current results support that conclusion using the broader constructs of parent-child "overall closeness" and the parent's "household management."[11]

The high correlation between parent-child closeness and parental management in our sample, however, also led to some counterintuitive results. For example, although mother-daughter overall closeness—when considered alone—was associated with less substance use for mother-resident girls, it was associated with *more* substance use when household management was included in the analysis. Thus when both constructs were used to predict substance use, the positive effects of closeness were captured in the degree to which mothers maintained an organized home in which the daughter's activities were monitored. Closeness in excess of that related to good supervision and management in the home appeared to be related to more substance use, and may reflect a more permissive parenting style.

To test this possibility, we looked explicitly at different patterns of closeness and management as they related to substance use among mother-resident girls. Results indicated that when high overall closeness was accompanied by high management (an "authoritative" parenting style; see Baumrind, 1991b, and Lamborn et al., 1991), substance use was, in fact, low—as we would expect—but not significantly lower than when high management was accompanied by low mother-daughter closeness (see Figure 6.2). When overall closeness was high but management was low—a more "permissive" parental style—mother-resident girls tended to use alcohol and other substances more frequently, indeed at about the same level as for girls whose mothers were low in both closeness and control. Substance use among mother-resident girls was thus much more strongly influenced by household management than by mother-child closeness—when management was high, whether closeness was high or low, substance use was low.

Another counterintuitive result that emerged concerning parent-child closeness occurred for daughters in father residence: father-daughter closeness was associated with more school deviance among these girls. We therefore investigated patterns of parent-child closeness and parental management in relation to school deviance for father-resident girls. In this case, low levels of father-daughter closeness when coupled with high levels of management (akin to "authoritarian" parenting) were associated with the lowest levels of school deviance. High levels of management coupled with close relationships, however, were unaccountably

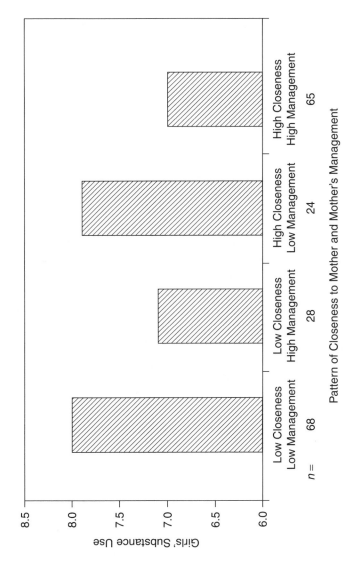

Figure 6.2 Substance use in mother-resident girls, by patterns of mother-daughter closeness and maternal household management. Means are adjusted for age of adolescent.

associated with high levels of school deviance. This finding goes sharply against the vast literature on the benefits of authoritative styles of parenting.

Thus we find that an authoritarian style of parenting may in fact discourage minor forms of deviant behavior among father-resident girls, although there is no indication in the rest of the data that such a style of parenting was otherwise particularly beneficial (with the exception noted above that an "authoritarian" style of parenting was as "good" as an "authoritative" style with respect to substance use in mother-resident girls). Furthermore, although we have argued that girls and boys may need or benefit from somewhat different kinds of parenting from mothers and fathers, we have no reason to believe that an authoritative parenting style by fathers, in and of itself, should be detrimental to girls' development. We are therefore inclined to believe that the relation between father-daughter closeness and school deviance, though significant, represents a chance occurrence among this relatively small group of father-resident girls. In other words, despite this one counterintuitive finding, we do not believe that girls living with their fathers are exempt from the overall benefits of authoritative parenting. As we noted earlier, affective closeness in the father-child relationship did have benefits with respect to daughters' substance use and use of compromise. Otherwise, father-daughter closeness was simply not a strong direct predictor of adjustment. We do not want to underestimate its indirect importance, however; as we reported in Buchanan, Maccoby and Dornbusch (1991) and emphasized above, parent-child closeness has indirect benefits for adjustment, because close relationships appear to facilitate successful parental monitoring of a child's activities.

Less Important Aspects of Family and Household

We have summarized those aspects of the family and home that had the most powerful and consistent links with adolescent adjustment. What aspects of family and home did we investigate that did not turn out to be important, at least with any consistency? First, family size. The number of children in the original family had only sporadic relations with adjustment; the relations that did emerge indicated a possible benefit to adolescents of having at least one sibling, perhaps especially for boys living with their mothers. Although research by Hetherington and colleagues (for example, Hetherington and Clingempeel, 1992) indicates that siblings are not altogether supportive of one another after their parents divorce, it is possible that simply having a sibling who is also going through the family transition is ultimately helpful. Given the sporadic nature of our results on this point, however, further investigation of this hypothesis is needed.

A second factor that did not turn out to be important with respect to adjustment was the number of hours the residential parent worked outside the home. This "nonfinding" may be important, as parents may wonder whether working outside of the home is detrimental to adolescent adjustment, especially in situations where there may not be a second parent at home. Our data suggest that the number of hours worked outside of the home by the residential parent is not directly related to adjustment problems among adolescents.

We were interested, however, in whether working hours had an indirect link to problems such as adolescent deviance, through interference with a parent's control and management of the household. We were especially interested in this question because of the finding, reported in Chapter 4, that higher levels of income were related to higher levels of deviance. We thought that higher income might be related to longer working hours, which would interfere with parenting control and management, giving adolescents more opportunities to participate in deviant activities. We found a very modest relation between more working hours and less adequate parental monitoring, but the strength of the relation varied by residence and sex of the adolescent. It was strongest for girls living with mothers in sole ($r = -.16, p \leq .05$) or dual ($r = -.68, p \leq .05$) residence, and boys living in father residence ($r = -.18$, not significant). Shorter working hours thus enhance parents' knowledge of their adolescents' activities only modestly and sporadically. Furthermore, because controlling for the number of working hours did not eliminate the link between parental income and deviance, a greater number of hours worked does not explain why adolescents of high-earning parents are more likely to be involved in deviant activities. Overall, then, our data do not indicate that the number of parental working hours, in and of itself, is important to an adolescent's well-being. Other research (for example, Galambos et al., 1995) suggests that when employment is stressful for a parent, it affects adolescent adjustment by interfering with the quality of the parent-adolescent relationship. Although one would expect working many hours per week to increase the odds of a parent feeling stressed and the resulting "spillover" effects, our data indicate that absolute number of hours worked is not the only, nor even the most important, factor to consider.

Finally, the amount of responsibility adolescents had for chores in the home, in contrast to household management more generally, had very little to do with adjustment. The only consistent finding with respect to "chores" was that adolescents who had more chores assigned were also more likely to compromise when in conflict with peers. Other research has documented that having chores and responsibility in the home contributes to prosocial behavior (Mussen and Eisenberg-Berg, 1977; Whiting and Whiting, 1975); perhaps we are seeing some small evidence of this link in our sample. We do not want to overinterpret either our scanty significant finding or our more pervasive absence of effects, however. Chores may have benefits in areas of adjustment other than those we have focused on in this study.

Dual-Resident Adolescents

Up until now, we have been considering the relation between conditions in the major residential home and adolescent adjustment. Adolescents in dual residence, by definition, spend substantial amounts of time in both parental homes, and the conditions that prevail in each home ought to have a noticeable impact on the adolescent's functioning. Perhaps the two homes have an equal impact, or perhaps one is more salient in the adolescent's life than the other. A possible approach to exploring the role of the two households would be to examine them jointly: for example, to put closeness to mother and closeness to father together into an analysis predicting adjustment. We encountered a major problem with this approach, however. The conditions in the two homes—at least as reported by the dual-resident youth—were surprisingly similar. For example, adolescents who reported high levels of conflict with one parent usually also reported high levels of conflict with the other ($r = .72$).[12] We do not know to what extent these high correlations reflect a real similarity between the two households, or to what extent they simply mean that the adolescents perceived the two households to be similar. Whichever is the case, it was not legitimate to use such highly correlated variables as independent predictors. We therefore averaged the scores of the two parents and used the average scores in examining the links between processes and adjustment. Our averaged scores tell us whether, taken together, the two households are characterized by high or low positive affect, high or low management, and so on.

Before we summarize the findings for the dual-resident adolescents, two factors are important to keep in mind: to begin with, the group is the smallest of our residential groups, having only 32 boys and 19 girls (together, approximately 10 percent of our sample). These small numbers do not allow us to consider as many household characteristics simultaneously as was possible for the other residential groups, especially when considering the two sexes separately. But the small numbers mean something else, too. Many of the families maintaining dual residence four and a half years after parental separation were "survivors," people who had managed to sustain the arrangement against the odds. Dual residence has proved to be an arrangement that is especially difficult to sustain when either parent moves (Maccoby and Mnookin, 1992), and it calls for a higher level of communication between the parents than some divorced couples are able to manage. As we saw in Chapter 3, although 4 percent of the sample had moved into dual residence during the life of the study, over 10 percent had moved out. Thus the 10 percent of the sample sustaining dual residence at Time 4 are matched by another 10 percent of adolescents who had tried it and dropped out for a variety of reasons. The "survivors" must be seen as a highly selected group of families, although we do not know all the conditions that help some families to stick with the arrangement while others leave.

The small number of adolescents who moved into dual residence after having initially lived with only one parent are also, very likely, a select group. As we reported in Chapter 3, when people adopted dual residence after initially having a sole-residence arrangement, they generally did so for positive and "child-centered" reasons. So the "choosers" as well as the "survivors" are select groups in which both parents and children may be closer and better functioning, and in which parents may be more highly motivated than other parents to have children maintain good relationships with both parents.

Having said this, we begin by considering some of the contextual factors that we examined above for sole-resident families. Table 6.3 displays the correlations between an adolescent's "worst problem" and characteristics of the context, family relationships, and household processes for dual-resident adolescents; as with the sole-resident adolescents, these correlations serve to illustrate some of the major findings we will discuss.

With regard to the adjustment of father-resident adolescents—but not mother-resident adolescents—it mattered whether they had lived in the same arrangement since their parents had separated or instead had moved at least once from one parental household to the other. The meaning of residential instability is somewhat different for dual-resident youth than it is for sole-resident youth, however. It means that an adolescent has moved from primary residence in one of the parental households into an arrangement where substantial time is spent in both households. In such cases the adolescent has not "moved out" of either parent's

Table 6.3 Correlations of selected measures of context, family relationships, and household processes with "worst problem," by sex, for dual-resident adolescents[a]

	Boys (32)	Girls (19)
Maximum *n*		
Set 1: Context		
Stability of residence	−.18	−.37
Life stress	.23	−.14
Mother's working hours (T3)[b]	.55**	−.08
Father's working hours (T3)[b]	.07	−.07
Set 2: Interparental Relations		
Maximum hostility (T3)[b]	.33	−.01
Set 3: Parent-Child Relationship (Average of Two Parents)		
Overall closeness	−.24	−.15
Child disengaged from household	−.11	.40
Parent-child conflict	.53**	.72**
Parent confides in child	.05	−.02
Child nurtures parent	.16	−.14
Set 4: Parental Control and Management (Average of Two Parents)		
Household management	−.49**	−.13

a. Correlations are controlled for adolescent's age and average parent's education.
b. Based on a sample of only one adolescent per family, selected randomly.
**$p \leq .01$.

household, but has simply begun spending more time with the parent who was formerly only visited. Thus the change may, overall, be more positive in the sense that it strengthens or renews ties to a less-seen parent. Still, any residential change may be stressful in some sense. We found, however, that residential instability had few connections with adolescent adjustment among dual-resident youth. It was not related to performance in school, or to deviance. Only in the small group of girls was there any indication of a link; for them, instability was associated with an attacking style of conflict resolution and with depression, and although not significant, the link with a higher "worst problem" score was equal in magnitude to the link among sole-resident adolescents.

Life stress, too, was less strongly associated with adjustment in the dual-resident group than it was for sole-resident adolescents. Does maintenance of a close association with both parents mean that when stresses occur in one household—the loss of a pet, illness of a family member—the impact of these events is buffered because the adolescent can rely on the resources of the other household? We do not know, but it is a plausible explanation.

It would be desirable to know about the impact of stepparents and cohabiting new partners in the two parental households where dual-resident adolescents spend their time. We have too few cases in this residential arrangement, however, to permit subdividing them according to the repartnering status of each parent and sex of the adolescent. For example, only nine dual-resident mothers and six fathers had cohabiting new partners, and only eleven and fourteen, respectively, were remarried. Combining boys and girls, it appears that the presence of a stepfather in the mother's home may have beneficial effects similar to those documented for adolescents whose sole-resident parent had a remarried new partner. But given the low numbers we hesitate to speculate further; a good understanding of the impact of repartnering by dual-resident parents must await larger samples.

Number of parental working hours was perhaps somewhat more important among dual-resident adolescents than it was among sole-resident adolescents. There were no relations between fathers' working hours and the adjustment of their dual-resident children. Mothers' working hours were more strongly related, although the linkages were sporadic. For boys, mothers' long hours were associated with higher substance use, worse grades, and a higher "worst problem" score; for girls, they were associated with an attacking conflict-resolution style.

With regard to family relationships and processes, the adjustment of the adolescents in dual residence was generally linked to the same factors that proved important for sole-resident adolescents. A high level of household management once again emerged as a predictor of several aspects of adolescent adjustment: for boys, it predicted a compromising, rather than an attacking, mode of conflict resolution, as well as high school effort and low scores on "worst problem." For girls, it predicted avoidance in conflict situations and also low levels of deviance. A close positive affective tie between the child and parents appeared from the first-order correlations to be a strong predictor of good adjustment in boys, but when it was combined in analysis with household management, it was management, not closeness, that turned out to be most important for adolescents of both sexes. Thus, as was the case for sole-resident adolescents, the closeness of the relationship between the child and parents, in and of itself, proved not to be as strong a factor as we had expected. But management of the home was important, and, at least for boys, a close relationship enabled the parent to engage in more effective management and control.[13]

The amount of conflict the dual-resident adolescents reported having with their parents was a significant predictor of adjustment, although the specific aspects of adjustment it predicted differed somewhat for the two sexes. For boys, conflict with parents predicted deviance and an attacking rather than a compromising style of conflict resolution; in other words, it predicted "acting out" behaviors. For girls, although the same associations were present, they were weaker, and the stronger associations were with higher depression and lower school effort.

When dual-resident adolescents reported that they were "disengaged" from the parental households, they were also more likely to report symptoms of depression, as were sole-resident adolescents. We noted earlier that this correlation may simply reflect the fact that disengagement is another symptom of depression. It is, perhaps, more meaningful that, for girls, disengagement was related to lowered grades.

What we thought of as role reversal—parent confiding in the child, or the child feeling the need to take care of the parent—appeared to have little or no relation to adolescent adjustment for the dual-resident group. Although an adolescent's feeling the need to "nurture" a parent was associated with some negative adjustment indices among sole-resident youth, this did not occur in the dual-resident group. Indeed, among the small group of girls, there were tendencies in the other direction—toward an association with favorable adjustment.

Interparental hostility, as reported by parents one year before the adolescent interview, was associated with higher levels of depression among dual-resident adolescents, and for the girls, with lower school grades. In general, however, the effects of interparental hostility were not as pervasive as they were for adolescents in sole residence. It is possible that a number of the parents who have managed to sustain a dual-resident arrangement have found ways of insulating the children from their interpersonal conflict (see Chapter 11).

Understanding Residence Differences in Adjustment

In Chapter 5, we reported that different residence groups differed moderately on some of the very characteristics that we now have found to be most important in predicting adolescent adjustment: the number of life stressors, residential instability, parent-child closeness, and household management (in particular, parental monitoring). Is it because father-resident adolescents have less favorable environments on these dimensions that they also report somewhat more problems in adjustment (see Chapter 4)? In general, yes. The residence differences in adjustment drop out when these aspects of the family and home context are controlled, with the exception that father residence remains associated with poorer adjustment for two subgroups of adolescents: those that have moved in with their father after initially living with their mother or in dual residence, and those from families with high levels of hostility between parents (see Buchanan, Maccoby, and Dornbusch, 1991). Otherwise, the association of father residence with a somewhat higher "worst problem" score appears to reflect somewhat lower levels of closeness and, consequently, monitoring by the residential parent, although the issue is more complex than it may appear. As we have already discussed at length, we cannot completely rule out the possibility that more difficult children (especially girls) select themselves into father custody to begin with, and are subsequently more difficult to monitor and be close to. Furthermore, as we have noted, although emotional closeness appears to facilitate monitoring and subsequently adjustment among all groups of adolescents, the associations among other components of "overall closeness" and "household management" have some peculiarities among father- and dual-resident (see note 13) girls. These peculiarities may be an artifact of the small size of these groups, or they may have to do with characteristics of the kinds of girls that select themselves into father or dual residence.

In many respects, the adjustment of adolescents in dual residence was similar to that of adolescents in mother residence (see Chapter 4). There was, however, a tendency for dual-resident adolescents to have the best scores on some adjustment measures (depression, grades, worst problem), even if the differences were not statistically significant. We reported in Buchanan, Maccoby, and Dornbusch (1991) that this advantage is not completely accounted for by lower levels of interparental conflict in these families. The question of whether the small advantage of being in dual residence has to do with the fact that dual-resident adolescents were more likely to maintain close relationships with not just one, but two, parents will be taken up in Chapter 10.

Summary

In terms of understanding adolescent adjustment after divorce, we find that contextual factors as well as interpersonal family factors are impor-

tant. Several facets of family context were strongly and consistently related to adjustment. For adolescents as a group, the more life stresses
they experienced, the worse they did on a variety of indices. This is in line
with other research pointing to the cumulative effects of multiple stresses
for adolescents (see, for example, Rutter, 1979; Simmons et al., 1987),
and points to the toll taken by a variety of emotional and physical events
such as moving, financial stress, and illness. A related finding is that
changing residences one or more times since the parental separation had
fairly strong links to negative adjustment, although only for father-resident adolescents. Moving is a stressful event. Instability of residence may
itself have negative repercussions because it necessitates adaptation on
the part of the adolescent and the family, and some adolescents and
families will not be able to adapt easily or well. The fact that instability
of residence was linked to poor adjustment only for father-resident adolescents may indicate that these families have fewer resources available
to help them cope with the stresses of this transition. It may also indicate,
however, that instability is a symptom of problems as well as a potential
cause. As we have noted, shifts into father residence are likely to occur
under more difficult circumstances more often than shifts into mother or
dual residence.

Among adolescents living primarily with either the mother or the
father, we found that when the residential parent had remarried, this was
generally a positive factor for adolescent adjustment. When the residential parent had an unmarried cohabiting new partner, however, the implications were different: in these households, adolescent adjustment (for
boys, primarily) appeared to suffer. We will explore these matters further
in Chapter 7, where we take up the issue of parents' new partners in
detail. We had too few cases to determine whether similar patterns
prevailed for adolescents in dual residence.

What about the quality of the relationship between parents? On the
basis of a solid body of literature pointing to the harmful effects of
interparental conflict on children (see Amato, 1993; Cummings and
Davies, 1994; Depner, Leino, and Chun, 1992), we expected that higher
parental conflict would be related to negative adjustment in our adolescents. And indeed, there were some indications of such a relation, especially if we used adolescents' reports of T4 parental conflict. Our earlier
measures of parental conflict derived from the reports of parents themselves did not have a great deal of predictive power. The stronger associations between interparental conflict and adolescent adjustment when
using adolescents' reports of interparental conflict indicate that a report-

ing bias may be at work: adolescents who are not doing well see the world in more negative terms and therefore report more conflict between their parents as well as a number of other negative perceptions. However, adolescent reports may measure the conflict to which the adolescent is exposed better than reports from parents. Furthermore, the level of conflict reported by the adolescents was occurring at the same time that adjustment was being measured. Although having experienced conflict in the family in the past is expected to be a negative factor in children's adjustment, we also know that children's adjustment can benefit from reductions in conflict over time. It may be that some parents have become less conflictual between the T3 and T4 interviews (and that a small number may have become more conflictual), and that T4 adolescent adjustment is thus most closely related to the level of conflict that persists at T4.

The connections we did find between interparental conflict and adolescent adjustment were stronger for boys than for girls, and stronger for father-resident adolescents than for other residential groups. Other research has indicated that boys and girls do not differ so much in whether they react to interparental conflict, but in how they react. In line with sex-role expectations, investigators have found that boys are more likely to show externalizing problems (acting out, expressing hostility) and girls are more likely to show internalizing problems (withdrawal, emotional distress). We did not find this distinction, however. Although we did find associations between interparental conflict and deviance for boys, we also found boys reporting higher depression in situations of high conflict. And there were very few instances of association between interparental conflict and depression or any other problem among mother-resident girls. Cummings and Davies (1994) suggest that the diversity of findings concerning sex differences in response to parental conflict indicates considerable variability in response within each sex, and that no conclusions can be drawn about typical patterns. Our results appear to support this assessment.

Why should conflict be more detrimental for father-resident adolescents? Perhaps because, in father residence, the more hostile parent was usually the father, while in mother and dual residence, the more hostile parent was usually the mother. It may be more stressful for children to deal with anger and hostility exhibited by fathers than by mothers.

A close, intimate relationship between the residential parent and adolescent was generally associated with positive adjustment. However, when the overall closeness of the parent-child relationship and the residential parent's level of management and control were considered jointly, it was management and control that remained important, and parent-child closeness was no longer substantially related to adolescent adjustment (with the exception of depression among mother-resident adolescents). This implies that when the parent and adolescent have a close, intimate relationship marked by warmth, trust, and joint activities, the parent is able to stay in touch with the details of the adolescent's life and feelings. In turn, being informed about the child's interests, temptations, and relationships with friends enables a parent to be effective in averting negative outcomes by providing appropriate help, guidance, and discipline (see also Buchanan, Maccoby, and Dornbusch, 1991). The importance of "management/control," however, goes beyond successful monitoring. It also involves providing a structured milieu for the child, a milieu in which daily household events are predictable and family members can adapt readily to one another's routines. Such a structured environment reduces stress and permits other aspects of daily life to unfold more smoothly. Close affective relationships between parents and adolescents may also facilitate such a milieu by enhancing mutual respect and cooperation among family members.

Disengagement from the residential home (feelings of not wanting to be there, or not feeling at home there) was one of the strongest predictors of depression. Quite likely, withdrawal from the home is a symptom of an adolescent's depressed state. There were also links between disengagement and deviant behavior, and for these relations, disengagement might facilitate deviance as well as result from it. These findings are in line with a body of evidence indicating that disengagement or detachment from the family during adolescence is not associated with healthy developmental outcomes (Hill and Holmbeck, 1986; Noller, 1994; Rutter et al., 1976). We also found conflict between parents and children to be associated with some negative outcomes, but these associations were few in number.

Finally, we found little evidence that parents' confiding in their adolescents, at least to the extent that parents in our sample engaged in this kind of behavior, is associated with negative adjustment of any kind. Extreme cases of confiding in children may be detrimental, but within the range reported here, confiding appears harmless. However, when adolescent children—for whatever reason—feel that they need to take care of a parent or feel excessively worried about a parent's well-being, there are negative consequences, at least for sole-resident adolescents. When we speak of potential detrimental results of "role reversal" among children of divorce, therefore, it appears important to differentiate between two types of situations. In one type, the parent reveals personal feelings and needs to the child, but conveys a sense of competence in coping with those feelings and needs. In the other type of situation, conversations and other behavior take place in such a way that the adolescent feels insecure about the parent's own adjustment and feels responsible for making things better.

As is evident, many of the predictors of adjustment turned out to be similar for adolescents from different residential arrangements, and for boys and girls. With a few exceptions (for example, stability of residence over time, interparental conflict, disengagement from the home), what adolescents "need" to promote healthy adjustment, or what interferes with healthy adjustment, does not vary substantially depending on the sex of the adolescent or depending on whether the primary caretaker is the mother, the father, or both parents. There were indications, however, that the benefits of what would be considered "good parenting" (high parent-child closeness and high household management) were somewhat more tenuous in father residence—particularly for girls—than they were in mother residence. For example, father-adolescent closeness did not have direct links to positive adjustment for either sex (although closeness did facilitate father's monitoring and household management), and certain aspects of low management (high levels of youth-alone decision making and late curfews) were linked with better adjustment of girls. These anomalies suggest that although sole-resident fathers—like sole-resident mothers—can enhance their adolescents' chances for positive adjustment by engaging in effective parenting practices, these practices alone are not as effective as they are in mother residence. The difference in effectiveness, of course, may be due to the different characteristics of families and adolescents that select themselves into father residence. Another possibility, indicated in Chapter 10, is that father-resident adolescents need to maintain a relatively good relationship with their nonresidential mothers as well as with their fathers in order to benefit from a good relationship with their fathers.

In summary, in this chapter we have described the major characteristics of the residential home and relationships that appear to promote adjustment of adolescents after divorce. In the next chapter, we consider in more detail the impact of a new partner in the residential home.

7

Adaptation to
New Partners

We saw in Chapter 6 that the presence of a parent's new partner was related to adolescent adjustment. Over the sample as a whole, but especially for boys, a residential parent's remarriage was associated with positive outcomes, while the presence of an unmarried new partner in the household was associated with adjustment problems. Now we look in more detail at what happens in a family when a new partner enters the scene. We proceed from the assumption that when a new partner enters the household, family processes may change in ways that range from minimal to substantial. Some changes may be conducive to positive developmental outcomes for adolescents; others may present special difficulties for them. We want to examine in detail how new partners influence family dynamics.

There is a body of research on stepfamilies, focusing on the adjustment of children in remarried as compared with single-parent or nondivorced families (Bray and Berger, 1993a; Ganong and Coleman, 1984; Hetherington and Clingempeel, 1992; Zill, 1988). These studies have not examined the possible impact of new relationships in which men and women do not remarry but date or live with new partners. Most parents who have divorced do eventually remarry. However, there is usually an extended period during which one or both parents begin to date, focusing more and more on one person as a new partner. Some of these parents choose to live with a new partner for a period of time before remarrying. This series of events unfolds more rapidly for some individuals than others, of course, and some go through several intimate new relationships before settling down. We believe the different stages of parental repartnering may have different implications for children in the family. For example, when a biological parent regularly dates someone who is not living in the home, the parent may invest a great deal of time in the dating relationship while the family derives little benefit from the relationship in terms of help with parenting or management of the household. At the same time, a dating relationship may be less disruptive to family routines than the presence of a new person living in the household whose needs and participation in family processes must be accommodated.

In this chapter we contrast three types of new-partner relationships: (1) steady dating (the parent was seeing a new partner on a regular and usually exclusive basis, and the adolescent identified this person as the boyfriend or girlfriend of the parent in question); (2) cohabiting (there was a new partner living in the same household with, but not married to, the parent); and (3) remarriage. We also compare these three new-partner situations with situations in which the parent was not dating any one person on a regular basis. Because we studied a variety of relationships that did not involve marriage, we primarily use the term "new partner" (NP) rather than "stepparent," "stepfather," or "stepmother." When we refer to "new mothers" and "new fathers," we mean any new partner, whether married or not. Although there were a few cases in our sample in which a parent was living with a same-sex roommate, we have no way of knowing whether any of these arrangements involved homosexual relationships. When we speak of repartnering, our discussion will be concerned exclusively with the formation of heterosexual couples.

We first describe the repartnering status of the two parents of adolescents in our sample. We then examine what relation the presence of a new partner has, if any, to the characteristics of the family context and processes (the quality of relationships between the residential parent and the adolescent, and the nature of parental management and control). Next we look more specifically at the relationships between adolescents and their parents' new partners and at the conditions that affect the quality of the adolescent–new partner relationship, including how accepting the adolescent is of this new partner. Finally, we look at the relation between an adolescent's acceptance of the parent's new partner and the adolescent's adjustment.

Stages of Repartnering

Our adolescents' parents, having typically been separated from their former spouses for about four and a half years, were in various stages of the repartnering process (see Table 7.1).

Table 7.1 Mothers' and fathers' repartnering status by residential arrangement[a]

Repartnering status	Adolescents' residence		
	Mother	Dual	Father
Mother's NP status	(*n* = 241)	(*n* = 41)	(*n* = 81)
No new partner	37%	46%	27%
Dating regularly	18	12	17
Cohabiting	12	17	25
Remarried	33	25	31
	100%	100%	100%
Father's NP status	(*n* = 237)	(*n* = 41)	(*n* = 81)
No new partner	25%	32%	31%
Dating regularly	16	24	15
Cohabiting	21	12	15
Remarried	38	32	39
	100%	100%	100%

a. Percentages are based on a sample of only one adolescent per family, selected randomly.

The parents who were maintaining dual residence for their children were somewhat less likely to be remarried. This is not surprising, for when parents do remarry, joint physical custody becomes harder to maintain. In part this is true because remarriage often involves residential moves that place the two parental households farther apart (Maccoby and Mnookin, 1992). Among all residential parents—that is, those who had either primary or dual physical custody of their adolescent children—about one-third had remarried, about one-third had a "steady" new partner, and about one-third were either not dating at all or dating casually.

Repartnering and Family Context and Processes

In comparing families in different stages of parental repartnering with respect to family context and processes, we had to consider that a mother's repartnering might have a different impact on the family than a father's repartnering; furthermore, the repartnering of either parent might have a different impact on boys than on girls. Being most interested in the impact of a *residential* parent's new partner, we examined the impact of the mother's new partner in households where the adolescents lived with their mothers (in primary or dual residence) separately from impact of a father's new partner in households where the adolescents lived with their fathers (in primary or dual residence),[1] and we examined whether the impact of a new partner in each of these situations was different for boys than for girls.

We also recognized that some new partners had children of their own; these children may or may not have been brought into the adolescent's household. As reported in Chapter 3, stepsiblings were present in about 7 percent of mothers' households, and about 21 percent of fathers' households (these percentages include children of cohabiting new partners as well as remarried new partners). Although our analyses in Chapter 6 of the presence of step- or half-siblings in the home indicated that there were few overall relations with adolescent adjustment, it is possible that the impact of a new partner's children varies depending on the status of the new partner or other family factors. Unfortunately, however, to subdivide our four repartnering groups according to whether stepsiblings were present would have created subgroups too small for analysis. Therefore we have not included this factor in the analyses reported below.

Family Context and Demographics

Appendix Table B.7 shows the differences between new-partner groups on selected context variables. Adolescents living in the households of remarried parents tended to be somewhat younger than those in the households of unremarried parents. Mothers who were remarried also had somewhat lower levels of education, on the average, than did those with no new partner. There was a tendency for fathers who were cohabiting to have lower levels of education than other fathers, although the differences were not statistically significant. Because of these modest differences in adolescents' age and parents' educational attainment by parents' new-partner status, we controlled statistically for adolescent age and for residential parent's education in subsequent analyses.[2]

When a new partner had taken up residence in the mother's home, she worked fewer hours than did mothers still living singly, an average of nearly ten hours per week less. Mothers' average earnings were somewhat lower too, though not significantly so. It seems likely that the economic support provided by resident new partners enables many mothers to cut back on their working hours when they wish or need to do so. Alternatively, mothers who work only part time may have more time and inclination to develop new-partner relationships.

Having a live-in new partner (whether married or cohabiting) had quite a different meaning for fathers. Their working hours were higher, and to a modest extent, their personal earnings were higher as well, when they lived with a new partner. These data indicate that the burden of providing economic support for the household shifts toward men upon remarriage (and probably upon cohabitation as well), a process that is in line with other findings concerning employment and income changes of men and women after divorce and remarriage (Duncan and Hoffman, 1985; Espenshade, 1979).

Relationships between the Two Biological Parents

It is important to know whether, when parents acquire new partners, this affects their ability to cooperate with their ex-spouses as they deal with the children of the former marriage. At Time 3, a year before our study was done, cooperation was highest between ex-spouses who had not yet begun to date (or in the case of mothers, who were only dating casually). When a parent had remarried, disengagement between the parents, as well as a conflicted co-parental relationship, was more common than when parents had either not begun to date or were in the early stages of repartnering (Maccoby and Mnookin, 1992). At Time 4, we asked the adolescents how frequently their parents talked to each other, how often they argued, how much they cooperated, and how much they agreed about rules, discipline, and privileges for the adolescent. The reports of adolescents living with their mothers (in sole or dual residence) about these matters were not related to the mother's stage of repartnering. Father-resident adolescents, however, reported that their parents argued less if their father was remarried. The amount of parental agreement over the children's regimen was not seen by these adolescents as differing according to the father's repartnering status.

There were some indications that among fathers who had remarried by T4, hostility toward the ex-spouse and interparental conflict had been high in the past. We noted in Chapter 5 that there was a history of greater interparental hostility among the families in which the adolescent children lived primarily with the father. This problem appears to be found most commonly among the father-resident families in which the father had remarried. At the time we interviewed the adolescents, however, the remarried fathers did not appear to be in either an especially conflicted or especially cooperative relationship with the children's mothers. In general, at least as far as adolescent perceptions are concerned, the presence of a parent's new partner had very little impact on the relationship between the two parents.

Mothers' Repartnering and Parent-Adolescent Relationships

Literature on preadolescents' adjustment to remarriage has suggested that girls may have particular trouble with a mother's remarriage because it threatens an especially close relationship formed between mothers and daughters during the postdivorce period. Did we find evidence of particularly close mother-daughter relationships when a mother was not remarried, or disrupted relationships after remarriage? Yes and no, respectively (see Figure 7.1). Adolescents—particularly girls—appeared to have better relationships with resident mothers when the mother did

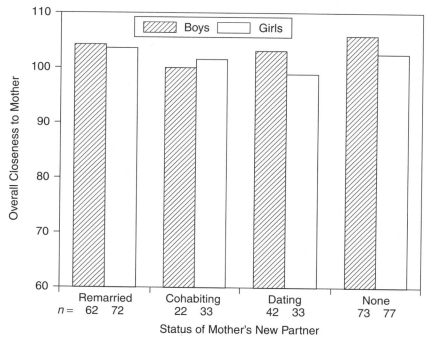

Figure 7.1 Overall closeness to mother among mother- and dual-resident adolescents, by status of mother's new partner and sex of adolescent. Means are adjusted for age of adolescent and mother's education.

not have a new partner or when she was remarried, and poorer relationships with her if she was just dating (especially for girls) or cohabiting (especially for boys). We also found that, for adolescents of both sexes, closeness to remarried mothers was greater the longer she had been remarried.

As further evidence of good mother-child relationships when the mother was remarried, disengagement from the mother's home was lowest in the remarried group, especially in contrast to the "dating only" group and, again, especially for girls. Average conflict between adolescents (both boys and girls) and their mothers was also lowest when the mother was remarried—lower than when she was either dating or cohabiting.

Remarriage *was* related to a certain level of distancing in the mother-adolescent relationship, as indicated by measures of role reversal (see Figure 7.2). For example, when a mother had a new partner living in the home, she was less likely to confide in her adolescent children. This effect was found primarily among boys.[3] It appears that a mother's new live-in partner takes the place of her children as a confidant, although daughters are less likely to lose that role than sons. Both daughters and sons were less likely to worry about their mother, or feel the need to take care of her, when the mother's new partner had moved into the household. The distancing indicated by these measures is likely to represent a move toward more healthy family functioning, although it is possible that the change is perceived negatively by the adolescents who are being "replaced."

In sum, our findings among adolescents indicate that relationships between children of both sexes and their resident mothers are as good when the mother is remarried as they are when she has no new partner. We do find, however, indications of more troubled relationships when the mother is involved in new relationships that do not involve remarriage. Relationships in families where the mother is dating seem to be especially strained; that is, these adolescents report feeling less close to their mothers, and they report higher levels of conflict and disengagement. Hetherington (1987) reported that mother-daughter conflict was elevated in families in which the mother had only been remarried for a short time (less than two years), but that the relationship improved over time. Our findings appear to fit this pattern, and extend it to show that the early stages of parental repartnering, even before remarriage, may be the most difficult for mothers and their children.

Does a mother's new partner influence adolescents' relationships with their fathers? For adolescents living with their mothers, the mother's

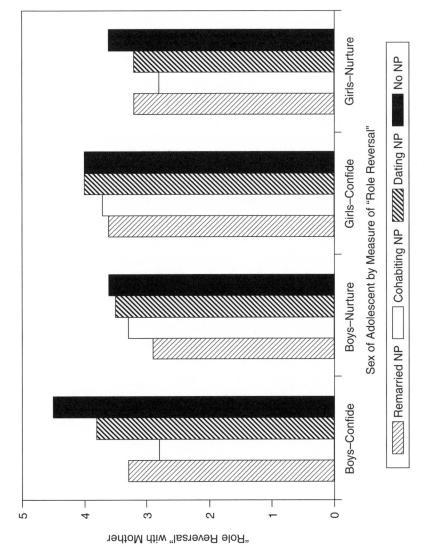

Figure 7.2 Mothers' confiding in adolescents and adolescents' feelings of nurturing mother among mother- and dual-resident adolescents, by status of mother's new partner (NP) and sex of adolescent. Means are adjusted for age of adolescent and mother's education.

remarriage did not appear to interfere with the adolescent-father bond. If anything, closeness was somewhat enhanced, at least for girls.[4] These findings are consistent with the report by Furstenberg, Morgan, and Allison (1987) that the presence of a stepfather did not hurt a child's relationship with an outside father. Our data suggest, in fact, that the father-child relationship may actually be better if the mother has remarried. Several factors may account for this finding. For example, when mothers remarry, nonresident fathers may make increased efforts to stay close to their children, in order not to be replaced. Alternatively, adolescents may idealize their nonresident fathers in contrast to their stepfathers. A further possibility is that remarriage may lessen the mother's emotional involvement with her former spouse, so that she less often undermines or derogates him in the children's presence.

Fathers' Repartnering and Parent-Adolescent Relationships

In contrast to the situation between residential mothers and their children, adolescents living with their fathers or in dual residence appeared to have the best relationships with "dating only" fathers (see Figure 7.3). Both boys and girls felt somewhat closer to fathers who were dating as compared with fathers who were remarried, cohabiting, or had no new partner.[5] Girls identified more with fathers who either had no new partner or were only dating, by comparison with those whose new partner had moved into the father's household. Fathers and adolescents also participated in more activities together when the father was only dating than in any of the other groups. The better quality of father-child relationships when the father was dating regularly was partially, but not completely, a reflection of the fact that these fathers worked fewer hours per week. Number of working hours was only modestly related to the quality of the father-adolescent relationship among father- and dual-resident adolescents. When we took the number of working hours into account, the differences between dating fathers and other fathers (in their relationships with their adolescents) were reduced slightly (and sometimes became nonsignificant), but relationships with dating fathers consistently had the highest means. So it seems that the enhanced father-child relationships between adolescents and fathers who are only dating may have other roots as well.[6] Perhaps when fathers begin to date, they make special efforts to prove to themselves and their children that their commitment to the children can continue unimpeded despite the new ties. Also, new partners who are women may be more inclined

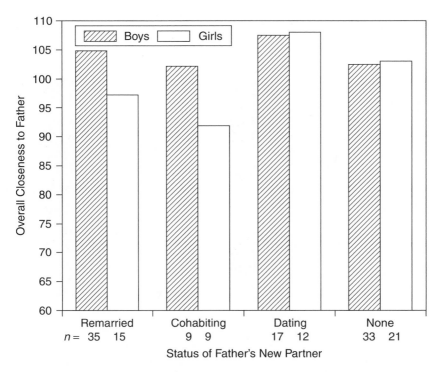

Figure 7.3 Overall closeness to father among father- and dual-resident adolescents, by status of father's new partner and sex of adolescent. Means are adjusted for age of adolescent and father's education.

than new partners who are men to become involved with the entire family even in the early stages of the relationship, and they may make greater efforts right off the bat to get to know the children. New partners who are men might require more time to become involved with the children of a new romantic interest. If this is true, a father's dating new partner would be less likely to distract the father from the children than a mother's dating new partner, and might even enhance the father's relationship with his children, at least initially. But this is speculation. We can only state that while a residential mother's dating is something of a negative factor for her children's relationship with her, a residential father's appears positive.

Fathers, like mothers, when remarried or living with someone, were less likely to confide in their adolescents (see Figure 7.4). In this case, the difference was especially apparent for daughters.[7] Stepmothers and fa-

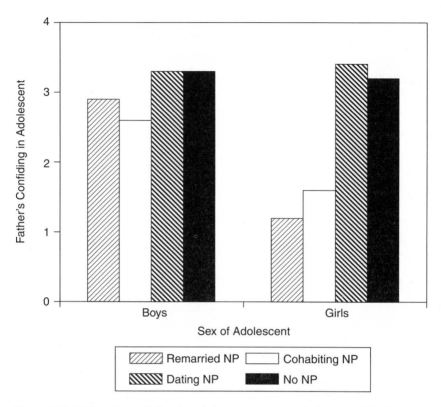

Figure 7.4 Fathers' confiding in adolescents among father- and dual-resident adolescents, by status of father's new partner and sex of adolescent. Means are adjusted for age of adolescent and father's education.

thers' new live-in girlfriends tended to take the daughter's place as the father's confidante, more than was the case for sons. This parallels the finding reported for mothers' households, where a stepfather or live-in boyfriend also tended to replace the opposite-sex adolescent as confidant.

When fathers either dated or remarried, this seemed to draw father- and dual-resident adolescents closer to their mothers. Underscoring this increased closeness, the father- or dual-resident adolescents whose fathers had remarried expressed more eagerness to see their mothers than did the adolescents in the other groups combined. The father's remarriage clearly did not weaken the relationship that father-resident children have with their mothers. If anything, the relationship with the mother was enhanced. As with mothers who remarried, this stronger connection may be the result of increased efforts by the nonresident mother not to be replaced, the adolescent's idealization of the nonresident mother in contrast to the stepmother, or a softened attitude toward the ex-spouse on the part of remarried fathers.

Parental Control and Management

In line with the hypothesis that dating a new partner may be more time consuming and present more of a distraction from the home, we found that adolescents reported lower overall household management in mother-resident homes when the mother was dating a new partner than when she was not dating at all or had remarried (see Figure 7.5a). The mother-resident households in which the mother was dating were also the least likely to have an adult home after school.

In fathers' households, the highest levels of parental control were found when the father was remarried. Remarried fathers were reported to have the highest levels of overall household management, significantly higher than fathers with no new partner or a cohabiting new partner (see Figure 7.5b).[8] Adolescents also had somewhat earlier weekend curfews and were more likely to report having an adult home after school when their father was remarried.[9] Neither the mother's nor the father's repartnering status was related to the locus of decision making with respect to issues affecting the adolescent's life. That is, parents were neither more nor less likely to be involved in joint decision making with their adolescents if they were remarried.

Other investigators have found that an additional adult in the home leads to increased supervision and better control and management of adolescents (Dornbusch et al., 1985; Hetherington, 1987). In some respects, we found this as well. The advantage, however, was limited to a remarried new partner. Cohabiting new partners did not appear to enhance household management or supervision of the adolescent for either mothers or fathers. Furthermore, a remarried new partner in the home for the mother was an advantage only in comparison with situations in which she was dating a new partner who lived elsewhere, and not in comparison with having no new partner at all. Single mothers who were not dating anyone more than casually appeared to monitor their adolescents and manage their homes as successfully as did remarried mothers. In contrast, a residential father's monitoring and management did benefit

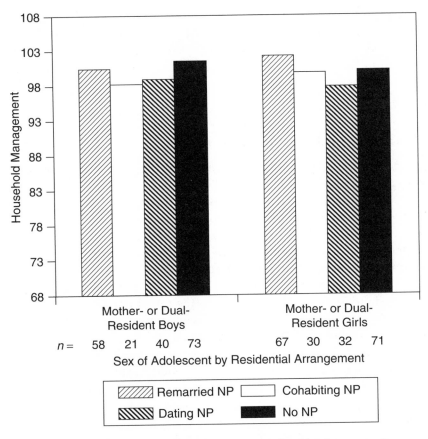

Figure 7.5a Household management by status of mother's new partner (NP) and sex of adolescent, for mother- and dual-resident adolescents. Means are adjusted for age of adolescent and mother's education.

from the presence of a remarried new partner in comparison with having no new partner.

Adolescents' Acceptance of Parents' New Partners

We focus now on the kind of relationships that adolescents developed with their residential parent's new partner. We assessed these relationships in several ways. First, the adolescents were asked a battery of questions about closeness to, and joint activities with, their parent's new partner; these questions were the same as those asked about the adoles-

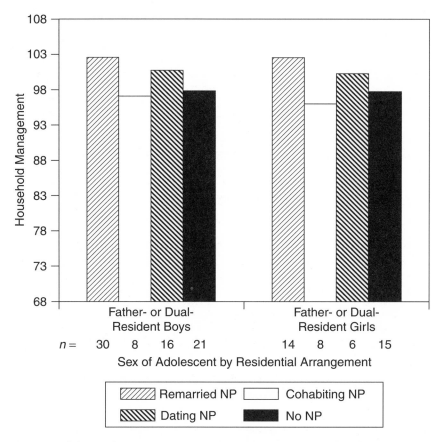

Figure 7.5b Household management by status of father's new partner (NP) and sex of adolescent, for father- and dual-resident adolescents. Means are adjusted for age of adolescent and father's education. Numbers are based on a sample of only one adolescent per family, selected randomly. See note 8.

cents' relationships with their biological parents. For both fathers' and mothers' new partners, the average level of closeness or activities reported by the adolescents was close to the mid-range of the scale (see Table 7.2). But more important, there was variability in the scores: some adolescents reported being very close to their parents' new partners; others reported hardly any intimacy at all. Similarly, some shared no joint activities with the new person, while some shared as many activities with the new partner as they did with the residential parent.

Table 7.2 Average closeness to, and joint activities with, parents' new partners[a]

Relationship measure	Mother's new partner	Father's new partner
Closeness to (range: 9–45)[b]	28.6	28.1
Number of joint activities with (range: 0–8)	3.3	3.4
Maximum *n*	(259)	(95)

a. These reports include only the adolescents' reports concerning their *residential* parent's new partners (in other words, the partners of primary- or dual-resident parents). Subjects whose residential parents did not have a new partner are excluded.

b. Ranges are possible, not actual, ranges.

In addition to the questions concerning closeness and joint activities, we asked two questions specifically focused on relationships with parents' new partners. The first was meant to examine the role of the new partner in the adolescent's life: "Is your (parent's new partner) mostly like a father (mother) to you? Like a friend? Just another person? Or someone you wish weren't part of your life?" The second inquired about the adolescent's willingness to accord authority to the parent's new partner: "In general, do you think your (parent's new partner) has the right to set up rules or tell you what you can or can't do?" Figure 7.6 displays the distribution of responses to each of these questions.

As Figure 7.6 shows, only about one-fourth of the adolescents accorded the parent's new partner full parental status. But at the other extreme, few adolescents appeared hostile or resentful toward their parent's new partner. Most commonly, the new partner was seen as a kind of friend. With regard to adolescents' willingness to accept the authority of a residential parent's new partner, a little less than half of the adolescents unequivocally rejected the idea of a parent's new partner exercising authority, answering our question about whether the new partner had the right to make rules or tell them what to do by saying simply, "No way!" or "Definitely not." Or as one late-adolescent boy elaborated more fully: "I don't think so, because . . . he's not really my father. I don't know, he's around a lot, but I think he just feels like kind of a friend. Usually I just ignore him . . . I would rather not have him set up things for me to do. My parents could pretty much take care of that."

But about as many adolescents as denied the new partner parental authority willingly accorded authority to the new partner. Willingness to accept the new partner's authority appeared to be somewhat more com-

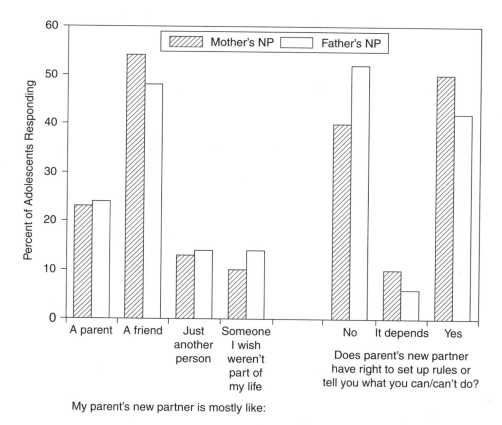

Figure 7.6 Percentage of adolescents indicating different levels of acceptance of residential (sole or dual) parent's new partner (NP). Adolescents whose parents did not have a new partner are excluded from this graph.

mon in cases where a parent and child had moved into a new partner's already-established home, as opposed to cases where the new partner had moved into the adolescent and parent's existing household. Here are some comments illustrating the bases on which adolescents accepted the new partner's authority:

(Early-adolescent[10] boy in mother residence): "When we bought our house it was pretty crappy; now it's really nice. He does a lot around the house, and he helped me fix up the house, so I guess he can tell me what to do."

(Late-adolescent boy in mother residence): "He doesn't do it that often, but yeah, because it's for my own good."

(Early-adolescent boy in mother residence): "I like him a lot and he's a friend and if he told me not to do this, no problem. I'd decide not to 'cause he knows more about it than I would."

(Mid-adolescent girl in father residence): "Well kinda, yeah, 'cause . . . she's an adult, and she's older, and I gotta, you know, respect what she says."

(Mid-adolescent girl in father residence): "Yeah, I think [new mother is] . . . a caring person . . . I know she cares about me."

(Early-adolescent boy in father residence): "Yeah, 'cause it's her home."

A small number of adolescents found our question difficult to answer, and expressed ambivalence or reservations concerning a new partner's right to authority. Less than 10 percent said that the new partner's rights depended on other factors, such as the type of rule or the extent to which that new partner contributed to the home financially. For example, one boy said explicitly that he would obey his stepfather on a family trip provided that the stepfather financed the outing. The following quotes further illustrate some of the ambivalence that was expressed:

(Late-adolescent girl): "No, but yes, because he pays for everything. I would like to say no, but in my mind I know 'yes.' I don't agree, no, that he should be able to give me rules on my life, but yes, to give me rules of the house and stuff like that." (Interviewer: "Would you say yes or no?") "I'm going to go for *no.*"

(Late-adolescent girl): "I think she has the right because this is her house—her and my father's house. If she has to help pay the bills and if she does most of the work around the house, but other than that, she really, I don't think she has any business at all. I mean I know she cares about me." (Interviewer: "So you're saying you don't think she should set up rules?") "It really depends on what situation. If it's something that I really don't care about, then fine; she can say whatever she wants. Usually she'll say it, and I'll just do whatever I'm going to do anyway."

Certain rights were accorded to a stepparent or cohabiting new partner simply because he or she was a member of the household and therefore deserved consideration in matters such as noise or clean-up. For example, one boy said: "Well, I say he has a right to say what time I come in at night, because, you know, he lives in the same house and he has to get up in the morning to go to work, and he doesn't want me coming in at one in the morning. I can see that. But that's about it: just curfew." Another boy said he refrained from practicing on his trumpet when his mother's new partner was home because the partner did not like the noise.

But a right to set rules of the household often did not extend to rights to control the adolescent's personal life and decisions. Certain areas of decision making were set aside as areas over which only the natural parents had rights, areas that were "not the new partner's place" to be involved. And adolescents often voiced acceptance of a new partner's authority if it was derived from or in line with the natural parent's authority ("It's okay if he checks with my mom first"), or voiced problems with authority that differed from that of a biological parent ("If my dad lets me do it, [my stepfather] should let me do it too").

As Figure 7.6 indicates, there were few differences in relationships with stepfathers (or mothers' boyfriends) compared with stepmothers (or fathers' girlfriends), a finding that is somewhat at odds with previous findings that relationships between children and stepmothers are more troubled than those between stepfathers and children (Furstenberg, 1987; Ihinger-Tallman, 1988). Adolescents in our sample were somewhat more willing to accept rule-making from the mother's new partner than the father's, but on the whole it made little difference whether the new partner was in the mother's or the father's household. More striking is the variation within each residential group, with some adolescents readily accepting their parents' new partners and forming close relationships with them, while other adolescents remained distant or even hostile.

Factors Related to Acceptance of New Partners

In this section we treat all measures of the relationship with and acceptance of the new partner as continuous measures. In other words, adolescents who said "Yes," they would accept a new partner's authority, were considered high in acceptance, and adolescents who answered "No" were considered low in acceptance. Those adolescents who said "It depends" were considered moderate in acceptance. With regard to the question about the new partner's role, answering that the new partner was "like a parent" indicated high acceptance and, at the other end, answering that the new partner was "someone I wish weren't a part of my life" indicated low acceptance.

Table 7.3 Correlations of new-partner acceptance with age of adolescent[a]

Measure of acceptance	Mother's new partner	Father's new partner
Closeness to NP	−.26****	−.23*
Joint activities with NP	−.34****	−.18+
Acceptance of NP's authority	−.34****	−.25*
NP's perceived role	−.25	−.18+
Maximum *n*	(260)	(95)

a. These reports include only the adolescents' reports concerning *residential* parent's new partners (in other words, the partners of primary- or dual-resident parents). Subjects whose residential parents did not have a new partner are excluded.

+p ≤ .10   *p ≤ .05.   ****p ≤ .0001.

Age and Sex of the Adolescent

Age was a major factor in the adolescent's acceptance of a parent's new partner. Younger adolescents accepted a parent's new partner more readily than did older ones, and this was true of both new fathers and new mothers (see Table 7.3).

Although we did not assess how willing our adolescents were to accept the authority of their natural parents, it is reasonable to expect that this, too, would decline with increasing age. We did assess closeness to both residential mothers and residential fathers, and there were similar age differences in closeness to parents and parents' new partners. The age differences in acceptance of a new partner reflect, no doubt, a general developmental trend of decreasing involvement with and increasing independence from adults in general, and are not necessarily specific to parents' new partners.

There has been some speculation, however, that early adolescence is the time of greatest resistance to new partners, on the grounds that the issues of adolescent sexuality and autonomy are emerging strongly at this time, and that these new developments create resistance that is moderated as the adolescent becomes more mature. Evidence from other research suggests that the entry of a new partner is, in fact, more difficult during early adolescence than at younger ages (Hetherington, 1993). In contrast, our findings suggest that new partners entering a family may have an advantage in forming positive relationships if the children are in early, rather than later, adolescence. There are limitations in our ability to draw this conclusion, however. First, although all new partners in our sample had entered the family less than four years before the time we talked with the adolescents, there was variability concerning when in that four-year period the new partner "arrived." Our results simply suggest that early adolescents are more accepting than are older adolescents of new partners, and do not speak directly to when it might be most difficult for a new partner to establish a relationship with the adolescent. Second, we assessed only limited aspects of the adolescent–new partner relationship; for example, we do not know how much active conflict took place between the adolescent and the new partner. It may be that early adolescents experience more conflict with parents' new partners than do older adolescents, whereas older adolescents experience less conflict but are more emotionally distant from the new partner. These possible relations need more explicit attention in future research.

With regard to the sex of the adolescent, we expected girls to be less accepting of both new fathers and new mothers. With regard to mother-resident children, a growing body of research suggests that girls put up more resistance than boys to the entry of their mothers' new partners into the family (see, for example, Bray and Berger, 1993a; Clingempeel, Brand, and Ievoli, 1984; Hetherington, 1993; Hetherington and Clingempeel, 1992; Hetherington, Cox, and Cox, 1982; Santrock et al., 1982). Hetherington has suggested that, at least among preadolescents, girls become closer than boys to their mothers during the postdivorce period, and therefore find the appearance of a stepfather or mother's boyfriend more threatening and more disruptive. Furthermore, boys are believed to be more welcoming of a new male role model or male companion in the family. Girls in turn are believed to be less accepting of their father's new partner, although for somewhat different reasons. Girls are thought to have stronger feelings of loyalty toward their biological mothers, thus being more likely to resent a stepmother for trying to "take the place" of the biological mother. It is also possible that, when fathers are not dating or married to a new partner, some girls fill a traditional female role in their fathers' households—cooking, shopping, cleaning, or entertaining. Even though household chores can be something teenagers would rather avoid, managing a household is nevertheless an adultlike role that conveys a certain status, so these girls may feel displaced when a father's new partner takes over these duties. We have also seen that the entrance of a new partner into the father's home takes the daughter's place as a confidante to some extent. Adolescent daughters who have enjoyed this status with their fathers may begrudge losing it.

Table 7.4 Acceptance of parents' new partners, by sex of adolescent[a]

Measure of acceptance	Mother's new partner			Father's new partner		
	Boys	Girls	*t*	Boys	Girls	*t*
Closeness to NP	29.7	27.6	+	29.6	25.6	*
Joint activities with NP	3.7	3.0	*	3.7	2.7	*
Acceptance of NP's authority	1.2	.97	*	.93	.86	n.s.
NP's perceived role	3.0	2.8	n.s.	3.0	2.6	+

a. These reports include only the adolescents' reports concerning *residential* parent's new partners (in other words, the partners of primary- or dual-resident parents). Subjects whose residential parents did not have a new partner are excluded.

$^+p \leq .10.$ $^*p \leq .05.$ n.s. = not significant.

In line with our expectations, boys accepted new partners somewhat more readily than did girls (see Table 7.4), although the differences were strongest for emotional closeness and shared activities, and less strong or consistent for acceptance of authority. In fact, with respect to accepting the authority of the mother's new partner, the sex difference was limited to early adolescents (see Figure 7.7),[11] suggesting that the age decline in acceptance of authority noted earlier occurs earlier for girls than for boys. Thus our results confirm previous findings comparing boys' and girls' relationships with new partners, although the mechanisms accounting for the differences are still in need of illumination. After all, mother-resident girls in our sample were not closer to their mothers than were mother-resident boys; why, then, would they view a new father more negatively? And if boys are eager to have a male companion in mother-resident homes, why do girls in father-resident homes not feel the same way about new mothers? Such questions are not answered by our study.

New-Partner Status

Did an adolescent's acceptance of a new partner depend on whether the new couple was remarried, cohabiting, or merely dating regularly? We have not been able to locate previous studies that examine this question, and we can imagine scenarios that would predict different outcomes. Remarriage may confer legitimacy on a parent's new partner; however, it also makes that partner's presence more permanent, more intrusive, and hence possibly more unwelcome to the adolescent. And it is not obvious whether

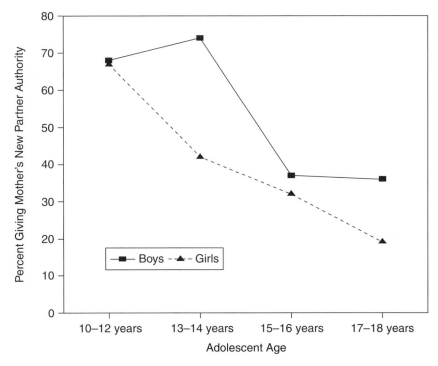

Figure 7.7 Acceptance of the authority of mother's new partner among mother- and dual-resident adolescents by age and sex of adolescent.

a cohabiting new partner would be more or less acceptable to an adolescent than someone the parent is merely dating. Regular dating partners are presumably less threatening in terms of their potential to "replace" a nonresident parent, but they may take a lot of the residential parent's time. The adolescent also has fewer opportunities to interact with and become attached to someone who is not living in the household.

We found that, especially in mothers' homes, remarried new partners gained the most acceptance from adolescents (see Table 7.5). The advantage of remarriage was especially apparent when it came to acceptance of authority. When asked about her mother's new boyfriend's right to exercise authority, an early-adolescent girl put it succinctly: "When he gets married to Mom, yes. [Interviewer: Now?] No." Furthermore, adolescents living with their mothers accorded somewhat more acceptance to a mother's boyfriend if he was living in the household than if he and the mother were merely dating.

Table 7.5 New-partner status and adolescents' acceptance[a]

Measure of acceptance	A. Acceptance of mother's new partner				
	Dating (D)	Cohabiting (C)	Remarried (R)	F	Significant differences
Closeness to NP	25.2	27.2	30.9	10.69****	R > C, D
Joint activities with NP	2.6	3.5	3.7	6.65***	R, C > D
Acceptance of NP's authority	.57	.94	1.4	26.48****	R > C > D
NP's perceived role	2.8	2.9	3.0	1.87	
Maximum *n*	(71)	(55)	(133)		

Measure of acceptance	B. Acceptance of father's new partner				
	Dating (D)	Cohabiting (C)	Remarried (R)	F	Significant differences
Closeness to NP	27.8	25.9	29.1	.86	
Joint activities with NP	3.3	2.6	3.7	1.81	
Acceptance of NP's authority	.38	.68	1.27	9.21***	R > C, D
NP's perceived role	2.9	2.5	2.9	1.37	
Maximum *n*	(27)	(18)	(50)		

a. Means are adjusted for age and sex of adolescent. These reports include only the adolescents' reports concerning *residential* parent's new partners (in other words, the partners of primary- or dual-resident parents). Subjects whose residential parents did not have a new partner are excluded.

***$p \leq .001$.　****$p \leq .0001$.

Acceptance of a father's new partner was less strongly related to marital status than was acceptance of a mother's new partner, and there were indications that adolescents' closeness to and activities with a father's new partner might be lowest for cohabiting girlfriends. But the major finding is that acceptance and positive feelings were consistently highest when a remarriage had occurred.

Was the greater acceptance of remarried new partners explained by the fact that the adolescents had known them longer? Not entirely. The differences associated with remarriage remained even if we controlled for the length of time the parent and new partner had been living together or dating. From the adolescents' standpoint, it appears that marriage confers legitimacy on a parent's relationship, giving the new partner a right to greater consideration and respect. Remarriage also probably gives the adolescent some confidence that the parent's new partnership will last, so that the adolescent can feel free to form an attachment with less fear of the loss often associated with more temporary liaisons. At the same time, we should not ignore the possibility that parents may be more likely to remarry if the new partner is someone the children can readily accept.

Closeness to the Residential Parent

Preadolescent children who have a close and involved relationship with a custodial parent are thought to have more difficulty accepting a stepparent (Furstenberg and Spanier, 1984; Hetherington, 1993). It would be understandable if children, including adolescents, who were closely bonded with a parent were jealous of his or her new partner and fearful that the adults' new love life would interfere with the close parent-child relationship. Yet it seems that adolescents, who typically want more independence from parents than do younger children, would be less likely to resent a new partner's intrusion in terms of its effect on the amount of time their parent spends with them. Thus, although previous work suggested that we might find that greater closeness between the adolescent and the resident parent would be related to less closeness to or acceptance of the new partner, we were not sure that those predictions would apply to our adolescent sample.

In contrast, there were many reasons to expect a positive correlation between adolescents' closeness to their residential parents and closeness to and acceptance of parents' new partners. For one thing, certain children—by virtue of temperament or training—are easier for everyone to get along with, and both natural parents and stepparents undoubtedly respond more positively to a pleasant and cooperative child than to a difficult and resistant one. Some adolescents are also undoubtedly more open than others are to the formation of positive relations with new adults, depending perhaps on their attachment history or other interpersonal experiences that have made them more or less wary of attachments. A strong bond with the residential parent may signify a positive interpersonal history that presumably could foster a child's readiness for new relationships. Furthermore, a parent who has a close relationship with a child also has a better chance of providing direct, concurrent support for the budding relationship between the child and the new partner.

Table 7.6 Correlations between closeness to parent and acceptance of parent's new partner[a]

Measure of acceptance	Closeness to mother		Closeness to father	
	Boys	Girls	Boys	Girls
Closeness to NP	.58****	.62****	.47***	.62****
Joint activities with NP	.26**	.36****	.11	.26
Acceptance of NP's authority	.05	.35****	.18	.39*
NP's perceived role	.24**	.28***	.26*	.41*
Maximum *n*	(122)	(138)	(59)	(36)

a. These reports include only the adolescents' reports concerning *residential* parents and their new partners (in other words, primary- or dual-resident parents and their new partners). Subjects whose residential parents did not have a new partner are excluded. Correlations are adjusted for age of adolescent.

*p ≤ .05.   **p ≤ .01.   ***p ≤ .001.   ****p ≤ .0001.

Our findings primarily support these latter hypotheses (see Table 7.6). The overall pattern of results suggests that the closer the relationship between an adolescent and a residential parent, the more likely the adolescent was to have a close relationship with the parent's new partner and the more likely the adolescent was to accept that person's authority. Our evidence certainly did not suggest that the two relationships were at odds with each other. The relation between closeness to the residential parent and acceptance of his or her new partner's authority was greater for girls than for boys in some instances, especially among children in father residence (the correlation between closeness to a father and acceptance of the authority of a new mother was .69 for father-resident girls and .16 for father-resident boys).[12]

Closeness to the Nonresidential Parent

The entry of a residential parent's new partner into an adolescent's life may affect the adolescent's relationship with the nonresidential parent. In turn, the kind of relationship the adolescent has with the nonresidential parent may influence that adolescent's acceptance of the residential parent's new partner. For example, children who are very close to the nonresidential parent may experience more loyalty conflicts and more resistance to having the residential parent's new partner "take the place" of the nonresidential parent. Presumably, too, the more time an adolescent spends with the nonresidential parent, the more opportunities there would be for loyalty conflicts to be activated. In addition, children who develop close relationships with the residential parent's new partner may become less dependent on their relationship with the nonresidential parent; indeed, the new partner may in some ways begin to take the place of the nonresidential biological parent (Bray and Berger, 1990, 1993b). Alternatively, as we argued above, some children—by virtue of temperament, social maturity, or family contexts that are more conducive to positive interaction—may have good relationships with most of the significant adults in their life, while others may have good relationships with few. Given these different predictions, we were not sure what to expect with regard to the relation between closeness to the nonresidential parent and closeness to and acceptance of the residential parent's new partner.

Contrary to speculation that greater amounts of time spent with a non-residential parent would interfere with a good relationship with the residential parent's new partner, and contrary to evidence from work by others (Cherlin and Furstenberg, 1994), we found that the amount of visitation an adolescent had with the nonresidential parent had no association with the nature of the relationship between an adolescent and the residential parent's new partner. This was true whether we were considering the effect of contact with a nonresidential father or a nonresidential mother.

Similarly, the various measures of adolescents' acceptance of their parents' new partners were almost entirely unrelated to the adolescent's closeness to the nonresidential parent (see Table 7.7). For girls living with their mothers, there was a small tendency for those who were close to the mother's new partner to be close to their nonresidential fathers as well (a relation in the opposite direction from what might have been predicted from considerations of loyalty conflicts), but other indicators showed no impact of closeness with nonresidential fathers on relationships with mothers' new partners.

In fathers' households, there were no statistically significant relations between closeness to the nonresidential mother and an adolescent's acceptance of the father's new partner. We should note, however, that three out of the four correlations for father-resident girls have a negative sign, and two of these are moderate in magnitude.[13] These data hint, then, that strong ties between a girl and her nonresidential mother may interfere somewhat with accepting a stepmother or father's girlfriend. This observation is speculative, of course, given the small number of father-resident girls who have new mothers; however, other authors have hypothesized just such a link (Clingempeel and Segal, 1986).

Table 7.7 Correlations between closeness to nonresidential parents and acceptance of residential parent's new partner for sole-resident adolescents[a]

Measure of acceptance	Closeness to nonresidential father		Closeness to nonresidential mother	
	Boys	Girls	Boys	Girls
Closeness to NP	.08	.29**	.07	−.05
Joint activities with NP	−.04	.03	−.17	.01
Acceptance of NP's authority	−.13	.13	−.09	−.20
NP's perceived role	−.06	.04	.08	−.32
Maximum *n*	(96)	(119)	(39)	(22)

a. Subjects whose residential parents did not have a new partner are excluded. Correlations are adjusted for age of adolescent.

**p ≤ .01.

Does the fact that we generally find adolescents' relationships with their nonresidential parents and residential "new parents" to be independent mean that we must abandon our hypothesis that "nice" children tend to have good relationships with everyone? Yes—or at least, the hypothesis must be modified. It now seems more reasonable to say that an adolescent's relationships with adults may be similar within a household. Each household may elicit different attitudes and behaviors on the part of the adolescent, that then influence all relationships within that home. As one example, consider an adolescent who strongly resists the presence of her mother's new partner. If that adolescent is rude, defiant, or cold toward the new partner, it will become difficult for the mother to maintain a good relationship with that adolescent. Thus low acceptance of the mother's new partner could very well weaken the child's closeness to her mother. The nonresidential father, in contrast, is not involved in the child's interactions with the mother or her new partner. Nor must he deal with the child's day-to-day behavior in the other household. Thus the adolescent's relationship with the nonresidential father can apparently continue, independent of the relationships in the other home.

Conflict between Biological Parents

In studies of divorce, little attention has been paid to the impact of discord between the biological parents on the kind of relationship a child develops with a parent's new partner. The possible nature of such a connection seems obvious enough: the left-over hostility between formerly married couples is often heavily tinged with jealousy and anger concerning the former spouse's new sexual relationships. If these feelings are conveyed to the child in the form of disparagement of the former spouse's new partner, it ought to become more difficult for the child to accept this new partner. We did not have information concerning the extent to which the conflict between former spouses centered on new partners, although certainly in some cases it was a fundamental problem. We found, however, no relations between interparental hostility, discord, or cooperation and the quality of adolescents' relationships with their parents' new partners.

Acceptance of New Partners and Adolescent Adjustment

Given that closeness to or acceptance of the new partner was strongly and positively related to an adolescent's closeness to the residential parent, we controlled for adolescents' closeness to their residential parent when we examined the associations between adolescents' acceptance of new partners and adolescents' adjustment. We wanted to know what impact a good relationship with the new partner might have above and beyond the impact of a good relationship with the residential parent.

Overall, we found sporadic relations between acceptance of the new partner and adolescent adjustment. Among the more promising relations, more acceptance was related to less depression/anxiety, less overall deviance, less school deviance, less severe "worst problem" scores, and more compromise in conflict resolution. It was also related to a measure of adjustment that we have not introduced yet: unstructured time use. Adolescents who were close to and accepting of parent's new partners were less likely to spend time just "hanging out" (as opposed to engaging in planned, organized activities). "Unstructured time use" has not emerged in our other analyses as a uniquely interesting aspect of adolescent adjustment, above and beyond the level of deviance. It did, however, emerge as particularly interesting in some of the subsequent analyses involving acceptance of the new partner, which is why we mention it here.

We reported in Chapter 6 that the presence of a parent's new partner in the adolescent's household was one of the stronger predictors of adolescent adjustment, at least among sole-resident adolescents. The presence of a stepparent was a positive factor for both sexes and in both parental households, although the relations were somewhat stronger and more numerous for boys than for girls. The presence of an unmarried parental partner, in contrast, was often a negative factor, again, especially for boys. In this chapter, we have seen that remarried new partners were also more accepted by adolescents than were unmarried ones. Thus we were interested in the extent to which the greater acceptance of remarried new partners explained the better adolescent adjustment in situations of remarriage.

To explore this question, we chose a subset of our adjustment measures to focus on: compromise in conflict resolution, school deviance, overall deviance, "worst problem," and unstructured time use. We chose this particular set of adjustment indices because each was related to the presence of a stepparent for all or most adolescents (as reported in Chapter 6), and each was related to acceptance of the authority of either the mother's or the father's new partner.

For each of these adjustment measures, we conducted a regression analysis in three steps. In the first step, the adjustment measure was predicted with the adolescent's closeness to his or her residential parent and the adolescent's age and sex. We needed to control for these three variables because each was related both to acceptance of the new partner and to adolescent adjustment. In the second step, we added a variable reflecting whether the residential parent (sole or dual) had remarried. Finally, in the third step, we added the adolescent's acceptance of the authority of residential parents' new partners.[14] What we wanted to see was whether adding the "acceptance of authority" measure would reduce or eliminate the relation between remarriage and adolescent adjustment. If so, we would have evidence that the level of acceptance of the new partner "mediated" or explained the link between marital status and adolescent adjustment. In other words, we would know that one primary reason that adolescents were doing better in situations of remarriage was because they were more likely to accept the new partner under such circumstances.

Was the association between remarriage and adjustment due to remarried new partners' having greater acceptance? In most instances, yes.[15] The results reported in Table 7.8 indicate that, for children living with their mothers or in dual residence, the greater acceptance of the mother's new partner's authority that occurs with remarriage accounts for at least some of the improved adolescent adjustment in situations of remarriage. Remarriage in and of itself, apart from its association with greater acceptance of the new partner, has a weaker (and in most cases, nonsignificant) relation to adjustment.

Table 7.8 Stepwise analyses of remarriage and new-partner acceptance in relation to selected aspects of adolescent adjustment[a]

Variables entered at each step	Mother as residential parent (mother and dual residence) (Maximum $n = 260$)	Father as residential parent (father and dual residence) (Maximum $n = 95$)
Compromise		
Step 1. Closeness to residential parent	.19**	.03
Step 2. Closeness to residential parent	.16**	.04
Residential parent remarried	.16**	.18+
Step 3. Closeness to residential parent	.14*	−.01
Residential parent remarried	.11+	.12
Acceptance of NP's authority	.13+	.14
School Deviance		
Step 1. Closeness to residential parent	−.15**	.13
Step 2. Closeness to residential parent	−.14*	.13
Residential parent remarried	−.05	−.12
Step 3. Closeness to residential parent	−.12*	.18+
Residential parent remarried	−.01	−.05
Acceptance of NP's authority	−.12+	−.16+
Deviance		
Step 1. Closeness to residential parent	−.17***	−.12
Step 2. Closeness to residential parent	−.16**	−.12
Residential parent remarried	−.10+	−.10
Step 3. Closeness to residential parent	−.13*	−.08
Residential parent remarried	−.04	−.03
Acceptance of NP's authority	−.17**	−.15+
Worst Problem		
Step 1. Closeness to residential parent	−.22***	−.11
Step 2. Closeness to residential parent	−.20***	−.12
Residential parent remarried	−.11+	−.14
Step 3. Closeness to residential parent	−.18**	−.10
Residential parent remarried	−.06	−.12
Acceptance of NP's authority	−.14*	−.04
Unstructured Time		
Step 1. Closeness to residential parent	−.01	.10
Step 2. Closeness to residential parent	.01	.10
Residential parent remarried	−.12*	−.07
Step 3. Closeness to residential parent	.04	.21+
Residential parent remarried	−.05	.08
Acceptance of NP's authority	−.21**	−.33**

a. The entries in this table are standardized regression coefficients (betas). Age and sex of adolescents were entered in each step of the analyses, although their betas are not shown here.
+$p \leq .10$.　　*$p \leq .05$.　　**$p \leq .01$.　　***$p \leq .001$.　　****$p \leq .0001$.

For adolescents living with their fathers, the evidence is weaker. There is some evidence for the mediation hypothesis with respect to school deviance, overall deviance, and unstructured time use: the relations between remarriage and these aspects of adjustment, though not significant to begin with, were reduced when acceptance of the new mother's authority was controlled, and acceptance of the new mother predicted lower levels of these problems. In the case of compromising as a means of conflict resolution, we could also make a case for mediation, although the evidence is even less strong.[16] There is no evidence that the beneficial effects of a father's remarriage on adolescents' "worst problem" result from the greater acceptance of the authority of that remarried partner. In sum, evidence that the beneficial effects of remarriage were due to adolescents' greater acceptance of a remarried new mother was less strong than it was for new fathers, but there were still hints of this effect.

The fact that adolescents spent less time simply "hanging out" when they accepted the authority of a residential parent's new partner was not predicted, but it is interesting. We originally had thought of unstructured time as a kind of way station to deviance. And indeed, more unstructured time use was significantly related to higher levels of deviance. Spending a lot of time "hanging out" might reflect either boredom or a lack of goals, either of which could increase vulnerability to the influence of deviant peers. As popular wisdom has it, the devil finds work for idle hands.

With regard to the reasons that acceptance of a new partner should protect against unstructured use of time, our first hypothesis was that children must be spending more time in joint activities with a new partner whom they accept, and so would have less time to spend in unplanned drifting. We found, however, that, although adolescents who accepted a new partner did spend more time in joint activities with that partner, the amount of such joint activity was not related to the amount of unstructured time (nor to the adolescent's level of deviance). Something else about the acceptance of the new partner is important, over and above the time spent with that new partner. Another possibility is that adolescents who accept the authority of this new adult are respectful of authority in general, and are therefore more likely to use their time in productive ways—ways that are encouraged and esteemed by parents, teachers, and other adults—and less likely to get into trouble. At present, all we can say is that having an accepted new adult partner is related to enhanced family bonds, and it may help to build barriers against deviance.

Summary

One of our most important findings is that the impact of a new partner on family functioning depends on whether that partner is married to the residential parent or is simply cohabiting or regularly dating that parent. In addition, the various forms of repartnering had somewhat different relations with family processes depending on whether we were talking about mother's homes or father's homes.

In homes in which the mother had sole or dual physical custody, remarriage was generally associated with positive family functioning. For example, when the mother was remarried, adolescents were closer to her, and there were higher levels of household management and control, in comparison with other forms of repartnering. On these aspects of family functioning, however, remarriage was no better or worse than having no new partner. The benefits of remarriage over not dating at all came primarily in the domain of "role reversal." Mothers who were remarried—in addition to those who had a cohabiting new partner—were less likely to confide in their adolescents (especially sons), and adolescents of these mothers were less likely to feel worried about their mother. Adolescents did not perceive a mother's remarriage to have any impact on the relationship between the biological parents. Furthermore, her remarriage did not appear to interfere in any way with the adolescent's relationship with the nonresidential biological father.

A father's remarriage also brought about some advantages in terms of family processes. In particular, the level of management and control in his home was highest when he was remarried. And remarried fathers, like remarried mothers, were less likely to confide in their adolescent children, especially their daughters. But adolescents were less close to remarried fathers than they were to fathers who were only dating or who did not yet have a regular new partner. Although we do not fully understand the reason, adolescents had the best quality of relationship with fathers who were regularly dating someone. This finding needs replication and more in-depth study and analysis in order to uncover what in these situations is beneficial for the adolescent.

Like mother-resident adolescents, father-resident adolescents did not become more distant from their nonresidential parent when the residential parent remarried. On the contrary, father-resident adolescents whose fathers were remarried were even closer to their mothers than were other adolescents. This finding, together with the slight evidence that father-resident girls were less likely to accept a new mother when their relationship with their own mother was close, provides some potential support for the view that a new mother is more threatening to adolescents than is a new father. In other words, adolescents—perhaps especially adolescent girls—may be particularly protective of their mother (even when they do not live with her) and particularly reluctant to have anyone take her place in their lives.

Our data also point to conditions under which acceptance of a parent's new partner is most likely. Early adolescents and boys were closer to and more accepting of parents' new partners than were older adolescents and girls. New partners who were married to the biological parent also received more acceptance than cohabiting new partners, or new partners who were dating the biological parent regularly but not living in the home. These results persisted after we controlled for the amount of time that the relationship had existed. In addition, adolescents who had close relationships with their residential biological parent were more likely to also be close to and accepting of that parent's new partner. Maintaining a relationship with the nonresidential parent did not appear to help or hinder adolescents' relationships with residential new partners, with the possible exception noted above of girls in father residence, who were somewhat less accepting of a new mother when they were close to their own mothers. Crosbie-Burnett (1991) also found that continuing involvement with a nonresidential parent did not interfere with relationships in stepfamilies, even in cases of high contact between former spouses.

When mothers or fathers acquire a new partner, they surely hope to win acceptance of that person by their children. Whether or not such acceptance has any concrete advantages for the adolescent in terms of adjustment, it surely makes home life more peaceful and happy than it would be in situations where the new partner is resented. Our results indicate, however, that the benefits may go beyond having more peace in the home. Adolescents who had better relationships with their parents' new partners were also somewhat better adjusted than were other adolescents (they had lower depression and lower deviance, and were more likely to work out compromises when faced with conflict). Of course, we cannot determine to what extent good relationships are the cause of better adjustment or a result of it, but the link is there, and worth further examination. Our results also indicate that the greater acceptance received by remarried new partners at least partially accounts for the better adjustment of adolescents who have stepparents.

Living in Two Homes

8

Living in Two Homes: Introduction

In Part II we described what life was like for adolescents and their families in different residential arrangements, and examined how different family experiences and processes were related to differential adjustment among the adolescents in those arrangements. We focused on the family life and background of the *residential* home. Because dual-resident adolescents really have two "residential homes," these earlier chapters touched on issues, and potential advantages and disadvantages, of going back and forth between two homes on a relatively frequent basis. For the most part, however, our concern was with what individual postdivorce homes (the home in which the adolescent spent the majority of his or her time) were like, and for dual-resident adolescents this was defined as the average of the two "residential" homes. What we have ignored to this point is that children in sole-resident arrangements often spend substantial time in both parental homes, and even when little time is spent with a nonresidential parent, the child remains, in some sense, a part of two families. In Part III, therefore, we explicitly consider issues of membership in two homes and two families.

When a divorce involves children, the now separated homes and families of the ex-spouses remain linked by those children. Although from an objective viewpoint—and even from the viewpoint of the divorcing spouses—divorce may split one family system into two separate family systems, the child remains a part of each of those new families (see Maccoby and Mnookin, 1992). In addition, the child may still view the original nuclear family as one family, a family that is now divided (Funder, 1991). Consider, for example, the following comments from adolescents in our study, when telling us what they did not like about their living or visitation arrangement. Even four and a half years after the divorce,

143

these children viewed the original family as the complete and whole family, and the postdivorce family as split, separated, "not together."

> (Mid-adolescent male): "I don't like being a partial family. I like being the 'great American 4' family: Mom, Dad, two kids, you know."

> (Early-adolescent female): "[I don't like that] the family is not together."

> (Early-adolescent male): "[I don't like that] I don't get to see both of [my parents] all the time."

Children's views of the postdivorce family—as one split family or as two separate families—may influence the ease with which they negotiate interactions or transitions between homes and, ultimately, adjust to the divorce. Regardless of the child's perception of the entire family unit, however, after divorce the child does remain a member of a subsystem with each parent, and each of these subsystems continues to be influenced by the nature of the other and by the nature of the postdivorce interparental relationship. Emotional ties between parents, and between a nonresidential parent and child, may endure in very real ways even when a child spends little or no time in one of the two homes. For example, if a child lives with a mother who maintains a high level of hostility toward her ex-spouse, and if that mother expresses her hostility openly in front of the child, the child's emotional—if not physical—membership in a subsystem that involves the father may be quite salient to both mother and child. Furthermore, the quality and intensity of the child's emotional ties to the nonresidential parent may have much to do with how adjustment to the divorce proceeds.

To the extent that a child does maintain contact with both parents, the child must negotiate not only the changes that take place within one home when a parent moves out and the lingering feelings of one sort or another about each parent, but the reality of life with each parent in two separate homes. Although we know something about the effects of varying amounts of time spent with a noncustodial parent in terms of a child's adaptation to divorce (see Chapter 9; Hess and Camara, 1979; Hetherington, Cox, and Cox, 1978, 1982; Kurdek, Blisk, and Siesky, 1981), we know little about the more intimate emotional and practical experiences of being an active member of two families. What are the specific challenges faced by adolescents who continue to see both parents, how prevalent and how difficult are those challenges, and how do adolescents handle them? On a practical level, how do they negotiate transitions between homes, and what is the extent of their input into the quantity and nature of their continuing involvement in both homes? What is the effect of an adolescent's ongoing relationship with one parent on the relationship with the other? How is the adolescent's experience of integrating and negotiating relationships with each parent influenced by the amount of time spent in each home, or by the nature of the interparental relationship? And how does the need to split time with one's parents influence or interact with other typical needs and desires of adolescence (for example, being available to peers, holding a part-time job)?

One of the central organizing questions in Chapters 8–12 has to do with the nature of family subsystems, and the boundaries between subsystems, after divorce. Family systems theorists and others have emphasized the importance for healthy family and child functioning of warm, child-focused parent-child bonds within the context of a strong parental alliance. What are the consequences of parents' maintaining—or not maintaining—an alliance when they are now part of new, separate, family systems? Under what conditions can the child maintain close relationships with both parents? And is this characterization of a healthy family system still important with regard to child adjustment when parents are no longer living together?

We investigated these questions concerning the experience of membership in two families mainly among those adolescents who actually spent time in two homes, although for some issues (for example, reasons for visiting a nonresidential parent), the time in the nonresidential home could be very slight and the issue still relevant. For other issues (for example, whether rules and expectations for behavior were different in the two homes), time spent in each home had to be more substantial for the issue to apply. We also considered, however, issues of continuing membership in two families that were relevant even to adolescents who no longer saw one parent. These issues were, of course, emotional rather than practical in nature, and our discussion of them is based on the premise articulated earlier that even an absent parent remains a child's parent and thus part of a family system for the child.

Plan for Part III

In this introductory chapter, we describe general levels of satisfaction with the way time is split between parents, and adolescents' feelings about their acceptance and comfort in two homes. Given this context, we then discuss some of what adolescents like and dislike about being part of two homes, and aspects of the situation that make membership in two homes more or less difficult.

In Chapter 9, we look at how the amount of time spent in the nonresidential household is related to the postdivorce experience. Our earlier discussions of how residential arrangements compared with respect to family processes and adolescent adjustment bear on the issue of how much time the adolescent spends with each parent; by definition, residential arrangements differ in this respect. Our previous discussion is extended, however, by examining the variety of visitation patterns adolescents have with the nonresidential parent. We look at how the amount of visitation is related to characteristics of relationships within the family: the interparental relationship and the adolescent's relationship with both the residential and the nonresidential parent. We also take up the question of how visitation may affect life in the residential home. Finally, we consider the relation between visitation and the adolescent's adjustment.

In Chapter 10, we move away from the amount of visitation, per se, to look in more detail at what goes on in nonresidential homes and at relationships between adolescents and their nonresidential parents. We begin by describing the nonresidential parent and home in comparison with relationships and processes in residential homes. Having set this context, we then address the question of how the nonresidential parent-child relationship is related to adolescents' adjustment. Does this relationship contribute anything to the adolescent's well-being, above and beyond the relationship between the adolescent and the residential parent? Central to questions concerning the effects of one home on the other is the question of how relationships with the two parents are linked. Does a close relationship with the nonresidential parent interfere with an adolescent's relationship with the residential parent? Can an adolescent maintain close relationships with two parents? If so, does closeness to both parents have positive consequences, or does it interfere with adjustment because it leads to feelings of tension and conflicts of loyalties for the adolescent (a question also addressed in Chapter 11)? We extend this inquiry by examining the broader question of whether the "effects" of being close to one parent vary depending upon how close an adolescent is to the other parent. For example, is it more beneficial, in terms of adjustment, to be close to a residential parent when one is not also close to a nonresidential parent? We also examine the effect of the co-parenting relationship on the parent-child relationships. Of most interest is whether ongoing conflict between parents after divorce interferes with the adolescent's relationships with one or both parents, and whether the impact of being close to a nonresidential parent depends on the nature of the relationship between the parents.

In Chapter 11 we examine adolescents' experience of feeling caught between their parents. The concept of feeling or being caught between parents may best typify how familial subsystems continue to interact after a family separates, even when a child spends little or no time with one parent. Regardless of whether the child sees the nonresidential parent, the residential parent can pressure a child to take sides in the conflict with the other parent, which may give rise to loyalty conflicts (Emery, 1988). Of course, when a child does see both parents, both may try to engage the child in alliances, or use the child to carry out what should be parental activities (for example, carrying messages to the ex-spouse or gaining information about the ex-spouse's home or activities). Family systems theory that has emerged from the study of nondivorced families suggests that such alliances and the erosion of boundaries between subsystems have potentially grave consequences for the child (Aponte and Van Deusen, 1981; Minuchin, 1974).

In Chapter 12 we examine discrepancies across households in parental rules and expectations for behavior. After divorce, opportunities and inclinations for parents to communicate about rules and expectations are greatly reduced, conceivably making inconsistent parenting quite common. We do not know, however, whether inconsistency is in fact common, or what the implications of inconsistency across homes are for the adolescent's experience.

Dividing Time between Households

In our study, most adolescents had spent at least some time in both homes within the year preceding their interview. Very few had not seen an outside parent in the previous year (twenty-six adolescents had not seen their fathers; four had not seen their mothers). Slightly fewer had not even talked to an outside parent over the telephone (twenty-five had not seen *or* talked to their fathers; only one had not seen or talked to mother). Thus continuing practical—as well as emotional—ties existed for the great majority of the adolescents whose parents had separated four and a half years earlier. In general, how satisfied were these adolescents with the amount of time they spent with each parent, and how comfortable were they in each home?

All 522 adolescents were asked to rate their satisfaction "with the time spent with each parent" on a scale where "1" meant "completely dissatisfied," and "10" meant "completely satisfied," and all but one adolescent responded. Mean satisfaction was almost 7, indicating that most adolescents felt fairly happy with their situation. Only 4 percent rated themselves as completely dissatisfied, and an additional 9 percent rated themselves as a "2" or "3" on this scale. Satisfaction had much to do with the amount of time adolescents spent with each parent. Adolescents in dual residence, who spent a great deal of time with both parents, had higher levels of satisfaction ($M = 7.8$) than did adolescents in sole-mother residence ($M = 6.9$) or sole-father residence ($M = 6.1$). Only one dual-resident adolescent gave a satisfaction score as low as "4"; all other dual-resident adolescents rated themselves at "5" or above. And although the absolute amount of visitation with a nonresidential parent (mother or father) for adolescents in sole-resident arrangements was not significantly related to degree of satisfaction, one of the most common complaints of adolescents who rated themselves as "completely dissatisfied" (a "1" or "2") with the division of time between parents—when asked what they did not like about their living or visitation arrangement—was that they missed their nonresidential parent, that they did not see him or her enough. Thus to a large extent, satisfaction had to do with getting to see both parents, and dissatisfaction was more likely to reflect wanting more—rather than less—contact with a parent.

The satisfaction of adolescents in mother residence was also higher than the satisfaction of adolescents in father residence, suggesting that it may have been harder for adolescents to be separated from their mothers than from their fathers. This finding is consistent with others (see Chapters 5 and 10) indicating that adolescents may have stronger emotional bonds with their mothers than with their fathers.

The greater the distance between parental homes, the lower was the satisfaction with the division of time, even after controlling for absolute amount of contact with the nonresidential parent. Perhaps because of the increased difficulty in making transitions, or because of the lessened flexibility with which an adolescent could go back and forth between homes, the distance between homes had an independent impact on adolescents' happiness with their arrangement.

We asked adolescents where they felt "at home"—at their mom's, dad's, both places, or neither place. About one-quarter (27 percent) of the adolescents living in one of the three major residential arrangements at the time of the interview (and who had at least seen both parents in the past year—$n = 463$), said they felt at home in both places. Adolescents in dual residence (43 percent) and father residence (35 percent) were more likely to say that both places felt like home than were adolescents in mother residence (22 percent). The majority of those living primarily with one parent said that their primary parent's residence felt most like home. For father-resident adolescents, however, this group (52 percent) was smaller than was the case for mother-resident adolescents, 71 percent of whom felt at home mainly in their primary residence.

A very small percentage of adolescents did not feel at home in either place (3 percent overall); slightly more father-resident adolescents (7 percent) than mother-resident (2 percent) or dual-resident (2 percent) adolescents chose this option. As with satisfaction, adolescents' comfort in each home appears related to having higher levels of contact with both parents, and additionally, to the gender of the nonresidential parent. When the mother was the nonresidential parent, adolescents were more likely to feel at home in the nonresidential home, but less likely to be satisfied with the division of time between parents, than when the father was the nonresidential parent. The differences between adolescents in mother and father residence were present even when controlling for the amount of contact with the nonresidential parent.

Several themes relevant to the experience of living in two homes and two families emerged when adolescents were asked what they liked and disliked about their living and visitation arrangements. Of course, for every theme, there is a "counter-theme." For example, although many adolescents felt that living in two homes made it difficult to do things with friends, there were others who said that having two sets of friends—one at each home—was a benefit of living in two homes. Obviously an individual's experience depends on many factors, including the temperament and personality of the adolescent and each of the parents, the family history before and after the divorce, and the communities in which each parent lives, among others. What we do here is to summarize some of the more prevalent responses that bear on adolescents' feelings about spending time in two homes or being a part of two families.

By far the most common type of remark that adolescents made about their living/visitation arrangements was a simple comment on their feelings about the amount of time they spent with both parents. Many adolescents who were in contact with both parents said that what they liked was that they could see both parents. Some of these adolescents went on to say that the time they now had with each parent was special, and that they currently spent more time with each parent than before their parents separated. They also liked being able to talk to each parent alone. For instance, one early-adolescent boy in dual residence said he liked "being able to see one parent at a time and talking to them without one or the other coming in . . . I like to be able to have private talks." A late-adolescent girl in mother residence said she got along better with her parents now that they were not living together, and an early-adolescent boy, also in mother residence, said, "I get to spend a lot more time with my mother than I used to because she's not with my father." These adolescents enjoyed the opportunity to receive attention from, and develop a relationship with, each parent individually.

Other adolescents, rather than enjoying special time alone with each parent, lamented the fact that they could not be with both parents together. When with one parent, they missed the other. One early-adolescent girl in dual residence said she didn't like the fact that "you miss the other one, and you don't really get to see them as much as if they both lived together." Another young adolescent, this time a boy in father residence, said, "I miss my mom when I'm over at Dad's and I miss my dad when I'm over at my mom's." An early-adolescent boy in dual residence said, "I wish they would be together still . . . I don't like having to see one parent one time and one parent the other time." Like the adolescents quoted earlier in the chapter, these adolescents still struggled with feelings that the family was not complete when they were not all together. Related to this, many adolescents also voiced real sadness over not having one or the other parent as a regular part of their lives. To these children, it did not seem right that they did not have ready access to both parents.

(Late-adolescent female in father residence): "[I don't like] not having [Mom] with me twenty-four hours a day—I don't like not being with her."

(Early-adolescent female in father residence): "[I don't like that] I can't see my mom whenever I want to."

(Mid-adolescent male in mother residence): "[I don't like that] he's not, like, always there. I can see him when I want to but, like, he's not in the house. It's not like walking distance to his house."

(Early-adolescent female in mother residence): "[I don't like] that I can't spend lots of time with my dad, . . . my dad used to play games with me."

(Mid-adolescent male in mother residence): "[I don't like that] I don't see my dad every single day. My dad can't be there every time I need him."

Feelings of enjoying time separately with each parent and of missing one parent when with the other are not mutually exclusive. Yet we infer that adolescents who generally feel one way or the other differ in the extent to which they have been able to accept the transformation of one family into two rather than still seeing the original family as their one true family. Parents' attempts to make access to each as easy as possible given the constraints of living in different homes undoubtedly help ease this transition for children.

Certainly, an adolescent's feelings about visitation and the experience of living in two homes reflect the quality of the adolescent's relationships and activities with each parent and in each household. For example, some adolescents said that their father slept a lot, or that their mother would go out with her boyfriend during their visit, and many commented on being bored at one house or the other. When parents spend their time predominantly in adult activities during times when they are responsible for their children, adolescents may be less likely to see the postdivorce situation as one that gives them positive access to both parents. Feelings also undoubtedly reflect the quality of family life before the separation. Among our adolescents were those who wished their parents had never divorced as well as adolescents who felt relieved that their parents were no longer living together. The latter adolescents, although they may have missed one parent or the other, clearly felt that their lives—including, for some, their own relationships with each parent—had improved since the divorce.

Another frequently voiced issue had to do with the flexibility (or lack thereof) of plans for spending time with each parent. Many of the older adolescents, and a few of the younger ones, mentioned flexibility as a plus:

(Early-adolescent male in dual residence): "[I like that] I can trade. If I don't want to go I can trade the next Wednesday or next Tuesday. And I don't have to go, and then the other parent gets that Tuesday or that next day."

(Mid-adolescent female in mother residence): "I like when it's not . . . scheduled for me to go visit [my father] at a set time every week 'cause it gives me a little more . . . freedom . . . I just have more of a choice."

(Mid-adolescent female in mother residence): "I like having the freedom to say yes or no if I want to see [Dad] or not. I like it better when it's not like every weekend or every other Saturday or something like that . . . It's nice that I can say, 'I'm busy this weekend. How about next week?'"

(Late-adolescent female in mother residence): "[I like that] I can do whatever I want. If I want to see my dad I can, but if I want to be at my mom's I can do that too."

(Late-adolescent female in father residence): "[I like that] if there's nothing else going on I can [see Mom]. There's no set appointment."

(Late-adolescent female in father residence): "[I like that] I have the freedom . . . my dad knows that I'm busy, and that I've got school and work . . . There's lots of flexibility."

(Late-adolescent male in father residence): "I like that I can go when I want and stay as long as I feel, and come back when I want."

(Late-adolescent female in mother residence): "I don't think it's fair that we can only have certain times when we can see our mother or father. I don't think it should be scheduled so strict."

Comments such as these point out the need to accommodate and adjust to older adolescents' increasingly busy lifestyle and extrafamilial interests. Younger children were more apt than older ones to like a set schedule, so as not to be put in the position of having to make decisions about when and when not to visit. Some adolescents felt that when it was up to them to decide, if they chose to spend time with one parent, the other would feel hurt. Even some of the older adolescents, who first mentioned flexibility as a positive, also pointed out its negative side, as did this older adolescent in father residence:

"Because I don't have set times sometimes my dad puts pressure on me to not go [to my mom's]. That's one thing about having set times. It wouldn't be up to me."

At least one young female, however, voiced concern over inflexibility, not because set visitation interfered with friends or other activities, but because she sometimes felt insecure about leaving her mother. This girl, who lived primarily with her mother, said:

"I like . . . seeing my father for the weekend, but . . . sometimes I feel sad, like the day before I leave, because . . . maybe I'd miss my mom a lot. You know, 'cause . . . I'm . . . attached to my mom a lot . . . Sometimes I don't want to go because, I guess, I'm scared or I just don't want to go."

The comments indicate that parents may have to strike a delicate balance between flexibility and scheduled visits. Having a set schedule not only promotes continued contact with both parents (Maccoby and Mnookin, 1992), but may relieve the child from having to make guilt-provoking choices between parents. Set schedules recognize and respect the ongoing relationship between the child and each parent. But especially as children get older and more involved with friends, work, and school, rigid adherence to a schedule may interfere with these other important aspects of adolescent development. Divorced parents face a special challenge in allowing their adolescents to invest time in developmentally appropriate extrafamilial activities without loosening the child's bonds with one or the other parent. Even when parents remain married, this particular challenge of adolescence may be difficult; when children must participate in two homes in order to maintain bonds with both parents, the challenge becomes even more difficult.

Not surprisingly, many adolescents talked of the difficulty in choosing between parents, and between parents and friends or other extracurricular activities. Many adolescents struggled with guilt over not spending "enough" time with one parent or the other. For instance, one mid-adolescent boy in mother residence said, "I feel like I should spend more time with my dad, but, you know, I'm at the age where I don't have to, so usually I don't. But . . . I've a pretty guilty conscience over it." Although adolescents in nondivorced families may also feel occasional guilt for choosing to spend time with peers or in other extrafamilial activities, the child of divorce may experience the tension between family ties and growing independence from family even more acutely, given the need to spend time with each parent separately. One boy in mother residence articulately voiced his frustration over being in a position that made him feel guilty:

"I know that I should at least go see [Dad] every once in a while. I don't like the guilt I feel when I don't go. And I don't like the fact that I'm at a total inconvenience just because they wanted to get a divorce. It's not like I didn't want to see them . . . I mean . . . you like your parents, you know, but it's not like you put out time to go visit them. . . . You think your parents are the people you are around, not people you have to go and visit. It kinda changes the relationship from being a parent almost to like going and seeing your grandma or something."

Many adolescents, without specifically mentioning guilt, simply commented on the difficulty in having to balance visitation with other activities. Even if parents allowed flexibility in scheduling visits around a child's activities, adolescents often found it hard to fit visitation in with everything else they wanted to do:

(Early-adolescent female in father residence): "Sometimes I have something I want to do, and the next weekend I might be going to [Mom's] house, and I might want to do that and when I do that, usually they switch weekends around, and sometimes things I want to do land on each weekend and I can't really do it because I have to spend the time with my mom."

(Mid-adolescent female in father residence): "I have friends, and if I go over to my mom's house, it's kinda hard to plan things with my friends and my mom."

(Late-adolescent male in mother residence): "[I don't like] trying to fit my dad in . . . I have my whole life here, and I have to take time out and drop everything to go there. It's kinda hard . . . Between work and my friends and everything like that . . . basically, it's just kind of hard to fit him into your schedule."

Conversely, other adolescents liked the fact that they did not feel guilty when they chose not to visit:

(Late-adolescent female in father residence): "With [an older adolescent] I don't think you can have any kind of a quality time unless I want it to be there. . . . I do like it because I don't feel like, when I go over to my mom's house, I'm pressured to stay two nights or one night or any amount of time . . . I know people who are supposed to spend every other weekend with their other parent. If you don't it's going to really hurt their feelings. I'm not in that position. You don't want to spend your weekend with your parents. You're going out with your friends."

Yet some adolescents who were allowed to choose friends over family still felt sad that they didn't have more time for their parents:

(Mid-adolescent female in mother residence): "Sometimes I wish it could be more. Maybe like four Saturdays or something, except that I have so many school things and I don't have enough time, but sometimes I wish it could be like a couple of more hours a week or something."

(Mid-adolescent female in mother residence): "I don't get over there much, because . . . I've got a lot of things going on, like friends and then activities, so actually, I don't get over there as much as I'd like to."

(Late-adolescent male in father residence): "I wish I . . . just wouldn't do some of the things . . . that I do now [so I could] just go over there and spend some time with [Mom]. It's kind of impossible."

Feelings of guilt over not spending enough time with one or the other parent were voiced less frequently by adolescents in dual residence than adolescents in sole-resident arrangements. In addition, dual-resident adolescents—regardless of age—were less likely to mention having to choose between parents and friends as something they disliked about their living arrangement. Perhaps because they typically saw both parents a great deal, it may have been easier for the dual-resident adolescent to choose to spend time with friends when a choice between the two arose.

Many adolescents enjoyed having "two different environments" in which to live. "I like being able to have a change . . . going from one house to another house" said one young female in dual residence. An early-adolescent male living primarily with his father liked having two different homes and two sets of friends; he summed it up with "I like change once in a while." For some, the availability of two homes provided an escape from unpleasant situations at one home or the other. Adolescents in all residential arrangements mentioned as a benefit of their living situation that when they were unhappy or bored at one house they could escape to the other house.

(Early adolescent in dual residence): "[I like that] I can get away from my dad's girlfriend. And that's about it. I get tired of one house and get to go to the other house."

(Middle adolescent in dual residence): "[I like that] you get a break from each parent . . . Sometimes one parent will be angry at you or something like that and you can go to the other parent's house . . . Basically, it's the fact . . . you can just trade off if one parent is getting on your nerves."

(Early adolescent in mother residence): "[Visiting] gives me a chance to get away from Mom 'cause if I'm with her alone too much of the time we get at each other's throats."

(Early adolescent in mother residence): "I don't have to deal with Mom if I don't want to. I can go to my dad's and I get to see him."

(Middle adolescent in father residence): "If you get sick of one parent, there's always the other one."

In some homes, where methods of dealing with conflict might otherwise be violent or abusive (emotionally or physically), having an avenue of escape might be adaptive. And being able to escape conflict or boredom by going to another parent's home may have better long-term consequences than escaping to friends or other nonfamilial establishments—an option that might be used by adolescents who are unhappy while living in a nondivorced family. There may be many instances, however, where the opportunity to escape cuts off more positive resolutions to conflict or more creative solutions to boredom before they can be reached. The frequency and destination of "escapes" from the parental home owing to conflict or boredom merits more detailed investigation among both divorced and nondivorced families.

The practical aspects of moving back and forth between homes were seen as a hassle by some of the adolescents, especially in dual-residence but also in sole-resident arrangements. Several adolescents told us of situations in which things they needed were at the other home; sometimes they could be retrieved and sometimes they could not. Remembering schedules was also difficult for some adolescents and their parents. The movement from one home to the other also contributed to feelings among some adolescents of always being on the go, of being unsettled.

(Early adolescent in dual residence): "[I don't like] moving. Just having to pack up every week."

(Early adolescent in dual residence): "It's kind of a hassle because sometimes you forget when you have to leave, and packing up all the time."

(Late adolescent in dual residence): "Things I don't like are when I don't know where my stuff is . . . or just remembering my parents' schedules . . . what they're doing, not knowing when they are going to be home. Like I go over there and I don't remember where they went."

(Middle adolescent in mother residence): "[I don't like that] my parents get . . . confused on which weekend I was over there."

(Early adolescent in mother residence): "Sometimes I get confused about where I'm going if they have to switch nights."

(Early adolescent in dual residence): "[I don't like that] I'm with one parent one day and then all of a sudden I go to the other parent's. It's all chopped up going back and forth."

(Middle adolescent in mother residence): "[I don't like] feeling like a package that's being stamped 'return to sender.' It's not that I feel unwanted. It's just that it makes me feel so awkward being sent back and forth."

(Late-adolescent in father residence): "It's hard to pin down a schedule, or create a livable lifestyle . . . I forget things at the wrong house. I don't feel like I have a patterned lifestyle."

(Early adolescent in dual residence): "Another thing that I don't like is going from one house to the other and . . . it seems to me I'm always hurried."

The fact that moving presented difficulties must be countered by the knowledge that most adolescents liked seeing both parents; the hassles of moving may be seen as "necessary evils." Yet the frequency with which these sentiments were voiced suggests that whatever parents can do to ease the burden of remembering schedules and transferring belongings could make the experience of living in two homes more positive. For example, a child might have a minimum set of clothing and everyday necessities at each home. Lists of things that must be taken back and forth, or a special bag where such items are kept, might reduce the possibility of forgetting homework, permission slips, and other essentials.

Two other themes voluntarily articulated by adolescents will be only briefly mentioned here because they are explored in more detail in later chapters. The first involves having different sets of rules in the two homes and the second, feelings of being torn between parents. Having two different sets of rules and expectations was a boon to some adolescents and a problem to others. Not surprisingly, some adolescents liked—and took advantage of—the fact that they could get away with things in one home that wouldn't be allowed in the other. Others found it frustrating and confusing. And adolescents often voiced with strong emotion their frustration with behaviors on the part of their parents that put them in the middle of ongoing parental battles. Because both of these themes are central to understanding the nature and consequences of ongoing inter-parental and parent-child bonds after divorce, and because they were areas in which we had more extensive quantitative as well as qualitative information, they are taken up in detail in Chapters 11 and 12.

9

Visitation

In the past two decades, a number of states have modified their divorce statutes in order to encourage decisions about custody and visitation that will allow children to sustain relationships with both parents. For example, the revised California custody code that became effective in 1980 included the following preamble:

> Section 4600 (a) The Legislature finds and declares that it is the public policy of this state to assure minor children of frequent and continuing contact with both parents after the parents have separated or dissolved their marriage.

The statute further included a "friendly parent" provision:

> Section 4600 (b) (1) In making an award of custody to either parent, the court shall consider which parent is more likely to allow the child or children frequent and continuing contact with the noncustodial parent.

The change represented an effort to be "fair" to both parents, and was part of the general trend toward making divorce laws more gender-neutral. But in addition, several then-current pieces of research indicated that children living with their mothers seemed to adjust better to the divorce if they had generous visitation with their nonresidential fathers (Hess and Camara, 1979; Wallerstein and Kelly, 1980). Hetherington, Cox, and Cox (1978, 1982) reported benefits from continued contact with fathers, except in cases where conflict between the parents was very high or the father was emotionally disturbed. But these studies were all based on relatively small and selective samples.

As we discussed earlier with regard to custody arrangements, children may derive several benefits from continued contact with both parents. First and foremost is the knowledge that they have not been abandoned by a parent. Continued contact with both parents should shield children from at least some of the grief or guilt over the loss of a parent that can occur when a parent simply disappears. In addition, a nonresidential parent with whom the child has a continuing relationship should be able to provide a variety of supports, such as emotional support when the residential parent is functioning poorly or when the residential parent and child are in serious conflict. A nonresidential parent who continues to be involved in the child's life may also be more willing to provide financial support, particularly in later years when college costs become an issue. And in the case of the illness, death, or institutionalization of the residential parent, the child who has continued to see the outside parent presumably has a viable alternative residence. The availability of the nonresidential parent for visitation may also provide support for the residential parent: much-needed time off from child care and, in the best case, a continuing united front between parents with respect to the rules and values by which the child is expected to live.

Continuing visitation has potential risks, however. One concern is that visitation for children necessarily involves some degree of continued contact between the divorced parents, and such contact may create opportunities for sustained, overt conflict—conflict that may well be harmful to the children. Furthermore, the more time the child spends in the nonresidential parent's household, the more the child may be exposed to two different sets of values, to conflicting demands, or possibly to weakened parental control because each parent is unable to monitor or supervise the child's activities in the other home. The continued involvement of the nonresidential parent in the child's life may also disrupt or intrude upon the functioning of the residential parent's family. The negative effects of these factors might neutralize, or even outweigh, the potential benefits to children of high levels of visitation.

After the original studies mentioned above were completed, several other studies assessed the functioning of children who had varying degrees of contact with the nonresidential parent. The findings of these studies have been mixed (see Amata and Rezac, 1994, for a review). Although many still indicated a positive link between visitation and child functioning, the links were often small. And in contrast to the earlier studies, several of the more recent—and larger—studies indicated no link at all between children's adjustment and how much contact they had with their father. For example, Furstenberg, Morgan, and Allison (1987) selected, as a subsample of the National Survey of Children (NSC) conducted in 1981, a group of 227 children aged eleven to sixteen who were living with their divorced mothers. The investigators found that the amount of contact children had with their fathers was not related, for either boys or girls, to any of the major adjustment dimensions studied (problem behavior, emotional distress, or academic difficulties). In another study of several hundred children from the National Longitudinal Survey of Youth (NLSY), contact with fathers was similarly unrelated to children's well-being (King, 1994); what was more important was a father's payment of child support.

Using yet another large national sample, Zill (1988) looked at the question of continued contact with a nonresidential parent among children of remarried divorced parents—that is, children living with one natural parent and a stepparent. This is one of the rare studies that includes children living with their fathers ($n = 216$) as well as a larger group of children living with their mothers ($n = 1084$). Still larger groups of single-parent and nondivorced families were available for comparison. The children ranged in age from three to seventeen years, although most were over age ten. Zill found that for children living with their mother and stepfather, the frequency of contact with their biological father was unrelated to the incidence of behavior problems in the children. By contrast, among children living with their father and a stepmother, problems were more frequent the less often the children saw their mothers. Indeed, the incidence of behavior problems was twice as high among children who never saw their mother as it was among children who saw her on a weekly basis.

In summary, recent studies are not as clear in establishing the importance of continuing contact with the nonresidential parent as were earlier studies, and the mixture of findings in the current literature suggests that the impact of visitation probably depends on additional factors such as the sex of the nonresidential parent, the level of conflict between the parents, or the quality of the relationship between the child and the nonresidential parent (Amato, 1993; Amato and Rezac, 1994; Bray, 1991; Kelly, 1993).

In the interviews with the parents of the adolescents in our study (Maccoby and Mnookin, 1992), some findings on visitation emerged that will help to set the stage for the present analyses of visitation among adolescents. Considering all the children from the earlier study—regardless of their age—it was found that the frequency of overnight visitation remained fairly stable over the three postseparation years for both mother-resident and father-resident children. Fathers who started out with only daytime visitation, however, tended to drop out over time. By

Time 3, a substantial proportion (42 percent) of nonresidential fathers were seeing their children seldom or not at all. For nonresidential mothers, however, daytime visitation increased with time, and the proportion having little or no contact with the children decreased (by T3, the proportion was 23 percent).

In the first year after parental separation, children between three and eleven years of age visited the nonresidential parent more frequently than did younger or older children. However, a child's age did not affect whether the amount of visitation increased or decreased thereafter (Maccoby and Mnookin, 1992). We expected, on the basis of these trends, that in the sample of adolescent children reported on here visitation should be somewhat lower than the levels reported for T3 from the parent sample as a whole, for two reasons. First, the adolescent follow-up sample did not include children who were under six years when their parents separated, and who were more frequent visitors with their nonresidential parents throughout the first three postseparation years than the oldest children (twelve to fourteen years old at parental separation). Second, the passage of an additional postseparation year was expected to bring additional decline in rates of visitation for children of all ages, at least for children living with their mothers.

We had information about the amount of current (T4) contact with the nonresidential parent for 347 mother-resident adolescents and 98 father-resident adolescents. Not included in these groups are the young people who had moved out of both parental homes by the time we interviewed them (and therefore current contact information did not reflect what it may have been when they were living at home), and those who were in dual residence. Within both mother and father residence, there was considerable variation in the amount and timing of visitation with the nonresidential parent. In the discussion that follows, we first compare mother-resident and father-resident adolescents with respect to the incidence of different patterns of visitation with the nonresidential parent, and examine whether visitation is related to demographic factors and the distance between the two parental households. We then turn to the following issues:

1. What visitation arrangements seemed most satisfactory to adolescents? How flexible were the arrangements, and how much voice did adolescents have in negotiations about visitation?
2. How is the amount of visitation related to the kind of interaction the two parents have with each other?

3. Is the amount of visitation related to the closeness of the relationship adolescents maintain with the nonresidential parent? Is visitation related to the closeness of the relationship with the
   residential parent?
4. Does the amount of visitation appear to have an impact on the
   functioning of the residential parent's household?
5. What is the relation between visitation and adolescent adjustment?
6. For each of the above questions, we consider whether the relation
   of interest depends on a variety of other factors. Where reasonable to do so, we consider modifying effects of: age or sex of the
   adolescent; parent's remarriage status; amount of conflict between
   parents; and adolescent's relationships with either the residential
   or the nonresidential parent.

Recognizing that the answers to these questions might not be the same
for adolescents living with their fathers and visiting their mothers as for
adolescents living with their mothers and visiting their fathers, we analyzed these two groups separately.

The Amount and Kind of Visitation

The adolescents in our sample were asked "When did you last see your
(nonresident parent)?" The large majority of adolescents who lived primarily with one or the other parent had seen the nonresidential parent
quite recently—about 70 percent had seen the nonresidential parent
within the previous month for both residence groups (see Figure 9.1). For
only a very few adolescents, 7.5 percent among mother-resident and 4.1
percent among father-resident, more than a year had elapsed since the
last contact. It is especially interesting that the length of time since the
nonresidential parent was last seen was very similar for father-resident
and mother-resident adolescents.

For the adolescents who had seen the nonresidential parent within a
year but not within the past month (approximately one-fourth of the
sole-resident adolescents), the contact was sometimes brief. In a few
cases, the nonresidential parent had come to Christmas or Thanksgiving
dinner, or to the celebration of a child's birthday, but had not been in
contact otherwise. In other cases, the child had spent some vacation time
with the nonresidential parent but had not been in contact during the
regular portions of the school year. More detail about visitation was thus

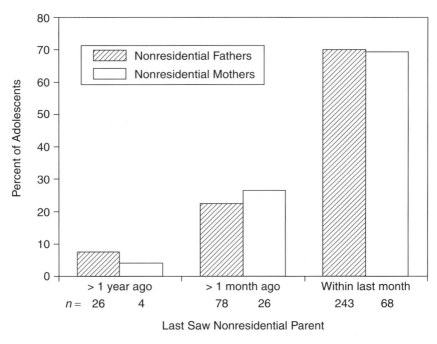

Figure 9.1 Time of most recent contact with the nonresidential parent for sole-resident adolescents, by residential arrangement.

obtained by asking separately about vacation time and visits during the regular school year.

In earlier parent reports, certain differences between overnight and daytime visiting had emerged. Overnight visits almost always occurred on a regular schedule; daytime visiting was frequently sporadic and less planned. Daytime visiting was also less stable from one year to the next than was overnight visiting. As we already noted, among mother-resident adolescents, overnight visits to the father were quite well maintained over time, while daytime visiting dropped off. So we also asked about overnight versus daytime visitation. For school-year visiting, adolescents were asked how many overnights they usually spent in a two-week period, not including vacations. If they said they never stayed overnight, they were asked about daytime visits: how many hours they spent in such visits during a usual two-week period during the school year. Then they were asked how many days (over and above the usual school-year pattern) they spent with the nonresident parent during their last summer's vacation, and the most recent spring and Christmas vacations.

In devising a scale for the amount of visitation, we gave vacation visits
less weight than regular visitation every two weeks during the school
year, and we gave overnight visits more weight than daytime visits. On
the basis of their answers to the series of questions, adolescents were
grouped into four visitation categories:

1. "Little or no visitation" ($n = 139$). No overnights, and less than
   eight hours of daytime visitation during typical two-week periods
   of the school year; less than two weeks of vacation time.
2. "Vacation only" ($n = 91$). Two or more weeks of vacation time,
   but no overnights and less than eight hours of daytime visitation
   during typical two-week periods of the school year.
3. "Moderate visitation" ($n = 97$). One overnight, or eight hours or
   more of daytime visitation, during typical two-week periods of the
   school year.
4. "Frequent visitation" ($n = 118$). Two or three overnights in typical two-week periods of the school year.

Adolescents who spent four or more overnights per two-week period
with each of the parents were considered to be in dual residence (see
Chapter 3) and, as noted, have not been included in the analysis of
visitation that follows.

The "little or no visitation" group includes those few adolescents who
had not seen the nonresidential parent in the past year. Nearly half of the
adolescents in this group, however, had done some daytime visiting during the school year, ranging from one hour to six hours per two-week
period. (The mean hours of daytime visiting per two weeks for the "little
or no visitation" group was 1.2 for mother-resident adolescents, and .84
for father-resident adolescents.) About half of these adolescents also
spent some of their vacation time with their nonresidential parent, with
fourteen adolescents reporting a one-week stay. The average amount of
vacation time spent by these adolescents was 2.8 days.

Some of the adolescents in the vacation-only group also did small
amounts of daytime visiting during the school year: .65 hours per two
weeks was the average for mother-resident adolescents, and .30 hours for
father-resident adolescents. These adolescents did not typically spend
overnights with the nonresidential parent.

We recognized that our four-step "scale" might not be linear. That is,
there is no way of knowing how much importance to give to a two- to
four-week stay with the nonresident parent during the summer, com-

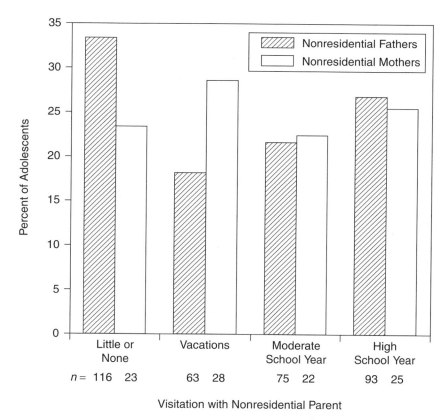

Figure 9.2 Level of contact with the nonresidential parent for sole-resident adolescents, by residential arrangement.

pared with spending every other weekend (Friday and Saturday nights) during the school year. Most of the analyses using visitation in this chapter and subsequent chapters, therefore, have been done in the form of analyses of variance, which do not assume linearity.[1]

With regard to the amount of visitation, there was somewhat less visitation with nonresident fathers than with nonresident mothers (see Figure 9.2). One-third of the adolescents living with their mothers seldom or never visited their fathers, while slightly under one-fourth of the father-resident adolescents were similarly out of touch with their mothers. In contrast, more father-resident adolescents (28.6 percent) than mother-resident adolescents (18.2 percent) were in the vacation-only group. The similarity between the two residential groups in terms of the two highest visitation categories, however, was striking: exactly 48 percent of the adolescents in each group visited with their nonresidential parents moderately or frequently during the school year.

Visitation and Demographic Characteristics

The amount of visitation with nonresidential parents was related to a number of characteristics of the adolescents and their families (see Appendix Table B.8 for details of visitation and demographics). Adolescents who had frequent overnight visitation with their nonresidential parents were younger, on the average, than adolescents with lower levels of visitation; adolescents who seldom or never saw their nonresidential parent were the oldest group, and this held true for both mother- and father-resident adolescents. Although the percentage of boys and girls in each visitation group was not significantly different, there was a somewhat higher concentration of boys in the highest visitation group (for both mother and father residence). We considered this association strong enough to make it wise to control for both age and sex of subjects in the analyses that follow. For both residential groups, father's education was significantly associated with the visitation patterns. For father-resident adolescents, it was the vacation-only group that had fathers with the highest levels of education. For mother-resident adolescents, both the vacation-only group and the frequent-visitation group had fathers with the highest levels of education. The average of mother's and father's education levels showed a similar pattern as that for father education; thus, mid-parent education was controlled in subsequent analyses as a way of taking into account the education levels of both parents. As we noted in Chapter 7, the frequency of visitation was not related to the remarriage status of either mother or father in either residential group.

When children started out living with their mother following the parental separation, they usually continued to do so over the next several years. Father residence was much less stable, however, and a majority of the adolescent children who were living with their fathers at the time of the adolescent interview had not lived with him continuously since the separation, having been in either mother or dual residence at some point in the interim (Maccoby and Mnookin, 1992; Chapters 3 and 5). Within each of the residential groups, however, the amount of visitation was not significantly related to whether the adolescent had continuously remained in the same residential arrangement.

Visitation and Travel Distance

As might be expected, adolescents reporting higher levels of visitation also reported living geographically closer to the nonresidential parent. Approximately two-thirds of the adolescents whose parents lived within an hour's driving time from each other's houses visited the nonresidential parent during typical two-week periods throughout the school year. These fairly high levels of school-year visitation were found in both mother-resident and father-resident families, so long as the two parents lived within what might be considered reasonable weekend driving range. This proportion dropped to 50 percent for those living between one and two hours apart. Differences between mother-resident and father-resident families emerged when the distance was even greater: nearly half the father-resident adolescents who lived from two to eight driving hours away from their mothers visited her (or were visited by her) on at least a biweekly basis during the school year, while only a fifth of the mother-resident adolescents visited their fathers this frequently when they lived so far apart. The vast majority of mother-resident adolescents who lived over two hours away from their fathers either visited primarily during vacations or visited hardly at all. Because most of the driving for visitation purposes tends to be done by the nonresidential parent (Maccoby and Mnookin, 1992), the difference in visitation between nonresidential mothers and nonresidential fathers when distances are great may reflect a greater willingness on the part of nonresidential mothers to drive longer distances to pick up and return children. Instead, or in addition, it may reflect a greater effort on the part of children to see nonresidential mothers over nonresidential fathers. The difference in contact with non-residential mothers versus nonresidential fathers remains when the non-residential parent's working hours are accounted for; thus the difference is not simply due to the fact that fathers work longer hours and therefore may have less time or less freedom to get away from work to travel longer distances.

Phone Calls to the Nonresidential Parent

Adolescents who visited their nonresidential parents most frequently also talked to them most frequently on the telephone. The average was four to five times a week for adolescents in the two highest visitation categories and one to two times a week for adolescents in the two lowest visitation categories. The difference was especially strong for mother-resident adolescents, but held for father-resident adolescents as well. Presumably the higher rate of telephone calls for adolescents with frequent visitations reflects in part the need for more contact to arrange visits and the lower likelihood that the phone call would be a long-distance one. It is likely, however, that adolescents and nonresidential parents who see one another more often also feel freer to call one another to talk about a variety of things other than visitations, especially when a regularly scheduled visit cannot take place.

Adolescents' Reports of Their Experiences in Visitation

Adolescents gave us their perceptions concerning the reasons they visited their nonresidential parents, how flexible their visitation arrangements were, whether they could exercise any influence over the visitation plans their parents made, how much they looked forward to visiting, and how satisfied they were with their visitation arrangement. The large majority of adolescents (87 percent), when offered a series of possible reasons for visiting (from which they could choose as many as applied), said they visited because they wanted to (see Figure 9.3). About one-third also said that they did not want to hurt the nonresidential parent's feelings by not going. Older adolescents were more likely to express this latter kind of sentiment, which may reflect the older adolescents' higher levels of involvement outside the home. A little over one-fifth of adolescents felt that they were required to go, and had no choice. Males were slightly more likely than females to say they visited because they had to, and less likely to say they visited because they wanted to. Adolescents living with their fathers were more likely than those living with their mothers to say that visitation provided a way to get away from the residential parent. Older adolescents also more often selected this reason for visitation than did younger adolescents.

We looked at whether boys and girls or older and younger adolescents had different reasons for visiting nonresidential mothers versus nonresidential fathers. In only one case did the proportion of individuals using a reason for visiting mother versus father differ by group: among older adolescents (aged fourteen years and older), fewer father-resident adolescents (78 percent) gave "because I want to" as a reason for visiting the nonresidential parent than did mother-resident adolescents (88 percent).[2]

Visitation schedules can become an arena of conflict between adolescents and their parents. Although in some families the distance between

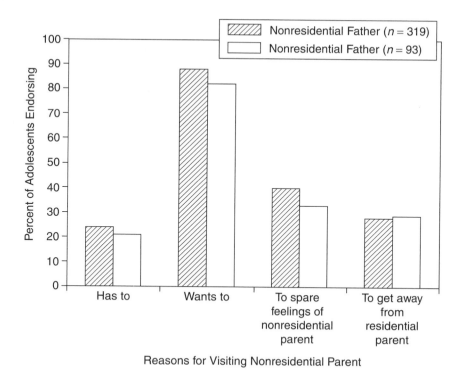

Figure 9.3 Percentage of adolescents in sole residence endorsing various reasons for visiting their nonresidential parent, by residential arrangement. Means are adjusted for age and sex of adolescent, the average education of the two parents, and amount of contact with the nonresidential parent. Excludes adolescents who had not seen their nonresidential parent in the past year.

parents places rather strict limits on visitation, especially during the school year, for families who live close enough for regular visits, situations may arise in which parents and children don't see eye to eye on visitation. In particular, such conflicts arise when either a parent or a child wants to change the visitation schedule. On the one hand, children sometimes resist visitation, even though nonresidential parents truly want to spend time with them and even though residential parents support that visitation. Especially among adolescents, conflicts arise between activities with friends or extracurricular activities in school and scheduled visitation times, and children may lobby with the residential parent to cancel a visit. On the other hand, children sometimes are eager to go for visits at times that are inconvenient for the parents, or when the residential parent wants to block visitation, feeling that the visits are not in the child's best interests (or the residential parent's own interests). The adolescents in our sample were asked about occasions when they were scheduled to visit the other parent but did not want to go, and about occasions when they wanted to visit the nonresidential parent but could not. A substantial number of adolescents in both residential arrangements had had such experiences. The links between residence or visitation and having had such experiences were the same for boys and girls. Overall, mother-resident adolescents were somewhat more likely to say they did not want to go on a scheduled visit than were father-resident adolescents (see Table 9.1); there was no difference in the desire to be with the nonresidential parent at unscheduled times between mother- and father-resident adolescents. This latter sentiment was more dependent on the level of visitation for mother-resident adolescents than for father-resident adolescents. Among mother-resident adolescents, frequent visitors and vacation visitors were more likely to say they wished they could be with their fathers at unscheduled times than were those who visited relatively seldom.

Feelings of not wanting to visit the nonresidential father when one was supposed to visit were reported more often by moderate and frequent visitors—a fact that probably reflects the greater frequency of scheduled visits, and hence more opportunities for conflicts to arise between visiting and other activities the child might want to participate in. Although father-resident adolescents with moderately high levels of visitation also reported feelings of not wanting to visit when they were supposed to, it is surprising to note that adolescents who had the highest levels of visitation with their mothers seldom reported such conflicted feelings—about as infrequently as adolescents with the two lowest levels of visitation.

Whether adolescents were actually able to go to a nonresidential parent's home when they wanted to differed more among the visitation groups than did simply having the desire: adolescents in the two low-visitation groups were usually not able to go. It is not surprising that the adolescents in the vacation-only group would not be able to make an unscheduled visit on short notice, considering that the nonresidential parent lived quite far away in many cases. In the two groups of more frequent visitors, about half went when they wanted to. When adolescents did not want to go on a scheduled visit, about two-thirds said that they had been able to cancel or reschedule on at least some occasions.

The ability to change plans did not differ depending on whether the adolescents were in mother or father residence. We also found no sex differences, either overall or within each residential arrangement, in the ability to change plans, although the numbers of cases in some of these analyses—especially when considering father residence—became too small for our tests to be meaningful.

Often the reasons given for not being able to change visitation plans had to do with parents' work schedules or other commitments that parents could not change. For example, one girl in mother residence said: "I can't just call up and say I want to come over 'cause [my father] . . . has a lot of work to do. I usually can't see him because he doesn't have time." Similarly, one boy in father residence told us: "My mom couldn't have me over . . . she had to work." Some adolescents couldn't visit a parent because he or she didn't have living accommodations big enough for them to stay over. Still others said that a residential parent worried that visits to a nonresidential parent would lead the adolescent to "run away" to that home.

Adolescents are not always aware of the considerations that determine their parents' decisions about visitation schedules, and situations may arise that seem arbitrary to the adolescents. One boy in mother residence told us that he couldn't visit his father when he wanted to, because "my mom made up some excuse. We were supposed to go visit my father . . . We didn't go." Although standing by an agreement made in the divorce proceedings may make a lot of sense to the parents, adhering rigidly to a schedule because "it's what we agreed on" may also seem arbitrary to adolescents. An early-adolescent female in mother residence told us, "I'm not allowed to see [Dad] during school . . . It wasn't his time to see me . . . it wasn't in the divorce papers." Another girl in mother custody said that she went to her father's even when she didn't want to, because "it's in the custody agreement so I have to . . . There was one week where I had tons of tests and everything and I didn't want to go there just to work and I really didn't want to go . . . but I had to . . . It's in the agreement and I have to go see him."

In response to a more general question about how much influence they felt they could have over changes in the visitation schedule, most adolescents placed themselves at about the midpoint of a five-point scale running from "not much say at all" to "a great deal." There were no sex differences in adolescents' answers to this question, but older adolescents felt they had more control over whether they would visit, and when, than did younger ones.

Table 9.1 Adolescents' reports of their experience with visitation, for adolescents in sole residence[a]

| Measure | Level of visitation | | | | F values |
	Little or none (1)	Vacation only (2)	Moderate (3)	High (4)	
"In the past year, has it happened that you were at your (residential parent's) house and wanted to be with your (nonresidential parent)?" Percentage responding "yes":					
Mother-resident adolescents (visit father)	42.9 (n = 115)	68.6 (n = 63)	52.2 (n = 75)	66.3 (n = 93)	Residence: 3.72[+,b] Visitation: 1.10 (n.s.) Residence × Visitation: 2.10[+]
Father-resident adolescents (visit mother)	67.6 (n = 23)	58.5 (n = 28)	74.2 (n = 22)	73.2 (n = 25)	(Mother res.: 1 < 2,4; 3 < 2) (Father res.: n.s.)

"In the past year, has it ever happened that you were supposed to go to your (nonresidential parent's) but you didn't want to?" Percentage responding "yes":

Mother-resident adolescents (visit father)	21.9 (n = 115)	27.5 (n = 63)	43.9 (n = 75)	51.3 (n = 93)	Residence: 1.22 (n.s.)[c] Visitation: 4.22** (3 > 1,2) Residence × Visitation: 1.91 (n.s.)
Father-resident adolescents (visit mother)	24.5 (n = 23)	22.1 (n = 28)	49.7 (n = 22)	24.4 (n = 25)	

a. Means are controlled for age and sex of adolescent and mid-parent education.
b. This effect was nonsignificant in three random samples.
c. This effect became significant in three random samples.
$^{+}p \leq .10.$　　**$p \leq .01.$　　n.s. = not significant.

On the whole, most of the adolescents in our sample seemed to take the visitation arrangements in stride. They were asked: "When you are at your (residential parent's) house, and thinking about going to (or seeing) your (nonresidential parent), how do you usually feel?" The five-point scale from which they could choose an answer ran from "very reluctant" to "very eager." Overall, adolescents expressed more eagerness than reluctance. Adolescents living with their fathers were more eager to visit mothers ($M = 3.6$) than were adolescents living with their mothers to visit fathers ($M = 3.3$), and this difference did not vary by sex or age of adolescent. In both residential arrangements, younger adolescents were more eager to visit than were older adolescents: for mother-resident adolescents the correlation between age and eagerness was $-.23$, and for father-resident adolescents it was $-.22$.[3]

Eagerness to visit *was* related to the level of visitation: for both mother-resident and father-resident adolescents, those who seldom saw the nonresidential parent were the least eager to visit (see Figure 9.4). For mother-resident adolescents, only those adolescents who saw their fathers little or none of the time had lower levels of eagerness; those in the vacation-only group looked forward to their visits with their fathers as much as the more frequent visitors. For the father-resident adolescents, high-frequency visitors were more eager to visit mother than the adolescents who rarely visited. Although the relation between visitation and eagerness is statistically weaker for the father-resident adolescents, in part this is a result of the lower number of children in this arrangement. Of course, we don't know to what extent adolescents who initially had low levels of contact with a nonresidential parent became less eager to visit over time, or to what extent adolescents who were not eager to visit were subsequently less likely to do so.

After answering all the specific questions about their visitation situation, adolescents were asked a global question: "Think of a scale from 1 to 10, where 1 is completely dissatisfied and 10 is completely satisfied. How satisfied are you with the time you spend with each parent?" As noted in Chapter 8, adolescents living with their mothers were somewhat more satisfied than adolescents living with their fathers. We also noted there that satisfaction appeared to be linked to time spent with each parent, with satisfaction highest among adolescents who had high levels of contact with both parents (the dual-resident adolescents), and with adolescents who were very dissatisfied typically citing their failure to see one parent or the other as the reason for their dissatisfaction. To our surprise, then, within each sole-residence group, satisfaction was unrelated to the frequency of

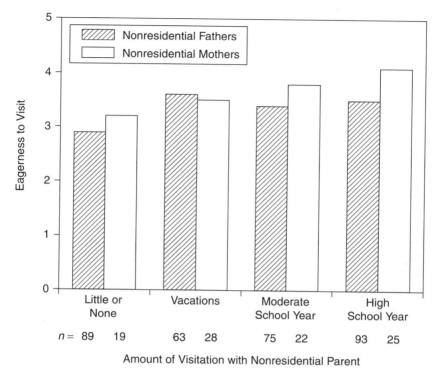

Figure 9.4 Sole-resident adolescents' eagerness to visit their nonresidential parent, by residential arrangement and level of contact with the nonresidential parent. Means are adjusted for age and sex of adolescent and the average education of the two parents. Excludes adolescents who had not seen their nonresidential parent in the past year.

visitation. Most adolescents appeared to have adapted themselves to whatever pattern of visitation the family had adopted.

Visitation and the Interparental Relationship

One might expect that visitation would covary with the amount of conflict or hostility between parents. On the one hand, after four and a half years, visitation might be lower for adolescents whose parents are not on good terms. On the other hand, as we noted earlier, some people believe that ongoing visitation can foster continued high levels of conflict between ex-spouses. Interestingly, what we found was that visitation with the nonresidential parent four and a half years after divorce—for both

mother- and father-resident adolescents—was related only to the
mother's earlier level of hostility, not to the father's (see Table 9.2). For
mother-resident adolescents, mother's hostility was highest in the lowest
visitation group and lowest in the highest visitation group. Mother's
hostility was also high right after the divorce (T1) in the moderate visitation group, but by three and a half years after the separation, it had
dropped to levels similar to the vacation-only and high-visitation groups.
It appears, then, that residential mothers function as gatekeepers: if they
remain hostile toward their ex-spouses, they can cut off (or minimize)
their children's visitation. The father's level of hostility had little or no
bearing on whether he received visits from mother-resident adolescents.

For father-resident adolescents, it was once again the mother's hostility, not the father's, that mattered. And here there was some evidence
that visitation could maintain or exacerbate parental hostility. Mothers
were especially hostile in the highest, as well as the lowest, visitation
group, and cooperative communication between the parents at T2 had
been especially low for these two groups. So for some families, maternal
hostility either led to the termination of her visitation or resulted from
being shut out, but for other families, frequent visitation may have kept
the flames of maternal anger and hostility burning. Our data indicate that
for both mother- and father-resident adolescents, it is the mother's feelings about her ex-spouse that are more closely linked to the nonresidential parent's continuing contact with the child.

Visitation and Adolescents' Relationships with Each Parent

Advocates of measures that foster continued contact between children
and their nonresidential parents have emphasized that such contact fosters
a close relationship with these parents, and that having a close relationship
is beneficial to children in the long run. Skeptics have urged that it is mainly
the residential parent that matters in children's development, and have
raised the question of whether continued involvement by the nonresident
parent may interfere with the major relationship. We compared adolescents who had different levels of visitation with their nonresidential parent
on several measures of their relationship with each parent, and the patterns are very clear. On average, adolescents who visit have better relationships with their nonresidential parent than adolescents who do not
visit (they feel closer to them—as shown in Figure 9.5—they trust them
more, they identify more with them, and the two share more joint activities). Adolescents who rarely visit their nonresidential parent are also less

Table 9.2 Relation of visitation frequency to the interparental relationship[a]

Measure of interparental relationship	Level of visitation				$F_{visitation}$
	Little or none (1)	Vacation only (2)	Moderate (3)	High (4)	
Mother-Resident Adolescents (visit father)					
Maximum *n*	(67)	(31)	(44)	(57)	
Mother's hostility (T1)	6.5	5.0	6.5	4.7	7.27**** (1,3 > 2,4)
Father's hostility (T1)	5.4	4.2	4.7	5.3	1.75[b]
Mother's hostility (T2)	6.0	5.4	5.1	4.6	3.02* (1 > 4)[c]
Father's hostility (T2)	5.3	4.6	4.6	4.9	.46
Mother's hostility (T3)	5.6	5.0	4.8	4.4	2.83* (1 > 4)
Father's hostility (T3)	5.0	5.0	4.1	4.6	1.04
Father-Resident Adolescents (visit mother)					
Maximum *n*	(15)	(19)	(16)	(16)	
Cooperative communication (T2)	3.6	4.7	5.8	3.2	9.02**** (3 > 1,4) (2 > 4)
Mother's hostility (T1)	6.5	4.0	4.8	6.3	3.69* (2 > 1,4)
Father's hostility (T1)	6.0	6.5	5.4	5.9	.62
Mother's hostility (T2)	6.3	5.6	4.8	5.8	.78
Father's hostility (T2)	7.1	5.4	5.0	6.1	1.98
Mother's hostility (T3)	6.3	5.5	4.2	6.6	3.06* (3 < 1,4)
Father's hostility (T3)	5.8	4.5	5.3	6.2	1.88

a. Statistics are based on a random sample. Means are controlled for age and sex of adolescent and mid-parent education.
b. In two other random samples, 1,4 > 2 (at $p \le .10$ and $p \le .05$).
c. Effect weakens to trend level ($p \le .10$) in random samples.
*$p \le .05$. ****$p \le .0001$.

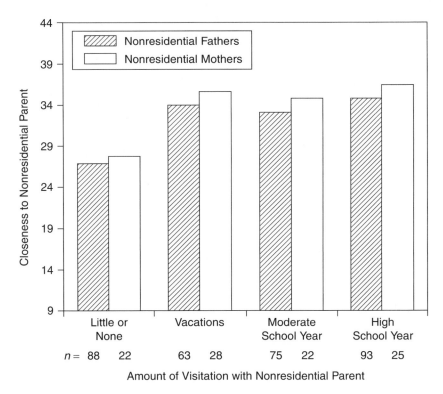

Figure 9.5   Closeness to the nonresidential parent among sole-resident adolescents, by level of contact with the nonresidential parent and residential arrangement. Means are adjusted for age and sex of adolescent and the average education of the two parents. Excludes adolescents who had not seen their nonresidential parent in the past year.

likely to have that parent confide in them and less likely to feel the need to nurture that parent (see Figure 9.6),[4] no doubt due to the lack of exposure to what is going on in the seldom-seen parent's life.

The link between more contact and a better relationship with the nonresidential parent is not at all surprising; very likely, the better relationship adolescents have with their nonresidential parent, the more they keep up visitation. Subsequently, the higher levels of visitation likely promote continued better relationships over time. What *is* surprising is that adolescents who see their nonresident parent as seldom as our lowest visitation group still report considerable closeness (above the midpoint of a scale that ranges from 10 to 45 points). And it is especially interesting

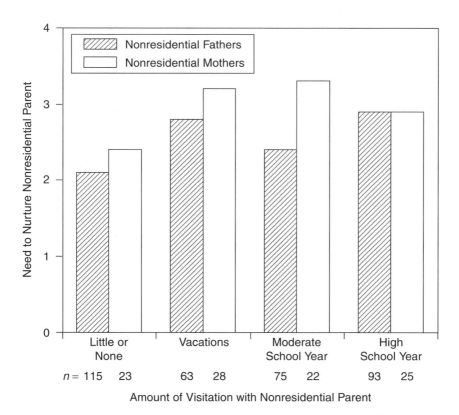

Figure 9.6 Sole-resident adolescents' reports of feeling the need to nurture their nonresidential parent, by level of contact with the nonresidential parent and residential arrangement. Means are adjusted for age and sex of adolescent and the average education of the two parents. Excludes adolescents who had not seen or talked to their nonresidential parent in the past year.

that even a small amount of visitation—only a two-week or longer vacation visit—appears sufficient to sustain a close relationship from the adolescents' perspective—nearly as close as that maintained by adolescents who spend two or three overnights with the nonresident parent every two weeks during the school year. This pattern is found among adolescents in both residential arrangements, and for boys as well as girls. In general, the relation between visitation and closeness is the same for older and younger adolescents as well, although for adolescents in mother residence the association is somewhat stronger for adolescents under age fourteen.

Our data also show that the gain in closeness to the nonresidential parent is *not* made at the expense of the relationship with the residential parent. Adolescents who visited their nonresidential parent frequently were extremely similar to adolescents who hardly ever visited the nonresidential parent in their relationships with their residential parent, and once again this was true regardless of whether the primary parent was the mother or the father, or whether the adolescent was male or female, old or young. We were particularly interested in whether adolescents would become more disengaged from the residential parent's household—in the sense of spending more time alone in their own rooms even when others were present in the house, or in spending more time away from the residential house—if they visited their nonresidential parent frequently. This did not turn out to be the case.

The only instance in which amount of visitation with the nonresidential parent was associated with the relationship between the residential parent and the child concerned the adolescents' felt need to nurture their mother. Adolescents who saw their nonresidential father rarely were more likely than other mother-resident adolescents to feel the need to nurture their mothers. Perhaps a lack of visitation itself leads to feelings of higher responsibility for one's mother because the mother-child relationship is more isolated, thus leading mother and child to depend on each other more than they would otherwise. Alternatively, this association may reflect some other aspect of families in which the fathers maintain little contact (for instance, lower levels of practical or financial aid) that may make life more difficult for mothers in this group, leading adolescents in this group to feel sorry for and worry about them.

Visitation and the Functioning of the Residential Parent's Household

Even though closeness to the residential parent may not be affected by the amount of visitation, it is still possible that residential parents may find it more difficult to manage households in which the children come and go frequently between the two parental households. Or, to the extent that the sharing of parenting has positive benefits (for example, a regular "break," support from the ex-spouse on parenting matters), high visitation might be linked with better household functioning. We examined whether the adolescents in our sample were reporting closer or looser monitoring by the residential parent, tighter or looser household organization, greater or less youth autonomy in decision making, or earlier or later curfews depending on the amount of visitation with the nonresidential parent.

We found no evidence that high levels of visitation interfered with or enhanced control and management in father-resident homes. Among mother-resident adolescents younger than age fourteen, regular school-year visitation was linked to somewhat more opportunities for the youth to make decisions alone—with or without discussion with parents—than was lower visitation (see Table 9.3). Among the older adolescents, however, high levels of visitation were associated with a lower likelihood that youths made final decisions concerning a range of issues, as well as a higher likelihood of earlier curfews on both school nights and weekends, than was less frequent visitation. Thus among older adolescents in mother residence, higher levels of visitation either allowed the parent to maintain a tighter rein at home or reflect a pattern of more controlled parenting (in other words, the very parents who maintain more control in the residential household may also be more likely to insist on regular and frequent visitation, even among older adolescents).

Visitation and Adolescent Adjustment

We noted earlier the questions that have been raised concerning the impact of visitation on the well-being of children in divorcing families, with the early research having indicated that mother-resident children were benefited by visits with their fathers and more recent work having called this finding into question. There has been very little work examining the effects of visits to mothers upon children who live with their fathers. We thus examined the relation between the level of visitation and adolescent adjustment.

As Table 9.4 shows, the amount of visitation with fathers had virtually no relation to the adjustment of mother-resident adolescents. A very modest exception initially was found in relation to grades—the group who saw their fathers primarily (or only) for a two-week or longer vacation period had the lowest grades—but this result weakened in random subsamples. It is puzzling that the vacation-only group should be different both from adolescents who see their fathers less often and from those who see them more often. As far as grades are concerned, it would be reasonable that fathers could only help with homework and otherwise support children's school effort if they see the children during the regular school year. But fathers' unavailability for help with schoolwork did not

Table 9.3 Relation of visitation frequency to mother's control and management in mother-residence homes, by age of adolescent[a]

Measure of control/management	Level of visitation				F_{visit}	F_{age}	$F_{interaction}$
	Little or none (1)	Vacation only (2)	Moderate (3)	High (4)			
Youth decides							
Adolescents under 14 years	.47	.43	.61	.51	5.95***	40.99****	6.89***
Adolescents 14 years and older	.77	.71	.71	.51		Older: 4 < 1,2,3 Younger: 3 > 1,2	
School night curfew							
Adolescents under 14 years	.75	.67	1.32	.79	3.49*	178.36****	4.12**,b
Adolescents 14 years and older	3.84	3.32	3.18	2.47		Older: 4 < 1,2,3; 3 < 1 Younger: n.s.	
Weekend night curfew							
Adolescents under 14 years	1.60	1.66	2.18	1.80	2.53+	223.50****	4.15**
Adolescents 14 years and older	5.65	5.53	4.99	4.07		Older: 4 < 1,2,3 Younger: n.s.	

a. Means are controlled for age and sex of adolescent and mid-parent education.
b. Effect weakens in random subsamples.

$+p \leq .10$. $*p \leq .05$. $**p \leq .01$. $***p \leq .001$. $****p \leq .0001$.   n.s. = not significant.

Table 9.4 Relation of visitation frequency to adolescent adjustment[a]

Measure of adjustment	Level of visitation				
	Little or none (1)	Vacation only (2)	Moderate (3)	High (4)	$F_{visitation}$
Mother-Resident Adolescents (visit father)					
Maximum *n*	(115)	(63)	(75)	(93)	
Depression/anxiety	15.9	15.8	15.2	14.4	.84
Deviance	21.3	22.3	21.3	20.3	2.28+,b
School grades	5.9	5.3	6.0	5.9	3.01*,c (2 < 1,3,4)
School effort	14.8	14.3	15.0	14.5	.74
Worst problem	110.9	112.8	109.4	110.3	.78
Father-Resident Adolescents (visit mother)					
Maximum *n*	(23)	(28)	(22)	(25)	
Depression/anxiety	17.2	13.7	17.6	13.6	2.59+,b
Deviance	24.8	22.1	22.4	23.0	1.00
School grades	5.2	5.5	5.4	5.5	.14
School effort	14.1	14.5	14.2	14.4	.05
Worst problem	119.2	111.9	116.8	111.2	1.17

a. Means are controlled for age and sex of adolescent and mid-parent education.
b. This result does not hold up in random samples.
c. This result weakens in random samples.
+$p \leq .10$.   *$p \leq .05$.

appear to affect the competence of adolescents who spent little or no time with their fathers. Overall, the differences in adjustment measures for adolescents with different amounts of visitation with fathers were remarkably small.

We examined whether the group averages might conceal countervailing trends in which visitation affected boys one way and girls another; or whether visitation might have different effects on adolescents of different ages. We found no interactions of visitation with age or sex of adolescent. We also did not find that the relation between visitation and adjustment differed by either parent's remarriage status, with one exception: if nonresidential fathers were remarried, adolescents were most depressed if they rarely saw him and least depressed if they saw him frequently. Perhaps when adolescents have the opportunity to spend time with fathers and their new wives, they can more easily feel a part of this new family; adolescents whose fathers remarry and also discontinue visitation may leave adolescents feeling abandoned or "left behind."

The relation between father visitation and adjustment did not differ depending on how close the adolescent felt to either parent. We also did not find that more visitation was linked to worse adjustment in situations of high parental conflict. There were only a small number of instances in which the relation between visitation and adjustment differed depending on the interparental relationship, and these instances generally pointed to a differential impact of vacation-only visitation. Vacation-only visitation was associated with poor adjustment if parental cooperation was low or hostility was high, but relatively good adjustment if parental cooperation was high or hostility was low. The low number of instances where such differential relations occurred leads us to view this particular set of findings somewhat skeptically, but it may indicate that infrequent (but regular) visitation is especially difficult for children when parents do not get along. Given that previous research concerning divorce and children's contact with the nonresidential parent has not looked in detail at the implications of visiting a parent infrequently but for substantial periods of time (such as summer vacations), this may be a form of visitation that deserves more focused attention.

The amount of visitation with mother also had very little relation to the adjustment of father-resident adolescents. And the effect of visiting mothers did not depend on the age or sex of the adolescents, on mother's or father's remarriage status, on adolescents' feelings of closeness to either parent, or on the degree of interparental conflict or cooperation.

Summary

In our sample of adolescents, few adolescents had "drop-out" nonresident parents; most had had at least some contact with their nonresidential parent within the past year. For many of the adolescents (a third of the mother-resident adolescents and a quarter of the father-resident adolescents), however, the contact was fairly minimal and not very regular. Adolescents were, not surprisingly, less likely to see parents who lived over two hours away (by car), but visitation was more often maintained despite long driving distances for father-resident adolescents visiting their mothers than for mother-resident adolescents visiting their fathers.

Whether visitation was being maintained at T4 was related to the amount of hostility the mother maintained toward her former spouse, but not to the father's hostility. It seems, then, that mothers function as gatekeepers who are able to exercise some control over the amount of visitation that will occur.

The amount of visitation, in and of itself, was related to very little about the adolescents or their primary residences. Visitation did not interfere with the residential parent's ability to monitor the adolescent or manage the household. If anything, older adolescents who visited their fathers frequently experienced more control by their residential mothers. And in line with some other studies (Furstenberg, Morgan, and Allison, 1987; Hess and Camara, 1979; King, 1991; Kurdek, Blisk, and Siesky, 1981; Luepnitz, 1982), there were few direct links between visitation and adolescent adjustment. But unlike some other studies (Amato and Rezac, 1994; Hetherington, Cox, and Cox, 1978, 1982; Zill, 1988), we did not find that the impact of visitation for sole-resident adolescents varied depending on the quality of the interparental relationship or the parents' remarriage status.

The primary finding with regard to visitation and its possible benefits is that when adolescents did visit the nonresidential parent—even if only for a couple of weeks in the summer—they were able to have a closer relation with the nonresidential parent than if visitation did not occur. Given that some visitation occurred, the amount of visitation mattered very little: vacation-only visitors were as close to their nonresidential parents as were more frequent visitors. The pattern of visiting only during vacations often occurred when the parent and adolescent lived a substantial distance apart. Thus even under circumstances of geographic distance and infrequent but regular and sustained contact, adolescents appear to be able to sustain a close relationship with the nonresidential parent. As we have already noted in detail, this is most likely due to a circular process. Adolescents and nonresidential parents who have close relationships are, no doubt, more likely to spend time together, but in addition, closer relationships can be maintained or enhanced when adolescents and parents continue to see each other. In the next chapter, we examine whether this enhanced closeness with the nonresidential parent provides benefits to the adolescent.

10

Life in the
Nonresidential Home

In this chapter we consider the impact of the nonresidential parent and home on the adolescent. First, however, we need to set a context for the nonresidential household. How do the relationship with the nonresidential parent and the kind of home that parent maintains compare to those of the residential parent? And does the answer to this question depend on which parent is residential and which is nonresidential, or whether the adolescent is a girl or boy? We address these questions before examining the relations between the quality of the nonresidential home and adolescent adjustment.

The Nature of the Nonresidential Home

Parent-Child Relationships

Two trends emerged concerning adolescents' relationships with their parents (see Appendix Table B.9 for means for both nonresidential and residential parents on the various constructs used to measure parent-child relationships). The first trend has to do with a comparison of relationships with a given parent (say, the mother), depending on whether that parent was a residential or a nonresidential parent. Not at all surprisingly, adolescents usually reported closer relationships with a parent of a given gender if they lived with that parent than if they just visited him or her. This was especially true of father-child relationships: both boys and girls who lived with their fathers—in sole or dual residence—reported better relationships with them on several indices (trust, identification, remembering special days, and to a lesser extent, closeness itself) than did adolescents who only visited their fathers. Living with one's mother was associated with better relationships with her as well, but only for girls. Unexpectedly, boys reported feeling equally close to, and equally likely to share activities with, residential and nonresidential mothers. The lack of a difference for boys indicates a particularly good relationship with the nonresidential mother, and not a poor relationship with the residential mother.

Along with closeness, and living with a parent, often comes conflict (Flanagan, Schulenberg, and Fuligni, 1993; Furman and Buhrmester, 1985a, b; Hartup et al., 1993; Youniss and Smollar, 1983). Accordingly, adolescents who lived with their father not only felt closer to him, but also reported more conflict with him and more disengagement from his household than adolescents who only visited their father. Surprisingly, however, conflict between adolescents and mothers did not depend on whether the mother was residential or nonresidential. Especially for girls, the level of conflict with nonresidential mothers was equal to that experienced with residential mothers,[1] one of the first indications we had that father-resident girls had more negative relationships with their nonresidential parent than did other groups of adolescents.

The second trend we noted, which was in line with previous research comparing relationships with mothers and fathers in nondivorced families (see, for example, Youniss and Smollar, 1983), was that adolescents tended to have somewhat closer relationships with their mothers than with their fathers. In Chapter 5, for example, we reported that adolescents were somewhat closer to residential mothers than to residential fathers. A comparison of adolescents' relationships with nonresidential mothers and nonresidential fathers revealed that, in some respects, adolescents also enjoyed better relationships with a nonresidential parent if that parent was a mother than if that parent was a father (see Appendix Table B.9).[2] For example, nonresidential mothers were reported to be more likely to remember special days, and adolescents reported more eagerness to visit them, than was the case for nonresidential fathers. These differences held for both boys and girls. But for girls, this is where the differences favoring nonresidential mothers ended. Only boys trusted nonresidential mothers more[3] (see Figure 10.1), and only boys identified more with nonresidential mothers than with nonresidential fathers. Girls in father residence, in contrast, experienced higher conflict with their mother (see Figure 10.2) and more disengagement from their mother's home than girls in mother residence experienced with their father. For boys, then, we see a somewhat more positive relationship with nonresidential mothers than nonresidential fathers, a positive relationship not accompanied by higher conflict. In contrast, girls had very similar relationships with nonresidential mothers

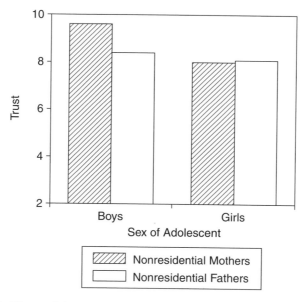

Figure 10.1 Trust of the nonresidential parent among sole-resident adolescents, by residential arrangement and sex of adolescent. Means are adjusted for age of adolescent and nonresidential parent's education.

and nonresidential fathers on most positive dimensions, but had more conflict with nonresidential mothers. Together with the finding reported earlier that the conflict between girls and nonresidential mothers is as high as that between girls and residential mothers, these results indicate that girls living with their fathers have more difficult relationships with their nonresidential mothers than other adolescents have with their nonresidential parents. Father-resident girls do not appear to be more distant, necessarily, from nonresidential mothers than one would expect on the basis of the mother's nonresidential status, but their emotional relationship appears to have a larger negative component. This is in line with previous speculations (see Chapters 3, 4, 5, and 6) that problems in the mother-child relationship represent one reason why children, especially girls, end up living with their fathers after divorce.

The two trends just described—greater closeness to residential parents than nonresidential parents and greater closeness to mothers than fathers—combined to create the following phenomenon with regard to a comparison of relationships between individual adolescents' residential and nonresidential parents (for the means for these comparisons, see

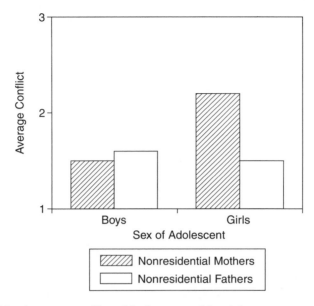

Figure 10.2 Average conflict with the nonresidential parent among sole-resident adolescents by residential arrangement and sex of adolescent. Means are adjusted for age of adolescent and nonresidential parent's education.

Appendix Table B.9): adolescents in mother residence were quite a bit closer (across several measures) to their residential parent (mother) than to their nonresidential parent (father); adolescents in father residence, particularly the boys, were about equally close to their residential parent (father) and their nonresidential parent (mother). The closer relationship with mothers for mother-resident adolescents emerged on every measure of parent-child relationships, and is demonstrated for closeness in Figure 10.3. Adolescents in mother residence also had higher levels of conflict with their mother and higher levels of disengagement from their mother's home than they had with their nonresident father.

For father-resident adolescents as a group, as already noted, relationships with mother and father were very similar. Adolescents in father residence, particularly boys,[4] felt equally close to their mothers and fathers and trusted them equally. Nonresidential mothers were as likely as residential fathers to remember special days, and adolescents were equally eager to see residential fathers and nonresidential mothers. The amount of conflict also did not differ by the parent's residential status for

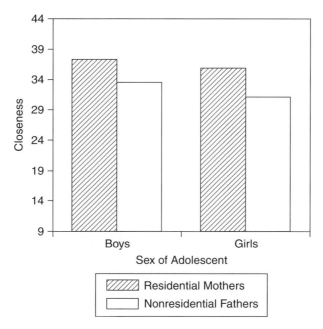

Figure 10.3 Closeness to mother versus father for mother-resident adolescents, by sex of adolescent.

father-resident adolescents.[5] And nonresidential mothers actually confided more in their children than did residential fathers. Only joint activities and disengagement were higher for residential fathers than for nonresidential mothers. Although identification with the residential father was higher than identification with the nonresidential mother among girls, father-resident boys identified with their mothers somewhat more than with their fathers (as did boys in the other residential arrangements). This sex difference in identification with each parent supports the earlier findings indicating a more troubled relationship between the nonresidential mother and girls, compared with boys, in father residence. The finding also points to a particularly positive relationship between boys and nonresidential mothers.

Parental Management and Control

There were few differences in the type and extent of parental management and control depending on residential status (see Appendix Table

B.10 for means). There were some small differences indicating more control on the part of a residential parent, as one might expect. For example, adolescents, especially in mother residence, were more closely monitored by the residential parent. And father-resident adolescents were less likely to have decision-making authority in their residential father's home than in the home of their nonresidential mother. There were no differences in decision-making practices between residential mothers and nonresidential fathers for mother-resident adolescents, however. Father-resident adolescents rated the rules in the nonresidential mother's home as more fair and consistent than those in the residential father's home, whereas mother-resident adolescents reported no difference in the fairness and consistency of rules between residential mothers and nonresidential fathers. Not surprisingly, adolescents spent more time doing chores in the residential home than in the nonresidential home, whether they were in mother or father residence, although this was slightly more true of mother-resident adolescents. The difference in chores between households was also greater among boys than among girls.

The Nonresidential Parent and Adolescent Adjustment

Of what importance are the nature of the nonresidential parent–child relationship and the processes within the nonresidential home? Does the nature of the relationship with or the home environment of the nonresidential parent have any impact on adolescent adjustment beyond the effect of the residential home? In the next section, we focus on the quality of the nonresidential parent–child relationship (how close it is, how conflictual) and its relation to adolescent adjustment after divorce. The impact of management and control practices in the nonresidential home is taken up in Chapter 12, in the context of consistency of parenting across households.

We have noted in earlier chapters that close, connected relationships between parent and child are important for healthy psychological and emotional adjustment of adolescents. But it is not clear from the available literature whether there are benefits from being close to two parents, or whether a strong, trustworthy relationship with one parent will suffice. If one parent is "enough," must the "good" relationship be with the residential parent, or can a close relationship with the nonresidential parent substitute for a more distant residential parent–child relationship? Can sustained closeness to the nonresidential parent after divorce ever be harmful? It is also not clear whether closeness to mother and closeness to father (or, conversely, the lack of closeness to one or the other) have different consequences. In situations of divorce, it is crucial to know whether the consequences of the nonresidential parent–child relationship depend on which parent is the nonresidential parent.

To examine these questions, we focused on five adjustment indices: depression/anxiety, overall deviance, school grades, school effort, and the adolescent's "worst problem." Aspects of the nonresidential parent–child relationship were used as predictors of adjustment: the overall closeness of the parent-adolescent relationship (the composite described in Chapter 5, made up of "emotional closeness," "trust," "identification," and "joint activities"), parent-child conflict, disengagement from the home, eagerness to see the parent, and whether the parent remembered special days such as holidays and birthdays.

First, we focused on whether the quality of the relationship between the nonresidential parent and adolescent was related in any way to the adolescent's adjustment, beyond the quality of the adolescent's relationship with the residential parent.[6] We examined the relation between various aspects of relationship quality and adjustment separately for male and female adolescents in each residential arrangement. In this way, we examined not only the general importance of the nonresidential parent but also whether the importance of that relationship varied as a function of who the nonresidential parent was—mother or father—and of the gender of the child.[7] Table 10.1 displays the relations that emerged.

Parent-Child Closeness

The closer the relationship between adolescents and their nonresidential parents, the less depression the adolescents experienced and the less severe was their "worst problem." In addition, adolescents who had closer relationships with their nonresidential parents tended to have higher grades. Although the strength of these associations varied among the different groups and depended on the measure of adjustment, the analyses indicated that the relation was basically the same for both boys and girls in both mother and father residence. The one exception is that for girls in father residence, but not boys, levels of deviance were lower if they maintained close relationships with their nonresidential mothers. Thus the overall closeness of the relationship with a nonresidential parent—whether mother or father—appears to be moderately linked with several aspects of better adjustment for both boys and girls.

Table 10.1 Associations between quality of nonresidential parent–adolescent relationship and adolescent adjustment for sole-resident adolescents[a]

Measures of relationship with nonresidential parent and adjustment	Mother-resident adolescents			Father-resident adolescents			Quality × Residence × Sex	Quality × Residence	Quality × Sex	Quality main effect
	Boys	Girls	All	Boys	Girls	All	β	β	β	β
Parent-Child Overall Closeness										
Maximum n	(151)	(184)	(335)	(61)	(38)	(99)				
Depression	−.05	−.13+	−.11*	−.05	−.12	−.11	n.s.	n.s.	n.s.	−.12**
Deviance	−.02	−.04	−.02	−.00	−.45***	−.18*	−.08+	−.09*,b	n.s.	n.s.
School grades	.07	.07	.07	.23+	.12	.18+	n.s.	n.s.	n.s.	.09*,c
School effort	.16+	−.01	.06	.09	.08	.11	n.s.	n.s.	n.s.	n.s.
Worst problem	−.11	−.14*	−.13*	−.01	−.33*	−.13	n.s.	n.s.	n.s.	−.13***
Parent-Child Conflict										
Maximum n	(89)	(74)	(163)	(30)	(14)	(44)				
Depression	−.31*	.11	−.06	−.08	−.51	−.26	−.14*	n.s.	n.s.	n.s.
Deviance	.27*	.07	−.13	.09	−.02	.07	n.s.d	n.s.	.12*	n.s.
School grades	−.04	−.02	−.01	−.26	.38	−.13	n.s.	n.s.	n.s.	n.s.

School effort	.09	.14	.14	−.11	−.21	−.19	n.s.	n.s.[e-g]	n.s.	n.s.
Worst problem	−.37**	.08	−.13	.17	.16	.16	−.11+	n.s.	.11+	n.s.
Disengagement from Home										
Maximum n	(106)	(101)	(207)	(44)	(21)	(65)				
Depression	−.05	.01	−.01	−.03	−.07	−.07	n.s.	n.s.	n.s.	n.s.
Deviance	.05	.13	.07	−.04	.25	.06	n.s.	n.s.	n.s.	n.s.
School grades	−.09	−.07	−.08	−.01	.01	−.01	n.s.	n.s.	n.s.	n.s.
School effort	−.10	−.10	−.10	−.04	−.55*	−.23+	n.s.	n.s.[d]	n.s.	−.14*[b]
Worst problem	.00	.06	.02	−.03	.43*	.10	n.s.	n.s.	n.s.[d-g]	n.s.
Eagerness to See										
Maximum n	(146)	(174)	(320)	(58)	(36)	(94)				
Depression	−.02	−.01	−.03	−.11	.10	−.04	n.s.	n.s.	n.s.	n.s.
Deviance	.04	.03	.04	.05	−.36*	−.13	n.s.	−.11*[f]	n.s.	n.s.
School grades	.09	−.07	−.00	−.04	.02	−.01	n.s.	n.s.	n.s.	n.s.
School effort	.16+	.01	.07	−.16	.09	.01	.09+	n.s.	n.s.	n.s.
Worst problem	−.05	−.02	−.03	.17	−.09	−.01	n.s.	n.s.	n.s.	n.s.

Table 10.1 (continued)

Measures of relationship with nonresidential parent and adjustment	Mother-resident adolescents			Father-resident adolescents			Quality × Residence × Sex β	Quality × Residence β	Quality × Sex β	Quality main effect β
	Boys	Girls	All	Boys	Girls	All				
Remembers Special Days										
Maximum *n*	(167)	(196)	(363)	(61)	(38)	(99)				
Depression	−.18*	−.07	−.13**	−.22+	−.01	−.10	n.s.	n.s.	n.s.	−.13**
Deviance	−.12+	−.07	−.09+	−.11	−.16	−.11	n.s.	n.s.	n.s.	−.08+,f
School grades	.22**	.09	.15**	.28*	−.12	.08	−.10*	n.s.	−.08+,g	.12
School effort	.24**	−.07	.06	.28*	−.17	.06	−.09+	n.s.	−.15**	n.s.
Worst problem	−.25***	−.06+	−.15**	−.18	−.06	−.11	n.s.	n.s.	.09*,b,g	−.14**

a. Numbers are standardized beta weights from regressions predicting adjustment with quality of the relationship with the nonresidential parent, controlling for quality of the relationship with the residential parent and age of adolescent. Sex is controlled in analyses not broken down by sex.

b. Effect is not significant in random subsamples.

c. Effect weakens in random subsamples.

d. Effect becomes significant in random subsamples.

e. Effect becomes marginally significant (*p* ≤ .10) in random subsamples.

f. Effect becomes more significant in random subsamples.

g. Although this particular two-way interaction was significant, the change in *R*² as a result of the three two-way interactions entered into the second step of the regression analyses was not significant. Because this particular two-way interaction was of interest in and of itself (and not just as part of the set of two-way interactions), we still note its individual significance.

p ≤ .05.　　**p* ≤ .01.　　***p* ≤ .001.　　+*p* ≤ .10.　　n.s. = not significant.

Remembering Special Days

Besides parent-child closeness, remembering special days like birthdays and holidays was the only other aspect of the nonresidential parent–child relationship that was consistently related to adolescent adjustment. The more likely a nonresidential parent was to remember special days, the less depressed and less deviant the adolescent, and the less severe the "worst problem." In addition, for boys—those in father residence, particularly—having a nonresidential parent who remembered special days was linked to higher grades and higher effort in school. Thus the more the nonresidential parent remembered holidays and birthdays, the more the son was invested in school. Why was the ability of the nonresidential parent to remember special days one of the most important predictors of adolescent adjustment? Perhaps the symbolic value of remembering holidays and birthdays is particularly important to children of divorce. By remembering such days a parent is communicating that the child is important and not forgotten, even in situations where parent and child do not often see each other or where the relationship cannot be characterized as emotionally warm or close.

Other Aspects of the Relationship

The more negative aspects of the relationship with the nonresidential parent—disengagement from the nonresidential home and conflict with the nonresidential parent—mattered little with regard to adolescent adjustment. Disengagement from the nonresidential home was not associated with any index of adjustment.[8] There were also no associations between nonresidential parent–child conflict and adjustment that held for all subgroups of adolescents, and the associations that did emerge were counterintuitive. For example, higher levels of conflict with nonresidential fathers (but not nonresidential mothers) were sporadically linked to better, not worse, adjustment for boys. Although we envisioned high levels of conflict between parents and children as a negative factor in children's adjustment, perhaps within the range of conflict experienced by nonresidential fathers and their sons conflict was indicative of a higher level of engagement with the father that was positive for those boys.

Adolescents' eagerness to see the nonresidential parent was also virtually unrelated to their adjustment. Among girls, greater eagerness to see the nonresidential mother was linked to lower levels of deviance.[9] And there was a slight tendency for boys in mother residence to report more school effort when they also reported eagerness to see their nonresidential father. These associations, however, are probably too weak and too sporadic to be meaningful.

Summary

It is important to make it clear that we cannot establish whether a better relationship with the nonresidential parent leads to better adjustment in the adolescent, or whether adolescents who are better adjusted maintain better relationships with their nonresidential parent. There is reason to believe that both processes are at work. A conservative interpretation of our findings is that a continuing positive relationship with the nonresidential parent, in general, does not pose risks for the adolescent. And in fact positive effects may be felt from closeness in the nonresidential parent–child relationship and from having a nonresidential parent who remembers special days—even among father-resident girls, who, on average, have more negative relationships with their nonresidential mothers. The strength of the associations we have reported is small, indicating that any impact is weak to moderate; nonetheless, the associations were consistently positive and, in the cases we have noted, strong enough to reject the notion of chance associations. Of course, the small magnitude of the associations also suggests that any impact of the nonresidential parent–child relationship is moderated by other factors (for example, the quality of the relationship between the parents or between the residential parent and child), and we consider this possibility in subsequent sections. Before considering other aspects of the context in which the relationship with the nonresidential parent is embedded, however, we need to address several issues concerning the findings thus far.

Do these data provide any support for the notion that adolescents need most to retain a good relationship with their same-sex parent? It has been argued that children benefit from sustaining a relationship with the same-sex parent (Santrock and Warshak, 1979; Warshak and Santrock, 1983; Zaslow, 1989), and Gunnoe (1994) provides some support for the importance of a relationship between adolescents and a same-sex nonresidential parent. Our own data on the adjustment of adolescents living with same-sex versus opposite-sex parents (reported in Chapter 4), however, did not indicate that, in general, living with the same-sex parent promoted better adjustment than living with the opposite-sex parent. Our data on nonresidential parents also do not indicate a special need to maintain a close relationship with the same-sex parent, with the possible exception that girls benefit slightly more than boys do from a sustained relationship with their mother. Although for most of our adjustment indices, boys and girls appeared to benefit equally from the continued relationship with a nonresidential mother, a close relationship with and eagerness to see nonresidential mothers was linked to lower levels of deviant behavior for girls only. Although conflict with the nonresidential father was most strongly linked to various adjustment measures for boys in mother custody, it was linked in a counterintuitive way: more conflict with nonresident fathers was associated with better adjustment. These sporadic findings certainly do not point to any special value of maintaining a relationship with the same-sex parent. The more important message seems to be that nonresidential parents have a small but positive role to play in promoting positive adjustment in their adolescents. This is true even for nonresidential mothers and their daughters, whose relationships tend to be more negative, on average, than other nonresidential parent–child relationships.

This message raises another important question. If a good relationship with the nonresidential parent can promote positive outcomes in adolescents, and if visitation promotes a good relationship with the nonresidential parent (as we reported in Chapter 9), why did we not find that visitation with the nonresidential parent, per se, promoted positive adolescent adjustment? The answer to this question is complex, but has to do with the fact that the associations between visitation and the nonresidential parent–child relationship, and between this relationship and adolescent adjustment, are small, and vary in strength depending on other factors. For example, low visitation interferes with closeness mainly at the extreme. Children cannot be close to a nonresidential parent if they never or almost never see that parent. But even modest levels of contact appeared to allow relationships between nonresidential parents and adolescents that were as close as those that occurred when contact was high. Furthermore, although visitation opens the door to a close relationship, it certainly does not guarantee one. Closeness clearly depends on many factors, including how committed and involved the nonresidential parent is, his or her personality, or the supportiveness of other members of the nonresidential household. Similarly, closeness to the nonresidential parent is of some benefit to most adolescents, but is no guarantee of better adjustment. As will be seen shortly, closeness to a nonresidential parent may help with adjustment more under some circumstances, such as when there is not too much discord between the residential and nonresidential parent. In the end, we conclude from these data that sustained closeness to a nonresidential parent is more important to adolescent adjustment than is visitation per se; visitation levels are not precise enough indicators of what happens in the course of visitation to capture the changes in adjustment that may occur as a result of those happenings.

Patterns of Positive Affect with Each Parent
and Adolescent Adjustment

We conclude from the results just reported that a good relationship with the nonresidential parent can sometimes be a positive factor in adolescent adjustment, beyond the relationship with the residential parent. In addition, however, we wished to know whether the effect of the relationship with the nonresidential parent varied as a function of the relationship with the residential parent. In other words, is there benefit to having a good relationship with two parents, or is a good relationship with one parent "enough"? Is a good relationship with a nonresidential parent of greater benefit when an adolescent is not close to the residential parent than when a good residential parent–child relationship already exists?

Before exploring the potential benefits of remaining close to both parents, we must ask whether children *can* remain close to both parents after divorce. Some argue that in situations of interparental conflict, it is very difficult for a child to maintain positive relationships with both parents; later in this chapter we will address the link between ongoing interparental conflict and closeness to each parent. Four and a half years after divorce, however, many parents are not actively in conflict; in fact, many parents shield their children from such active conflict throughout the divorce process. In general, what can one expect concerning the relationships a child of divorce can maintain with each parent? Some believe that the circumstance of divorce itself—the fact that parents are enough at odds to go through with a divorce—makes it difficult, if not impossible, for children to remain close to both parents. According to this controversial view, it is as if children's closeness to two people who are so different that they cannot remain married is a zero-sum game, in which increases in closeness to one of the opposing parties must be associated with decreases in closeness to the other (see Goldstein, Freud, and Solnit, 1979).

Other perspectives offer different predictions. For instance, an attachment perspective (for example, Bowlby, 1973) would predict that if children have a trusting and secure relationship with at least one parent they are more likely to be able to have close relationships with other adults, including the other parent. Or, from a personality perspective, the types of parents who develop and nurture truly positive relationships with their children are more likely to possess personality traits (sensitivity, warmth) or interpersonal orientations (maturely developed) that are conducive to allowing their children physical and emotional access to the other parent. These latter perspectives not only suggest that a child can be close to both parents, but that closeness to one parent will be predictive of closeness to the other.

Our data generally support the latter views. Overall, among our adolescents, having a close relationship with mother was positively, albeit moderately, related to having a close relationship with father ($r = .19$, $p < .0001$). The magnitude of this relation varied for different subgroups of adolescents, however. For example, the correlation between overall closeness with mother and overall closeness with father for adolescents in dual residence was .55 (as opposed to .20 in mother residence and .07 in father residence). Only among one group was the correlation between mother-child closeness and father-child closeness not positive: the correlation was −.15 (not statistically significant) for father-resident girls.[10] Thus a good relationship with one parent was generally predictive of a good relationship with the other, except for father-resident girls.

To begin to examine the relation between patterns of closeness with both parents and adjustment, we focused first on sole-resident adolescents. We examined whether the impact of a close relationship with the nonresidential parent differed depending on the level of closeness to the residential parent. We also investigated whether the answer to this question varied by residential arrangement (in other words, depending on the gender of the residential and nonresidential parent).[11]

For four out of the five adjustment measures (all except school grades), the relation of nonresidential parent–adolescent closeness to adjustment depended on the closeness of the residential parent–adolescent bond *for father-resident adolescents only.* In other words, the "effect" of a close relationship with a nonresidential mother depended on the degree of closeness to the residential father (see Figures 10.4 and 10.5). If adolescents reported being close to their residential father, a close relationship with their mother in addition was beneficial; the group of father-resident adolescents that were engaged in a close relationship with both parents were better adjusted than any of the other father-resident adolescents. In contrast, adolescents who had close relationships with their residential fathers and *not* their nonresidential mothers tended to have the lowest levels of adjustment. If adolescents were *not* engaged in a close relationship with their residential father, being close to their mother did not add consistent

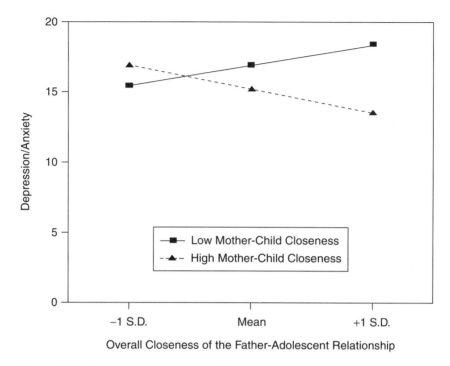

Figure 10.4 Depression/anxiety at different levels of father-child and mother-child closeness for father-resident adolescents.

benefits with regard to adjustment; adolescents who had a close relationship with their mother and those who did not were generally similar in their levels of depression, deviance, school effort, and "worst problem" in situations where the father-adolescent relationship was not close.[12]

In contrast, for mother-resident adolescents, the associations between closeness in the father-child relationship and adjustment did not vary depending on what the relationship with the mother was like. In general, closeness between an adolescent and the residential mother was the stronger predictor of several adjustment measures; the relationship with the father appeared to add modest additional benefits for selected measures of the relationship and selected measures of adjustment, sometimes for both genders and sometimes only for boys, but any relations were independent of the quality of the relationship between an adolescent and his or her mother. As a result, in instances where the relationship with the nonresidential father *was* related to better adjustment, adolescents who had good relationships with both parents were better off than ado-

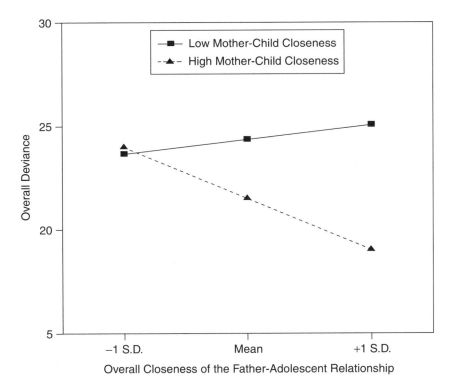

Figure 10.5 Overall deviance at different levels of father-child and mother-child closeness for father-resident adolescents.

lescents who had good relationships with only their father or with neither parent (see Figure 10.6). But the benefits of being close to both parents over being close to only the residential parent were not as great in mother residence as they were in father residence.[13] In addition, the relationship with the mother was clearly a stronger predictor of adolescent adjustment than was the relationship with the nonresidential father, and it predicted better adjustment regardless of the level of father-child closeness.

In sum, although having a close relationship with both parents was of some benefit to both mother-resident and father-resident adolescents, it was of more benefit to father-resident adolescents. For father-resident adolescents, in fact, a close relationship with their mother appeared to be necessary for adolescents to benefit from a close relationship with their father. Adolescents did not benefit, however, from being close only to the nonresidential parent in either mother or father residence.

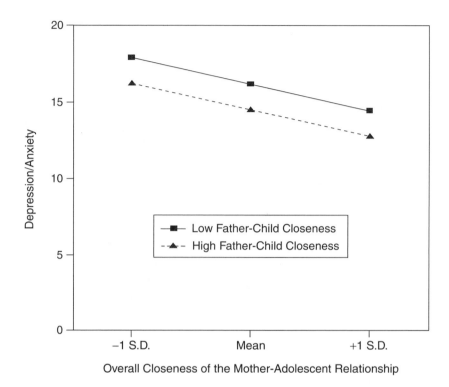

Figure 10.6 Depression/anxiety at different levels of mother-child and father-child closeness for mother-resident adolescents.

Thus far we have excluded dual-resident adolescents from analyses looking at the relations between closeness to the nonresidential parent and adjustment, because dual-resident adolescents do not have a nonresidential parent. In Chapter 5, however, we noted that adolescents in dual residence maintained close, positive affective bonds with both their mother and their father, remaining as close or closer to each parent as adolescents in sole-resident arrangements were with their residential parent. Is it the fact that adolescents in dual residence were more likely to have close relationships with two parents after a divorce than adolescents in sole residence that accounts for their somewhat better levels of adjustment (see Chapter 4)?

To test this, we looked at an adolescent's "total closeness" to both parents (to do this, we summed the reported closeness to two parents). We then examined whether any advantage of being in dual residence on the "worst problem" index remained when taking account of this total closeness.[14] When closeness to two parents was controlled, dual-resident adolescents no longer had better scores on "worst problem," indicating that their better adjustment was a reflection of their better relationships with both parents.

Interparental Conflict and the Parent-Child Relationship

Given that a continuing positive relationship with the nonresidential parent appears to carry some benefits for adolescents, it becomes important to know what factors enhance or interfere with that relationship. As we have already noted, continuing contact with the nonresidential parent—even at the level of summer visitation—is one such factor. Another that may be important for the quality of the nonresidential parent–child relationship is the amount of continuing conflict between the two parents. Earlier in this century, Fritz Heider (1958) proposed a balance theory of interpersonal relations that, applied to the social network of parent, parent, and child, predicts great difficulty for the child in remaining close to both parents when those parents are actively conflictual or hostile (see Johnston and Campbell, 1987, for such an application). In short, this theory predicts that instability in a social network (in this case the network of parent, parent, and child) will result if there exists an odd number of negative relations. If the bond between parents is negative, tension and instability in the network is expected to be resolved by the severing or souring of at least one parent-child bond.

In addition to Heider's formulation, several theoretical and empirical analyses suggest that an important mechanism by which parental conflict contributes to behavior problems and/or psychological distress in children is through the disruption of healthy parent-child relationships (Buchanan, Maccoby, and Dornbusch, 1991; Fauber et al., 1990; Patterson, 1982; Sessa and Steinberg, 1991). But what, exactly, is the impact of interparental conflict on the parent-adolescent relationship? Does it have an equally negative effect on the adolescent's relationship with each parent? Perhaps adolescents withdraw from both parents when those parents cannot get along, or perhaps neither parent has the energy to invest in the parent-child relationship under such circumstances. Alternatively, and more in line with Heider's prediction, interparental conflict may lead to alignment with a particular parent, an alignment that may be systematic in some fashion (for example, more often with mothers than with fathers; more often with a residential parent than with a nonresidential parent; more often with a same-sex parent than with an opposite-sex parent).

Given these unanswered questions, we looked at the relation of inter-parental conflict to adolescent-mother and adolescent-father closeness,[15] separately for each gender and residential arrangement, for sole-resident adolescents. The central question we sought to answer was whether interparental conflict was likely to interfere with the nonresidential parent–child relationship, and, if so, whether it was more likely to interfere with this relationship than with the relationship between the residential parent and child. We also wanted to know if the answers to these questions depended on the adolescent's sex or residential arrangement. In addition, we examined several indices of interparental conflict; in situations of divorce it might be important to distinguish between types and sources of conflict (for example, conflict specifically over co-parenting issues versus general parental hostility; or hostility toward the former spouse expressed by the residential versus nonresidential parent).

Table 10.2 displays the correlations between the various measures of interparental conflict and adolescents' closeness to their residential and nonresidential parents for all sole-resident adolescents combined, and for each sex by residence group.[16]

Interparental Conflict and Closeness to the Nonresidential Parent

In general, for adolescents living in either mother or father residence, a conflictual or noncooperative relationship between the parents was associated with a less close relationship between the adolescent and the nonresidential parent. Six of the seven measures of the interparental relationship (all except hostility of the nonresidential parent) were related to closeness to the nonresidential parent in the expected direction: higher conflict and hostility were linked to reduced closeness, and higher cooperation and agreement were linked with greater closeness. Hostility of the nonresidential parent was associated with less close relationships with the nonresidential parent only for girls in father residence.[17] Furthermore, the relation between several of the other conflict measures and closeness to the nonresidential parent was particularly strong for girls in father residence.[18] Thus girls' relationships with their nonresidential mothers appear especially vulnerable to interparental conflict. These findings also indicated that in father residence, girls' relationships with their mothers were more adversely affected by parental conflict than were boys' relationships with their mothers; in mother residence, any adverse impact of parental conflict on the relationship with father was similar for boys and girls.[19]

Table 10.2 Correlations between the interparental relationship and parent-adolescent closeness for adolescents in sole-residence arrangements at T4

Measure of the interparental relationship	All sole-resident adolescents[a]			Mother-resident boys[b]			Mother-resident girls[b]			Father-resident boys[b]			Father-resident girls[b]		
	n	NRP[c]	RP[d]	*n*	NRP	RP	*n*	NRP	RP	*n*	NRP	RP	*n*	NRP	RP
Parent Report															
Discord (T3)	287	−.16**	−.07	104	−.24*	−.11	122	−.14	−.02	38	.07	.07	23	−.26	−.27
Cooperative communication (T3)	286	.17**	.02	104	.14	−.07	121	.18+	.04	38	−.06	.09	23	.43*	.07
Residential parent's hostility (T3)	382	−.17**	−.02	137	−.25**	−.03	161	−.10	−.05	53	−.02	−.07	31	−.34+	.20
Nonresidential parent's hostility (T3)	317	−.09	−.08	108	.03	.02	136	−.10	−.16+	46	.11	.07	27	−.48*	.02
Adolescent Report															
Frequency of arguing (T4)	431	−.14**	−.00	148	−.06	.01	185	−.09	−.01	60	−.02	.08	38	−.57***	−.05
Parental agreement	437	.34***	.27***	151	.23***	.33***	187	.30***	.34***	61	.26*	.27*	38	.28+	.41*
Cooperation (T4)	282	.24***	.29***	109	.10	.23*	106	.32***	.25*	45	.17	.56***	22	.39+	.17

a. Correlations partial the effects of age and sex of adolescent and residential arrangement.
b. Correlations partial the effects of age of adolescent.
c. NRP = nonresidential parent.
d. RP = residential parent.
+*p* ≤ .10. **p* ≤ .05. ***p* ≤ .01. ****p* ≤ .001.

We also looked at whether the relation between interparental conflict and adolescents' closeness to the nonresidential parent differed for older and younger adolescents, or for adolescents with different levels of contact with the nonresidential parent. There were only a couple of selective instances where age or level of contact mattered. Within the age range in our sample, older adolescents' relationships with their parents appeared slightly more susceptible to the negative influences of discord at T3. In addition, in some instances the relation between interparental conflict and a less close nonresidential parent–child relationship held primarily for adolescents who rarely saw their nonresidential parent. In these instances (the associations between T3 maternal hostility and closeness to nonresidential fathers, and between T4 parental arguing or agreement and closeness to nonresidential mothers), if the adolescent was spending regular time with the nonresidential parent—even if only for several weeks in the summer—the quality of the relationship with that parent appeared to be unaffected by the problems between the parents. This indicates that continued visitation with a nonresidential parent may help children to maintain positive ties with that parent even in the face of continued interparental disharmony.

Does the association between interparental conflict and lower levels of closeness to the nonresidential parent occur because, under conditions of interparental conflict, the residential parent is more likely to restrict access to the nonresidential parent? Our results suggest not. Accounting for nonresidential parent contact does not eliminate the relation between better interparental relationships and a closer nonresidential parent–child relationship. The associations between various measures of the interparental relationship and contact with the nonresidential parent were, overall, quite weak and seldom significant (see also Chapter 9). Only in the case of mother-resident boys was there some evidence of an indirect link between interparental conflict (mother's hostility in particular) and less close relationships with father because of reduced visitation. It thus appears that negative interparental relationships interfere with the parent-child relationship for reasons that are more emotional and psychological than a product of the amount of contact. Clearly, the negative emotions expressed by the residential parent may influence the child to view the nonresidential parent more negatively. Alternatively, characteristics of the nonresidential parent may stimulate interparental conflict or hostility as well as difficulty in developing or sustaining a close parent-child relationship.

Interparental Conflict and Closeness to the Residential Parent

In contrast to the findings regarding closeness to the nonresidential parent, closeness to the residential parent was not related to the level of conflict or cooperation between parents as reported by the parents themselves, to the degree of hostility between parents, or to adolescent-reported frequency of parental arguing. Only adolescents' reports of parental cooperation or agreement at T4 were consistently associated with closeness to the residential parent. And only for older adolescents was hostility on the part of either parent—but especially the residential parent—associated with lower levels of closeness to the residential parent.[20]

Summary

For four of the seven conflict measures we used (T3 cooperation, residential parent hostility, nonresidential parent hostility, and T4 frequency of arguing), interparental conflict was most likely to interfere with the non-residential parent–child relationship.[21] This was true for boys and girls who were living with their mothers, but for adolescents living with their fathers, interparental conflict interfered with the relationship with nonresidential mothers primarily or only among girls (see Figure 10.7 for an illustration using residential parent's hostility).

Parental cooperation and agreement as reported by adolescents at T4, in contrast to the other parental relationship measures, were related as strongly to closeness to the residential parent as they were to the non-residential parent. Perhaps when both parents—in the adolescents' eyes—were trying to cooperate at the time of the final interview both enhanced their relationships with that adolescent. It is also possible, however, that adolescents' own reports of parental cooperation or agreement were biased by the adolescents' feelings of closeness to both parents; in other words, when adolescents felt close to both parents, they might also have been more likely to view them as cooperative. Even with these caveats, most of our results suggest that ongoing interparental conflict is more likely to interfere with the nonresidential parent–child relationship.

In sum, the circumstances of high interparental conflict appear to make it difficult for adolescents to develop or sustain close relationships to the nonresidential parent. To some extent, the adolescent's relationships with both parents may be vulnerable to the effects of conflict, but the vulnerability appears greatest for the nonresidential parent, particularly the non-

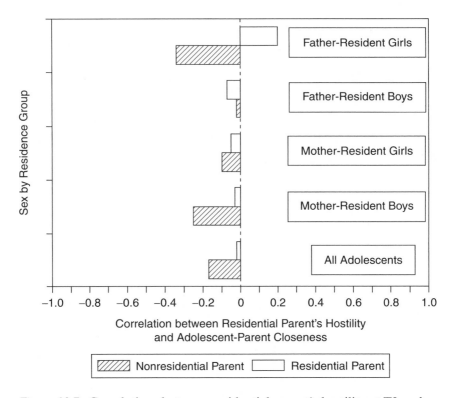

Figure 10.7 Correlations between residential parent's hostility at T3 and adolescents' closeness to both residential and nonresidential parents, by residence and sex of adolescent. Correlations are adjusted for age of adolescent.

residential mothers of girls who live primarily with their fathers. Is this evidence for alignment as a consequence of parental conflict? In a sense, yes, because adolescents may experience differential levels of closeness with the two parents, typically feeling closer to the residential parent under conditions of parental conflict. There is more evidence for alignment than there is for adolescent children's withdrawal from both parents.

Interparental Conflict, Closeness to the Nonresidential Parent, and Adolescent Adjustment

Earlier we reported generally positive findings regarding maintaining a close relationship with the nonresidential parent and adolescent adjustment. We wondered, however, if maintaining a close relationship with the nonresidential parent would be especially beneficial under conditions where parents got along with each other, and perhaps especially harmful when parents were still highly conflicted. Therefore we investigated how interparental conflict or cooperation interacted with parent-adolescent closeness in predicting adjustment. We also considered residential arrangement in order to see whether the effects of experiencing different patterns of interparental conflict and parent-child closeness depended on whether the adolescent's nonresidential parent was the mother or the father.[22]

We found little support for this interactive hypothesis. For example, using discord at T3 as the measure of interparental conflict, we found that depression was lowest among adolescents who reported both high closeness to the nonresidential parent and low interparental discord (see Figure 10.8). Under conditions of high interparental discord, the quality

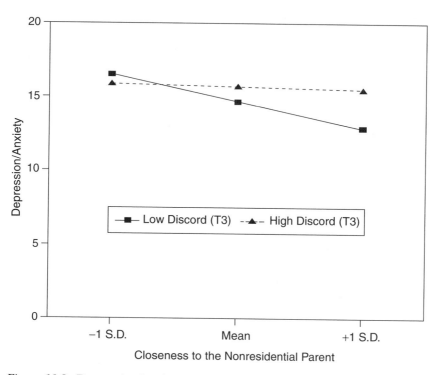

Figure 10.8 Depression/anxiety at different levels of interparental discord at T3, by level of adolescent's closeness to the nonresidential parent.

of the relationship with the nonresidential parent was of little consequence; being close to the nonresidential parent in conditions of high
conflict was neither detrimental nor beneficial. Thus in some cases adolescents may benefit from the combination of close relationships with the
nonresidential parent and positive interparental relationships even more
than they would from each factor independently. But there were many
instances in which no interactive effects of these two factors were found,
indicating that in most instances the two factors were independent.

Summary

The majority of the adolescents in our study continued to maintain some
kind of contact with their nonresidential parent after the divorce (see
Chapter 9). The quality of nonresidential father–child relationships was
lower on many indices than the quality of the relationship between those
children and their residential mothers. This is not surprising, because children—even in nondivorced families—are often closer to mothers
(Youniss and Smollar, 1983), and the greater contact with a residential
parent provides more opportunities to develop or sustain closeness, trust,
and intimacy. What is perhaps more surprising is the similarity in the
relationships with residential fathers and with nonresidential mothers
among boys. Even when boys were not living with their mothers, they
managed to stay almost as closely involved with them as they did with their
residential fathers. Girls in father residence, although similar on some
dimensions in their relationships with father and mother, were more likely
than boys to favor their relationships with their residential fathers.

In line with these observations, the quality of the relationship between
an adolescent boy and his nonresidential parent depended on whether
the nonresidential parent was a mother or a father. Father-resident boys
reported greater intimacy on a variety of measures with their nonresidential mothers than did mother-resident boys with their nonresidential
fathers. For girls, in comparison with boys, there was less evidence of
intimacy with the nonresidential mother; instead, these girls reported
higher levels of friction. Girls also reported more distance and somewhat
more conflict with nonresidential mothers than with residential mothers,
while boys' relationships with mothers were good regardless of their
residential status. Considered together, these results indicate a potentially troubled relationship between girls and nonresidential mothers
(particularly because of the higher levels of conflict) and a particularly
good relationship between boys and nonresidential mothers.

What is the role of the nonresidential parent in adolescent adjustment? Again, we have to begin by acknowledging that the causal direction of the associations that emerged is not clear. Our findings do, however, suggest that a continuing relationship with the nonresidential parent contributes positively to adolescent adjustment, although the magnitude of any general effect is modest. The aspects of the relationship that have this modest but positive relation with good adjustment are the overall closeness of the nonresidential parent–child relationship and the tendency of nonresidential parents to remember special days and holidays. Conflict with and disengagement from the nonresidential parent were less consistently related to adolescent adjustment. Furthermore, father-resident adolescents especially appeared to need a close relationship with both parents—having a close relationship with only one parent, father or mother, did not enhance adjustment. For adolescents in mother residence, in contrast, the relationship with their mother was clearly most strongly related to adjustment; adolescents were better off the closer they were to their mother,[23] regardless of their closeness to their father. The closeness of the father-adolescent relationship made an additional, though small, contribution to adjustment. As in father residence, however, closeness to the nonresidential parent alone was not especially helpful for adolescents.

We did not find that maintaining a close relationship with a nonresidential parent in situations of interparental conflict was especially harmful. We did find that ongoing conflict between parents can interfere with an adolescent's relationship with the nonresidential parent, however. Such conflict appears to have little or no bearing on the adolescent's relationship with the residential parent. These findings support the view that it is difficult for an adolescent to remain close to both parents when those parents are in conflict, and suggest that the most likely result of interparental conflict is a worsening of the relationship with the parent whom an adolescent sees least. Of course, it is also possible that adolescents have poor relationships with those same nonresidential parents with whom the residential parent finds it hardest to get along; only longitudinal data looking at the changes in the quality of the nonresidential parent–child relationship over time can distinguish between these possibilities.

11

Feeling Caught between
One's Parents

As we attempt to understand the experience of being part of two homes and two families, the issue of loyalty conflicts comes to the fore. It has been assumed by both popular and academic writers that feeling love and allegiance toward both parents after a divorce generates internal conflicts in children. Loyalty toward one parent is thought to preclude or interfere with the love for the other parent if the two parents do not love each other (Heider, 1958; Johnston and Campbell, 1987), so that when parents divorce, children are put in the position of having to choose between their parents and yet not being able to make such a heart-rending choice. Yet despite references to this concept in popular writing (for example, Rosemond, 1994) as well as in the scholarly divorce literature (for example, Clingempeel and Segal, 1986; Goldstein, Freud, and Solnit, 1979; Johnston and Campbell, 1987; Levy and Chambers, 1981; Shiller, 1986b; Wallerstein and Blakeslee, 1989; Wallerstein and Kelly, 1980), there has been little empirical research on loyalty conflicts. Detailed discussions tend to be clinical in nature (see, for example, Johnston and Campbell, 1987; Oppawsky, 1989; Wallerstein and Kelly, 1980) and based on clinical assessments or case studies. In our study, we attempted to study loyalty conflicts systematically in a broad sample of adolescent children of divorce, and examine both the predictors and the consequences of such conflicts.

It is a tenet of family systems theory that healthy family functioning requires the maintenance of clear boundaries between the parental sub-system and the children. These boundaries are obviously weakened when children are drawn into parental negotiations, tensions, or active conflicts; children can thereby feel pressure to take sides or form alliances with one parent or the other. Boundaries can be eroded in a number of

Table 11.1 Questions assessing adolescents' experience of feeling caught between their parents

---

How often do you feel caught in the middle between your mother and your father? (1 = never, to 4 = very often)

How often does your mother [father] ask you to carry messages to your father [mother]? (1 = never, to 4 = very often; maximum score between mother and father used)

Does your mother [father] ever ask questions about your father's [mother's] home that you wish she [he] wouldn't ask? (1 = yes, 2 = no; maximum score between mother and father used)

When your mother [father] is around, how often do you hesitate to talk about things concerning your father [mother]? (1 = never, to 4 = very often; maximum score between mother and father used)

---

ways, as for example when one or both parents use the child as a confidant or as a go-between. The consequences for children of playing such roles are expected to be stress, confusion, and anxiety (Aponte and Van Deusen, 1981; Emery, 1988; Minuchin, 1974).

We asked our adolescents several questions intended to capture the extent to which they felt caught between their parents (see Table 11.1). First, adolescents answered the direct question "How often do you feel caught in the middle between your mother and your father?," intended to assess subjective feelings of being caught. In addition, they were asked about aspects of parental behavior that might indicate potential triangulation or boundary diffusion (specifically, parents' attempts to use the adolescent as either a message carrier or an informer) as well as their feelings of needing to hide emotions or information regarding one parent from the other. Although all adolescents answered the first question ("how often do you feel caught"), the other questions were only asked of adolescents who had enough face-to-face or telephone contact with each parent to be able to answer the question. The answers to these questions were combined to create an overall index of the extent to which an adolescent felt caught between his or her parents (see Buchanan, Maccoby, and Dornbusch, 1991, for more details).

Adolescents' Comments

Almost two-thirds of the adolescents in our sample said that they felt caught between their parents at least sometimes. Ten percent said they felt caught "very often." For adolescents who said they felt caught at least sometimes, we then asked if they could give us an example of an instance in which they felt that way. Adolescents had little trouble answering these questions, and their responses helped us to understand the variety of situations that led to such feelings.

As anticipated, one commonly mentioned scenario involved parents asking their children to carry messages. Adolescents described a number of situations involving communication between their parents when asked to give an example of something that made them feel caught:

(Early-adolescent female): "When one parent tells me to tell the other one something, tell them this and tell them that. Tell her that I don't want you to do that anymore or something. Things like that."

(Early-adolescent female): "Like when they're arguing and my dad doesn't want to talk to my mom. I can't be all that specific, but . . . he's trying to yell at her through me, and I have to tell her these things, that, you know, kind of feel caught in the middle because . . . you're just telling her things you don't want to tell her."

(Early-adolescent male): "Like when my parents disagree on paying for . . . something, usually I have to talk on the phone for them 'cause they don't want to talk to each other."

(Mid-adolescent female): "Usually my father will say he doesn't have enough money to buy . . . something that [my sibling or I] need or that we want and he'll say, 'Tell your mother to get it,' and then we'll say, 'Mom, he said he can't 'cause he doesn't have enough money,' and she'll make that dissatisfied noise that all parents make."

Adolescents clearly had difficulty carrying messages that were angry, disparaged the other parent in some way, or touched on sensitive issues such as child support payments. It is easy to see why it would be hard to tell a parent, "Dad said to tell you you're money-hungry" or "Mom said to tell you you're just being stubborn." Yet comments from those we interviewed suggested that even being asked to carry seemingly harmless messages can be stressful. Adolescents do not feel comfortable with the responsibility of carrying adult messages, especially because they can then become the target of frustration for any confusion or misunderstanding in the messages relayed. For example, one boy said that he felt caught when he had to tell his mother about when he would visit her. If he got mixed up on the times, both parents would be angry with him. Because of this, he wished his father would make the arrangements directly with his mother.

We also had anticipated that children would feel caught between their parents if asked by either of them to report on the other home or parent. This expectation was supported by some of the responses to the question "Can you give me an example of what makes you feel caught?" One girl who lived with her mother expressed her frustration:

"[I feel caught] every time I go visit [my father]. I come home and I'm bombarded with twenty questions . . . I always get it because [my mother] thinks, you know, [my father's new partner] is going to try and turn me around, put me against her or something, but that's not going to happen. That's why she's asking 20 million questions."

Another girl complained:

"My father will tell my mom he's going to do something, and then she'll ask me if he's done it. I get caught in the middle."

One boy in mother residence did not mention the issue of parents asking questions in the context of feeling caught between one's parents, but he ended the interview by telling us:

"After I finish getting back from visiting my father, I get interrogated by my mom. You know what I mean? Like 'What happened?' This and that. 'Where did you go?' You know, 'Did he say anything about me?' [Interviewer: How did you feel about that?] Real uncomfortable. I don't like it."

Another commonly mentioned cause of feeling caught between one's parents was the denigration of one parent by the other in the child's presence. Many such instances were reported. This kind of behavior put children in the uncomfortable position of feeling that they needed to defend the parent being criticized. Here are some examples:

(Late-adolescent female): "My dad would cut down my mom for things she'd done, and I'd defend her. And my mom would cut down my dad for things he'd done and I'd defend him, and I was in the middle, and they both thought I was against them, and they'd always use me as an in-between instead of talking to each other. They'd tell me what they were upset at the other person for, and they'd expect me to tell them that, and then I was out of bounds."

(Mid-adolescent female): "My dad kinda knows that I am, you know, I'm with my mom, and he talks about her sometimes, and he tries to tell me not to say anything to her. Or my mom will complain about how much money Dad gives us. [Interviewer: He knows you're closer (to your mom)?] Yeah, we're closer, and sometimes he tries to cut her down."

(Mid-adolescent female): "My mom says things about my dad, and I don't know what to say . . . Sometimes my dad will say things about Mom is like, taking all this money."

(Mid-adolescent female): "Just when, like, I guess one of them mentions, 'I can't believe what he did' or 'what she did.' Or 'He's not such and such' or 'She's not such and such' like mature enough to handle it or something like that."

A final common thread was adolescents' experience of explicitly being made to choose between their parents in some way. Sometimes parents went so far as to ask the child whom he or she loved most; in many other cases they did not demand such a direct choice, but they taxed the child with decisions about with whom to spend the holidays, with whom to live, or simply with whom to spend time on a particular occasion. These latter kinds of decisions can be extremely difficult for children to make, because the choice is seen as an indication of preference for one parent over the other:

(Late-adolescent male): "Well, sometimes they used to try to put me on the spot and ask me about which one I'd rather live with in front of the other."

(Early-adolescent female): "Sometimes when they ask me who would I rather be with or who do I like most."

(Early-adolescent male): "[When] they were going to split up . . . we had to choose who we were going to go with . . . I didn't want to leave my mom or dad."

(Mid-adolescent male): "My mom wants me, and my dad wants me at the same time that weekend, and he's making us choose."

These excerpts summarize some of the main themes in the adolescents' comments concerning feelings of being torn between their parents. Other issues were mentioned as well. Many adolescents simply said that they felt caught when parents fought, and some felt especially uncomfortable when parents fought over something that had to do with them. Other adolescents felt caught when parents compared homes, or when parents told them conflicting stories concerning the divorce or the interparental relationship. What kinds of family circumstances increase the likelihood of these events occurring? And what aspects of children make them more or less vulnerable to feeling caught in response to potentially difficult situations?

Predictors of Feeling Caught between One's Parents

Characteristics of the Adolescent

It is possible that factors within the child, as well as from the child's environment, affect the likelihood that any particular child will experience loyalty conflicts. For instance, as others have pointed out (Kalter and Rembar, 1981; Wallerstein and Kelly, 1980), children's level of cognitive and emotional maturity will influence how they react to interparental conflict and divorce. Children's capacity to reason about parental conflict, including the ability to understand multiple perspectives or to understand in realistic terms one's own responsibility (or lack thereof) for parental conflict and its resolution, will certainly be related to their tendency to experience loyalty conflicts. Thus the age of the child is one "child" factor that is likely to be a predictor of feeling or being caught between one's parents.

Similarly, sex differences in the desire or willingness to take on responsibility for keeping parents happy, or to attempt to remain loyal to two "warring" parties, are likely to lead to sex differences in the tendency to become caught between one's parents. There is some evidence that females are more often concerned with maintaining harmonious interpersonal relationships and with resolving conflict in mutually satisfying ways (Gilligan, 1982; Maccoby, 1990; Miller, Danaher, and Forbes, 1986), and that their higher interpersonal caring orientation leads to greater emotional distress (Gore, Aseltine, and Colten, 1993). If this is so, we might expect girls to be more likely than boys to be caught between their parents.

Among our interviewees (who ranged in age from ten to eighteen), older adolescents were somewhat more likely to report feelings of being caught between their parents than were younger adolescents. The correlation between age and feelings of being caught was small but significant ($r = .12$). Girls ($M = 5.1$) reported more feelings of being caught than did boys ($M = 4.4$). The sex difference was virtually the same for older as for younger adolescents.

Characteristics of the Family Environment

Factors external to the child that might predict the extent of loyalty conflicts include the degree of interparental conflict, the level of contact with each parent, the quality of the adolescent's relationships with each

Table 11.2   Relations between the interparental relationship and feelings of being caught between one's parents[a]

	Relation to "feeling caught"	
Measure of the interparental relationship	β	*t*
Discord (T3) (*n* = 339)	.27	5.14****
Cooperative communication (T3) (*n* = 338)	−.19	−3.56***
Maximum hostility (T3) (*n* = 513)	.19	4.40****
Frequency of arguing (T4) (*n* = 514)	.33	8.07****
Cooperation (T4) (*n* = 334)	−.19	−3.48***

a. Statistics are from regression equations that control for age and sex of adolescent.

***$p \leq .001$.   ****$p \leq .0001$.

parent, and the existence of new romantic partners for one or both parents.

We expected loyalty conflicts to be higher when interparental conflict was higher, due to increases in parental pressure to take sides as well as to increased fear of negative consequences of loyalty to one or the other parent (Aponte and Van Deusen, 1981; Emery, 1988), and this is what we found. Regardless of the measure of interparental relationships used—whether level of conflict, hostility, or cooperation between the parents, and whether reported by parent or adolescent—the quality of the interparental relationship was associated with the tendency to feel caught between one's parents (see Table 11.2).

Although the extent to which parents disagree or argue after divorce and the extent to which they talk to each other and attempt to work together are related, they also represent two separate dimensions of parenting. The intersection of these two dimensions is likely to be important when considering effects on children. For example, Maccoby, Depner, and Mnookin (1990) identified four co-parenting patterns based on the degree to which parents disagreed and tried to undermine each other in parenting and the degree to which they tried to communicate and work cooperatively in co-parenting. "Conflicted" parents were high in conflict and low in cooperation. "Cooperative" parents were high in cooperation and low in conflict. "Disengaged" parents were low in both conflict and cooperation. The fourth combination—high in both conflict and cooperation—was relatively rare and will not be considered here. When we examined feelings of being caught among adolescents whose parents

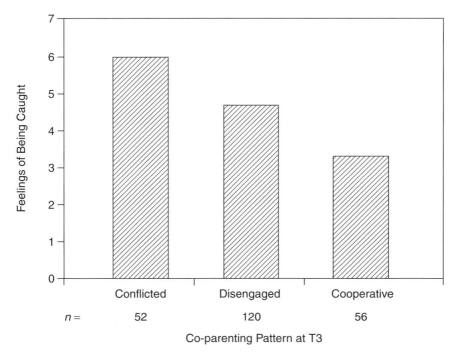

Figure 11.1   Feelings of being caught between one's parents by co-parenting pattern at T3. Means are adjusted for age and sex of adolescent and are based on a sample of only one adolescent per family, randomly selected.

displayed each of the three more common patterns, we found that adolescents from conflicted families were more likely to feel caught than adolescents from disengaged families, who were in turn more likely to feel caught than adolescents from cooperative families (see Figure 11.1).

The relation between interparental conflict and feelings of being caught was very similar for older and younger adolescents. There was some indication, however, that the relation was stronger for girls than for boys when using adolescents' own perceptions of the relationship between their parents as the index of parental interaction. Feelings of being caught were higher for both boys and girls under conditions of high arguing at T4 or low cooperation at T4, but the difference in feeling caught between those situations and more harmonious conditions was greater for girls (see Figure 11.2 for the findings for T4 parental arguing). Sex differences in the response to the quality of the interparental relationship did not emerge for any measures of relationship quality as re-

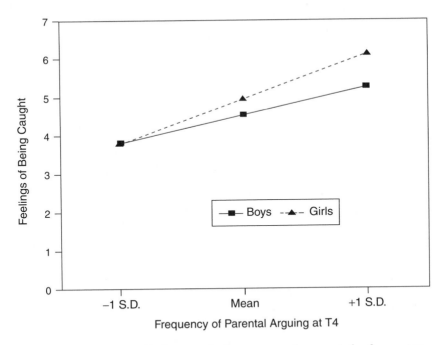

Figure 11.2 Feelings of being caught between one's parents by frequency
of parental arguing at T4 and sex of adolescent. Means are adjusted for
age of adolescent.

ported by parents. These results concerning adolescent-reported interparental cooperation and frequency of parental arguing also modify our
interpretation of the sex difference reported earlier. Sex differences in
feelings of being caught occurred mainly when parents were perceived as
being very uncooperative or argumentative. There was virtually no difference in boys' and girls' reports of feeling caught at low levels of
adolescent-reported conflict (or high cooperation); the sex difference
emerged when parents were reported to get along poorly.

One of the fears professionals have had about joint custody is that high
levels of contact with both parents after a divorce—especially when
parents maintain high levels of conflict—will lead to situations in which
children become caught between their parents, presumably because
there is greater opportunity for parents to use children as mediators in
their conflicts. To see whether feelings of being caught were related to
the amount of time spent with each parent, we examined both residential
arrangement (sole-mother, sole-father, and dual residence) and visitation

arrangements (for those adolescents in sole-residence arrangements). The amount of visitation for sole-resident adolescents was not related to feelings of being caught. Residential arrangement was marginally related to being caught between one's parents, but contrary to some predictions it was adolescents in father residence—rather than those in dual residence—who were most likely to feel caught.[1] The mean levels of feeling caught for mother residence, dual residence, and father residence were 4.7, 4.1, and 5.4, respectively. Thus we do not find that spending substantial time with both parents, in and of itself, leads to more feelings of being caught between their parents for adolescent children of divorce.

We looked next at whether the effects of level of contact on feeling caught between one's parents were dependent on the co-parenting relationship. In other words, we wanted to know whether adolescents who spent considerable time in both households (for example, dual-resident adolescents) were more likely than other adolescents to feel caught between their parents if those parents were in high conflict.[2] We found that when parents were in high conflict (or low in cooperation), dual-resident adolescents were more likely than sole-resident adolescents to report feeling caught between their parents. When parents got along well (didn't fight, did cooperate, were not hostile), however, dual-resident adolescents were less likely than sole-resident adolescents to feel caught between their parents (see Figure 11.3). This interactive effect of dual residence and interparental conflict was the same for boys and girls.

The very definition of "loyalty conflict" implies that children who feel strong emotional ties to both parents will be more likely to feel torn between those parents, particularly when they cannot get along with each other. To examine this assumption, we divided adolescents (at the median) into "High" and "Low" groups on both closeness to mother and closeness to father. Adolescents at the median were included in the "Low" closeness group. We then combined "High/Low" closeness to mother with "High/Low" closeness to father to form the following categories: "close to two parents," "close to only one parent," and "close to neither parent." Contrary to our expectations, adolescents who were close to both parents reported fewer feelings of being caught between their parents ($M = 4.1$) than adolescents who were close to only one parent ($M = 5.2$) or who were not close to either parent ($M = 5.1$). This was true of older and younger adolescents, and of boys and girls.

Was being close to both parents conducive to loyalty conflicts in situations where those parents were in high conflict? No. Regardless of level of conflict, the adolescents least likely to feel caught were those who felt

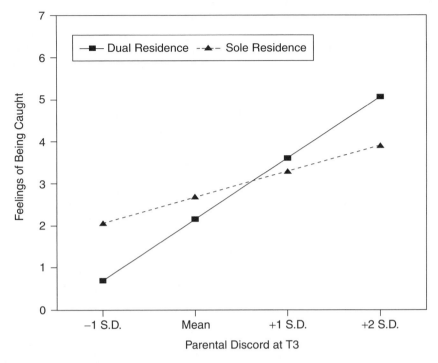

Figure 11.3 Feelings of being caught between one's parents by residential arrangement and level of parental discord at T3. Means are adjusted for age and sex of adolescent.

close to both parents. And the relation between parent-adolescent closeness and feeling caught did not vary depending on whether we considered the residential or the nonresidential parent: closeness to either parent was associated with lower feelings of being caught. These findings, of course, raise questions about the direction of effect. It very well may be that adolescents who feel caught between their parents are thereby precluded from feeling very close to one or both parents, whereas adolescents who do not feel caught between their parents are free to maintain good relationships with both.

Finally, does the presence of a new partner for one or both parents increase the likelihood of loyalty conflicts among adolescents? Lutz (1983) identified divided loyalties as the most stressful issue for adolescents in stepfamilies, and other authors have speculated about the importance of divided loyalties among children whose parents remarry. The entrance of new partners may lead to loyalty conflicts because these newcomers potentially represent new and additional parent figures; children may see these new partners as competitors for their affection with the biological parent of the same sex. Our findings suggest, however, that in the usual case a mother's remarriage does not alienate mother-resident children from their fathers (see Chapter 7), nor does it augment adolescents' feelings of being caught between their parents (see Figure 11.4). Rather than feeling more caught between their parents as a result of the presence of two—perhaps competing—father figures, adolescents whose mothers had remarried felt less caught than adolescents whose mothers had not remarried.[3] Among father-resident adolescents, those whose fathers were dating felt less caught between their parents than did those

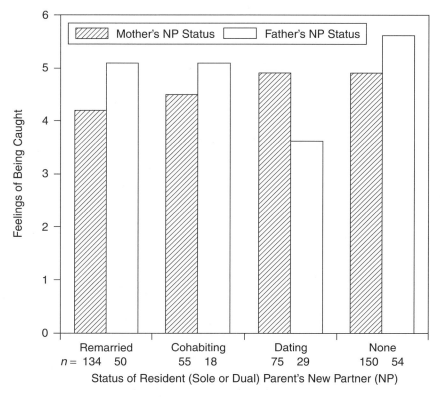

Figure 11.4 Feelings of being caught between one's parents by residential parent's new partner status. Means are adjusted for age and sex of adolescent and residential parent's education.

in the other three groups. Divided loyalties appear to be an issue faced by children of divorce regardless of whether their parents form new relationships; the residential parent's involvement with a new person per se does not appear to intensify those feelings—at least not four and a half years after parental separation.

Did a residential parent's involvement with a new partner lead to loyalty conflicts if the adolescent was especially close to the nonresidential parent? To the extent that we can address this question, the answer is no. In line with the findings just reported, greater closeness to a nonresidential parent was linked to a lower likelihood of feeling caught regardless of whether the residential parent had a new partner.

Feeling Caught between One's Parents and Adolescent Adjustment

In the absence of longitudinal data, we cannot truly talk about consequences of feelings of being caught. Conceptually, however, loyalty conflicts are presumed to lead to negative outcomes, particularly anxiety and emotional stress, for children. We expected, then, that more feelings of being caught between one's parents would be associated with poorer adjustment, especially "internalizing" aspects of adjustment. Indeed, we found this to be the case. Feelings of being caught were clearly related to higher levels of depression/anxiety ($r = .39$,[4] $p \leq .0001$). This link was the same for both genders (although somewhat stronger for girls than for boys) and in all residence groups. Feelings of being caught were also related to higher levels of deviant behavior ($r = .19$,[5] $p \leq .0001$), although the link between feeling caught and deviance was not as high as that for feeling caught and depression/anxiety. Feelings of being caught were not related to school adjustment as measured by grades or school effort.

Do feelings of being caught between one's parents help to explain why interparental conflict more often than not has negative effects on children's adjustment? In other words, do feelings of being caught "mediate" a relation between the quality of the interparental relationship and adolescent adjustment? We have some evidence that they do. Although the direct relations between measures of the interparental relationship and adolescent adjustment were not very strong in our sample—certainly not as strong as we had expected them to be based on previous work (see Chapter 6 for discussion)—we investigated whether the links that did exist were reduced or eliminated if we introduced feelings of being caught into analyses predicting adjustment with interparental conflict or

Table 11.3 Relations between the interparental relationship and adolescent adjustment, with and without controlling for feelings of being caught between parents[a]

Measure of the interparental relationship	Relation to depression		Relation to deviance	
	Without "feeling caught"	With "feeling caught"	Without "feeling caught"	With "feeling caught"
	β	β	β	β
Discord (T3)	.09+	−.01	.07	.02
Cooperative communication (T3)	−.00	.07	.01	.05
Maximum hostility (T3)	.02	−.04	.08*	.05
Frequency of arguing (T4)	.18****	.06	.19****	.15***
Parental agreement (T4)	−.16****	−.10*	−.10**	−.07+
Cooperation (T4)	−.09+	−.02	−.06	−.03

a. Statistics are from regression equations that control for age and sex of adolescent and residential arrangement.

$+p \leq .10$. $*p \leq .05$. $**p \leq .01$. $***p \leq .001$. $****p \leq .0001$.

cooperation. If introducing feelings of being caught into these analyses decreased the link between the quality of the interparental relationship and adolescent adjustment, we would have evidence that the effects of interparental conflict on children are due, at least in part, to the fact that conflict leads to loyalty conflicts (Baron and Kenny, 1986).

Table 11.3 shows the magnitude of the relations between various measures of the interparental relationship and both depression/anxiety and deviance, with and without the inclusion of feelings of being caught between one's parents in the same analysis.[6] The results suggest that feelings of being caught do partly explain the relation between frequency of parental arguing at T4 and depression, as well as the smaller relations between both discord at T3 and cooperation at T4 and depression. The evidence that feelings of being caught mediate the link between interparental conflict or cooperation and deviance is weaker, although there is a small reduction in the magnitude of the relation between deviance and five of the six measures of interparental functioning (all except cooperative communication at T3) when "feeling caught" is also included in the predictive equation.

Figures 11.5 and 11.6 depict the role of "feeling caught" as a mediator of discord at T3 (Figure 11.5) and frequency of arguing at T4 (Figure 11.6)

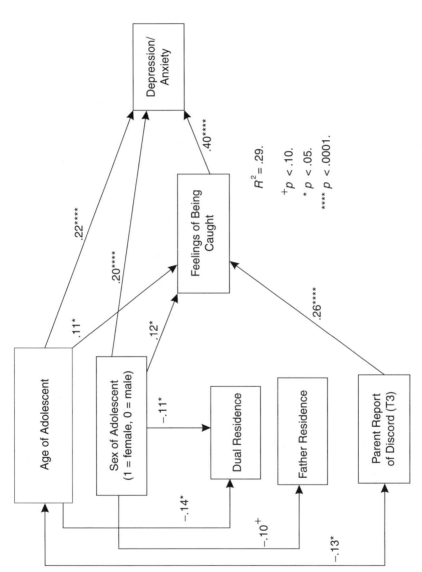

Figure 11.5 Model predicting depression/anxiety with feelings of being caught between one's parents and interparental discord at T3. Adapted with permission from Buchanan, Maccoby, and Dornbusch (1991), © The Society for Research in Child Development, Inc.

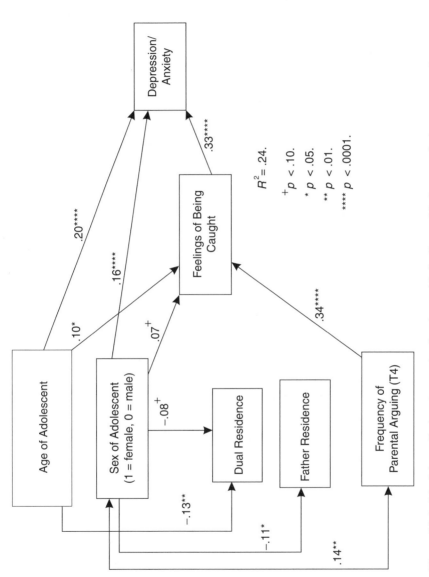

Figure 11.6 Model predicting depression/anxiety with feelings of being caught between one's parents and frequency of parental arguing at T4.

and adolescent depression/anxiety. These figures illustrate two of the instances in which we found no direct relation between the interparental measures and adolescent adjustment once feelings of being caught were accounted for, indicating that when interparental conflict does have an impact on adjustment, it does so by generating feelings in the adolescent of being caught between his or her parents.

Because the magnitude of the association between the interparental relationship and adjustment varied for boys and girls, and for adolescents in the different residential arrangements (see Chapter 6), we also looked at evidence for mediation in each subgroup of adolescents. We found more instances of mediation for girls than for boys, especially for girls in dual or father residence. Thus we did find some evidence that feelings of being caught mediate a relation between interparental conflict and adjustment, although we would expect this evidence to be stronger if we had better distinguished between general parental conflict prior to Time 4 and instances of conflict to which the adolescents were currently being exposed when we interviewed them at T4.

In summary, the fact that children (in this case, adolescent children) are more likely to feel caught between their parents when the adults have a great deal of conflict between them may help to explain why adjustment problems are often found among children in high-conflict situations. As we noted in an earlier report, parental conflict may change interactions among family members in such a way that "either the child is explicitly drawn into the conflict and/or becomes fearful of what effect a positive relationship with one parent will have on the other parent. Stress from the parent-parent relationship is, in this sense, shared with or diverted to the parent-child relationships, and this stress appears to have negative consequences in terms of adjustment" (Buchanan, Maccoby, and Dornbusch, 1991), particularly in regard to internalizing symptoms like depression or anxiety. These results also imply, however, that even if parents are in conflict, if they can avoid actions that lead children to feel caught—for example, avoid using the child as a go-between or an informer, or avoid denigrating the former spouse—the impact of that conflict on the child might be reduced.

Summary

Feeling caught between their parents is an issue many children face when parents divorce. A number of our adolescents told us graphically and in detail how difficult it was to deal with parents competing for their loyalty, using them as intermediaries or openly disparaging each other. The more intense the interparental conflict, the more likely it was that the children would feel caught up in the conflict in some way. And those adolescents who reported being caught between their parents showed more symptoms of maladjustment (depression and deviance).

What, besides interparental conflict, increases or diminishes the likelihood that adolescents will feel caught between their parents? Gender is one factor: girls are more likely to experience this problem. We expected that such feelings might be especially common among those children who had high levels of contact with both parents, either through dual residence or high levels of visitation, but this did not turn out to be the case. Dual residence was associated with higher levels of feeling caught if the parents were in high conflict, but dual-resident adolescents had the lowest "caught" feelings of all residential groups when their parents were cooperative. Spending substantial time with both parents thus does not automatically lead to being caught between them. Considering just the three residential arrangements by themselves, adolescents living with their fathers were the most likely to feel caught between their parents; this may have something to do with the unique circumstances under which father residence often comes about (see Chapter 5 for a more detailed discussion), in particular the higher levels of conflict in the history of these families. We also might have attributed the greater tendency of father-resident adolescents to feel caught between their parents to adolescents' stronger emotional ties to their mothers (see Chapters 5 and 10), except that we found no evidence to support a link between greater closeness to parents and greater feelings of being caught. The closer adolescents were to their parents—residential or nonresidential—the less likely they were to report feeling caught. In fact, adolescents were least likely to feel caught if they were close to both parents.

We conclude that loyalty conflicts, though common, are not by any means a necessary accompaniment of divorce. We have pointed to several individual and family factors that increase the likelihood that children will experience loyalty conflicts, the most important of which is the level of conflict parents maintain with each other during the postdivorce period and how careful they are to insulate the children from whatever conflict does continue to occur. In Chapter 12, we will see that inconsistencies in parental standards across the two households constitute another risk factor.

12

Inconsistency in Parenting

Consistency of parenting—with regard to how rules are created, what the rules are, methods of discipline, and expectations for behavior—is thought to be an important influence on a child's behavioral and emotional development. Consistency can be thought of as a within-parent phenomenon (how consistent is a mother over time, or a father over time?) or a between-parent phenomenon (how similar are a mother and father in their child-rearing behavior?). In keeping with our interest in adolescents' experience in two homes, this chapter is concerned with the latter: consistency between mother and father. Most research on consistency of parenting has been done with nondivorced families (see, for example, Block, Block, and Morrison, 1981; Deal, Halverson, and Wampler, 1989; Gjerde, 1988; Stoneman, Brody, and Burke, 1989; Vaughn, Block, and Block, 1988). Yet after divorce, opportunities and inclinations for parents to communicate about their rules and expectations are greatly reduced, raising the probability of inconsistent parenting. Among parents interviewed in the Stanford Child Custody Study at T3, only about one-third of the parents said that they were attempting to coordinate rules between the two households (Maccoby and Mnookin, 1992). When children interact with parents who live in separate homes, inconsistency between parents regarding rules and expectations for behavior may become a central issue in the child's life.

Consistency across parents might be important with regard to children's adjustment for several reasons. Disagreement between parents in their child-rearing may send confusing messages, so that the child does not know the true standards for appropriate behavior. One early-adolescent girl complained: "I don't like it 'cause all the rules are different," and went on to describe differences in expectations for how she dressed, what she ate, and the chores she had to do. Such confusion may be disconcerting to children who are trying to learn appropriate standards for behavior. In addition, it may be frustrating, even anxiety provoking, to try to remember or predict which behavior is appropriate in which situation as a child moves back and forth between homes.

Different rules on the part of each parent may also interfere with the child's relationship with one or the other parent—say, distancing the child from the parent whose rules or methods of parenting the child likes least, or creating conflict between the child and this parent. For instance, Stoneman and colleagues (1989) found that parental disagreement over discipline among married parents was related to increased conflict between mothers and daughters.

It is also possible that children, especially older children and adolescents, realize that they can manipulate parents who don't agree with each other. By using one parent against the other, children can end up setting their own standards and rules for behavior or at least evading discipline for deviating from parental standards. For example, if a parent establishes rules that the child does not like, children are more likely to be able to manipulate that parent into changing—or not enforcing—those rules if they can say that the other parent would not require the same behavior. Or, in situations of divorce, children may choose to spend more time with a more lenient parent. One late-adolescent male was quite open about how he took advantage of the situation:

> "I like that the supervision isn't so strong. I can get away with much more. I can take advantage of my parents. If one is being bad, I can go live with the other for a few weeks. It seems that parent tries harder to win your respect."

In nondivorced families where parents do not provide clear, consistent limits and expectations—where children are left to define their own limits—children are more likely to show both behavioral and emotional problems (Patterson, 1982). Adolescent children of divorce who are capable of manipulating parents in these ways may be more susceptible to becoming involved in the norm-breaking or risk-taking behavior common among adolescents who are not expected to abide by clear, reasonable expectations. Thus one might find higher levels of both minor and major forms of deviance among adolescent children in such situations, as they either openly or covertly manipulate parents' differences about rules and expectations to take part in those activities and behaviors that appear most appealing.

Finally, disunity between parents may cause a child to experience loyalty conflicts. Many of the elements of feeling caught between parents, described in Chapter 11, may be exacerbated by inconsistent parenting across homes. For instance, children may simply feel torn between the differing expectations of the two parents. Or they may be afraid to talk about one parent in front of the other for fear that disclosure of one parent's behavior or standards (or lack thereof) will anger the other parent. Parents who differ in their rules may also be more likely to use the child to carry messages or to spy on the other household. As seen in Chapter 11, feelings of conflicted loyalties are associated with more problems in adjustment among adolescents, especially higher levels of depression and anxiety.

Although the consistency of parenting across homes in which the child spends time after a divorce has not generally been considered by researchers, it seems that this aspect of a child's postdivorce experience might be a critical factor in understanding how the child adjusts. Consistency across homes in terms of rules and expectations would be expected to facilitate more quick and positive adjustment to the upheaval of divorce; inconsistency should make adjustment more difficult. Furthermore, consistency may be more important for certain children (for example, for boys) or in certain situations (for example, when a child spends a great deal of time in both homes).

In this chapter, we look first at how often consistency in parenting was present four and a half years after divorce. Second, we examine the relation between various demographic and family factors and consistency in parenting, including the age and sex of the adolescent, the level of the parents' education, the residential arrangement, and the quality of the interparental relationship. Third, we looked at whether consistency was related to better emotional and behavioral adjustment, and if so, whether consistency predicted adjustment by promoting better relationships and interactions between parents and adolescents, less manipulation of parents, or a lower likelihood of feeling caught between parents. Figure 12.1 shows our hypothesized model. Although Figure 12.1 does not indicate direct links between background variables (for example, age of adolescent or interparental conflict) and indices of the parent-adolescent relationship or adolescent adjustment, we know that these direct links exist and have discussed many of them in previous chapters. We did not include these in the figure in order to make it easier to focus on the links central to this chapter. Finally, we examined whether any links between inconsistency and either parent-child interaction or adolescent adjustment varied depending on age or sex of the child, parental education,

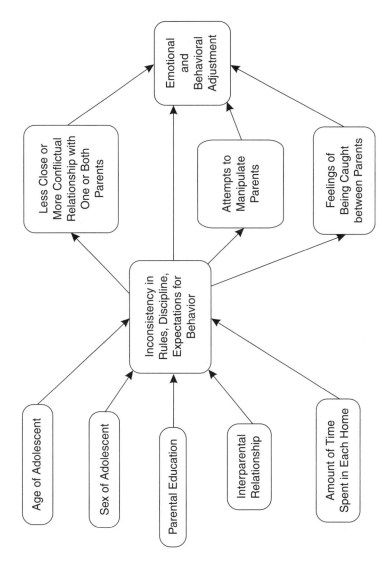

Figure 12.1 Hypothesized associations between inconsistency of parenting across homes, parent-adolescent relationships, and adolescent adjustment.

amount of time spent in each home, or the quality of the interparental relationship.

Defining Inconsistency in Parenting Practices

Inconsistency in parenting was measured from the adolescent's perspective. This represents an important divergence from previous data on the topic, which has measured inconsistency as the difference in parents' reports of their child-rearing practices (see Johnson, Shulman, and Collins, 1991, for an exception). Inconsistency in our study was measured by comparing adolescents' reports of specific parenting practices in the mother's home and the father's home.

The specific aspects of parenting used to examine differences were a subset of those we have referred to as indicators of parental management and control. Specifically, we compared adolescents' reports of mothers' and fathers' monitoring, youth-alone decision making (the practice of letting adolescents make decisions completely on their own, without discussion with parents), organization of the household and household routines, and each parent's use of consistent and fair rules. Scores were created by taking the absolute value of the difference in scores for the mother's and father's home on each of these four parenting variables and averaging these differences;[1] higher scores indicate higher inconsistency, or discrepancies, in parenting. We were only able to assess discrepancies for those adolescents who spent substantial time (at minimum, one month of vacation time) in both homes and who had, therefore, reported on the parenting practices of both homes ($n = 333$). Adolescents who rarely or never saw one parent could not report on specific practices for that parent's home and were excluded from analyses for this chapter.

Level of Inconsistency

To what degree were parents inconsistent in their parenting practices four and a half years after their divorce, from the adolescent's point of view? Reported inconsistency in actual parenting practices was quite low: the average score was only .91, on a scale that ranged from 0 to 5.17. Obviously the large majority of scores were toward the low end of the range. As another confirmation that parents were generally similar to each other in parenting practices, correlations between mothers and fathers on the four specific aspects of parenting that constituted the discrepancy score ranged from .51 to .85.

Correlates of Inconsistencies in Parenting

Demographic Variables

Of the demographic variables we examined, only sex of the adolescent was related to parenting discrepancy. Compared with boys, girls reported higher levels of parenting discrepancy (M_{girls} = 1.01, M_{boys} = .82). Neither age of adolescent nor level of parental education was related to discrepancies in parenting.

Time Spent with Each Parent

Two measures of contact were used to examine whether parenting inconsistency was related to the amount of time adolescents spent in each home. The first was residential arrangement. Using this measure, we found that parenting discrepancies were indeed related to the division of time in each home: parenting discrepancy was markedly lower in dual residence (M = .63) than in either mother (M = .93) or father (M = 1.04) residence. This is consistent with the results reported in Chapter 4, that dual-resident parents were seen as more cooperative at T4 than other parents—they talked with each other more frequently, and they tried to cooperate in making decisions concerning the child, including the rules in each home.[2]

The second measure of contact distinguished among levels of visitation within mother and father residence. Dual-resident adolescents constituted the individuals with the highest score on this measure of contact (a "5"); the remainder of the scale points indicated the amount of time spent with the nonresidential parent for adolescents in either mother or father residence. Specifically, a "2" indicated one month of vacation-time contact with the nonresidential parent but little or no contact throughout the school year; a "3" indicated low contact throughout the school year; and a "4" indicated high contact throughout the school year. (Adolescents with a "1" on this measure were those who had little or no contact with the nonresidential parent and were excluded from these analyses.) As indicated in Figure 12.2, parental inconsistency was generally lower the more time that adolescents spent with a nonresidential parent.[3] The biggest difference, however, was between the lowest-contact categories as a group and the highest-contact categories as a group. Adolescents who had high levels of school-year visitation or who were in dual residence reported more consistency between their parents than did adolescents with lower levels of contact.

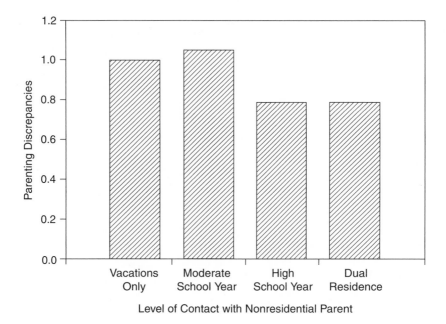

Figure 12.2 Parenting discrepancies by level of contact with the nonresidential parent.

Quality of Interparental Relationship

Parenting discrepancies were not related to any T3 parent-reported measures of conflict or cooperation (see Table 12.1). Adolescent reports of higher parental arguing and lower parental cooperation, however, were significantly correlated with more discrepant parenting. Although it is possible that parenting discrepancy is more highly related to current, rather than past, parental conflict and cooperation, it is also possible that the significant correlations only for T4 measures of the interparental relationship are due to the fact that adolescents reported on both the interparental relationship and parenting practices. In other words, an adolescent's tendency to view their parents as quite similar or quite different could have influenced both measures.

Predicting Parenting Inconsistency with Multiple Factors

Having described the relations between parenting inconsistency and each of the above factors individually, we were interested in (a) which of these

Table 12.1 Zero-order correlations between the interparental relationship and parenting discrepancies

Measure of interparental relationship	(*n*)	Parenting discrepancies
Discord (T3)	(260)	.02
Cooperative communication (T3)	(259)	−.05
Maximum hostility (T3)	(328)	.03
Frequency of arguing (T4)	(326)	.12*
Cooperation (T4)	(332)	−.24****

p ≤ .05.   ****p* ≤ .0001.

factors were the strongest predictors of parenting inconsistency, and (b) whether the relation between any one factor and discrepancy varied depending on any other factor.[4] Appendix Table B.11 summarizes the results of our analysis using multiple predictors simultaneously. Higher levels of adolescent-reported parental cooperation (T4) and higher levels of contact with the nonresidential parent at T4 continued to be directly related to fewer parenting discrepancies. In addition, parental arguing and parental cooperation were more strongly related to parenting discrepancy among parents with lower levels of education.[5]

Inconsistency in Parenting, Adolescents' Relationships with Parents, and Adolescents' Adjustment

In considering the relation of inconsistency to adjustment, we needed to account for the fact that greater discrepancies were related to a greater likelihood that at least one parent was using poor parenting practices (for example, not monitoring well, allowing the adolescent to make many decisions without parental input or discussion, maintaining a disorganized household). We needed to make sure that poor adjustment or poor parent-child relationships were related to inconsistency, not merely to poor parenting. To achieve this, we controlled for the quality, or level, of parenting in analyses relating discrepancy to aspects of relationships and adjustment.[6] Thus we are able to speak about the effects of parenting inconsistency over and above the quality of parenting being experienced by the adolescent in the two parental households.

High parenting discrepancies were related to more conflict with the residential parent and to a greater likelihood of feeling caught between one's parents (see Table 12.2). Parenting consistency was not related to the likelihood of using one parent against the other, at least as we measured it. This fact, together with the fact that using parents against each other was least likely to remain related to adjustment measures once the other relationship variables (feelings of being caught between one's parents and level of parent-child conflict) were controlled, led us to exclude "using parents against one another" from further analyses.

More discrepancies in parenting were also directly related to higher levels of depression/anxiety (see Table 12.2). Discrepancies were not related to overall deviance, but this was because they were related in different ways to different forms of deviance. The strongest association was between parenting discrepancy and antisocial behavior, with more discrepancies related to more antisocial acts. There were only very weak relations between discrepancies and school deviance or substance use, with more discrepancy marginally associated with higher levels of substance use but lower levels of school deviance. Neither school performance nor school effort were related to parenting differences.

Table 12.2 Associations between parenting discrepancies and various aspects of the parent-adolescent relationship and adolescent adjustment[a]

Measure of relationship or adjustment	β	n
Parent-Adolescent Relationship		
Conflict with residential parent	.16**	325
Using parents against one another	−.03	325
Feelings of being caught	.19**	333
Adjustment		
Depression/anxiety	.16**	333
Overall deviant behavior	.06	333
Substance use	.09+	333
School deviance	−.10+	333
Antisocial behavior	.24****	333
School grades	−.08	333
School effort	.05	316
Worst problem	.11*	333

a. The measures of association are standardized regression coefficients for parental discrepancy regressed on each of the parent-child relationships and adjustment measures individually, controlling for sex of adolescent and for absolute levels of parenting in each home.

+$p \leq .10$.   *$p \leq .05$.   **$p \leq .01$.   ****$p \leq .0001$.

A Closer Look at the Link between Parenting
Discrepancies and Adjustment

For depression/anxiety and antisocial behavior—the adjustment measures that were most strongly associated with parenting discrepancies—we
were interested in whether parenting discrepancy would continue to be
associated with adjustment once measures of the parent-child relationship
(parent-child conflict, feeling caught) were simultaneously considered or
whether the link would decline or disappear, indicating that discrepancies
affect adjustment by altering these aspects of the parent-adolescent relationship. In addition, we wanted to know whether the link between discrepancies and adjustment depended on any other factor. For example,
was parenting discrepancy more highly linked to depression for adolescent
girls, who are more prone to depression to begin with? And although
discrepancies did not appear to be related in a direct way to overall deviance, school grades, or school effort, we were still interested in finding out
whether discrepancies were linked to these aspects of adjustment for any
subgroup of adolescents.[7] The results for the central parts of the models
predicting depression/anxiety are presented in Figure 12.3.

Depression/Anxiety

As Figure 12.3 shows, both feelings of being caught between parents (primarily) and parent-child conflict (secondarily) were mediators of the relation between parenting discrepancies and depression/anxiety. In other
words, when parents were dissimilar in their parenting, adolescents were
more likely to feel caught between parents; in turn, adolescents who felt
caught were more likely to report being depressed and anxious. Similarly,
the more discrepant the parenting in the two homes, the more conflict
there was between the adolescent and the residential parent (especially for
older adolescents); this conflict was, in turn, related to higher levels of
depression/anxiety.[8] Apart from the fact that discrepancies interfered with
the parent-child relationship, discrepancies had no independent link to
depression/anxiety, except for certain subgroups of adolescents: girls,
younger adolescents, and adolescents whose parents were low in hostility.

Antisocial Behavior

Higher levels of parenting discrepancies were strongly related to higher
levels of antisocial behavior in a direct way, even when the indicators of

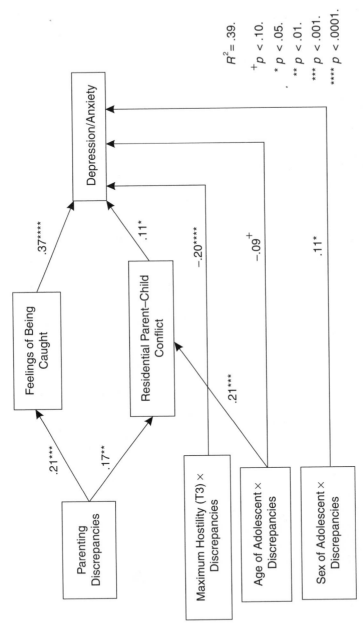

Figure 12.3 Model predicting depression/anxiety with parenting discrepancies, feelings of being caught between one's parents, and residential parent–child conflict. This figure depicts only the associations central to findings concerning the link between discrepancies and depression/anxiety; excluded are main effects of age or sex of adolescent, average parental education, interparental conflict or cooperation, contact with the nonresidential parent, and parenting quality on the main variables of interest.

the parent-adolescent relationship were taken into account. Unlike with depression, we had little evidence that discrepancies led to antisocial behavior by creating conflict between residential parents and their adolescents or by increasing the likelihood that adolescents would feel caught between their parents. Including these "mediators" in the analysis did not alter the strong relation between discrepancies and antisocial behavior (see Baron and Kenny, 1986). Dissimilarity in parenting was especially likely to be related to antisocial behavior for adolescents who had relatively low contact with their nonresidential parent.

Overall Deviance and School Adjustment

Parenting discrepancies were in fact related to higher levels of deviant behavior for adolescents who had low levels of contact with the nonresidential parent, and under conditions of high parental arguing (T4). Similarly, grades and school effort were also lower when parenting was discrepant and there was frequent parental arguing.

The Relative Importance of Discrepancy and Quality of Parenting

Our results thus far suggest that discrepant parenting after divorce has negative implications for certain aspects of adolescent adjustment. A question not directly addressed by our discussion up to this point, however, is whether consistency in parenting is beneficial even when parents are consistently *poor* in their parenting. Is a situation in which only one parent is using positive parenting practices better or worse than a situation in which neither parent does? To more directly address this issue, we classified our families into "high-discrepant" (scoring in the top third on the discrepancy scale) and "low-discrepant" (scoring in the bottom third on the discrepancy scale) families. We further classified these families according to the kind of parenting practiced by mothers and by fathers. If both mother and father had high scores on quality of parenting (in other words, they scored in the top half on the composite measuring levels of monitoring, decision making, household organization, and fairness and consistency of rules), the family was classified as "both parents good." Families in which both mother and father scored in the bottom half of the parenting measure were classified as "both parents poor." If one parent scored in the top half and the other parent scored in the bottom half of the parenting measure, the family was classified as "mixed." Table 12.3 shows the number of families in our sample that fell

Table 12.3 Number of adolescents in each category of parenting discrepancy by parenting quality

Level of parenting discrepancy	Quality of parenting of the two parents		
	Both parents good	Both parents poor	Mixed parenting
High discrepancy	20	46	47
Low discrepancy	72	28	

into each of the five possible categories. Note that it was possible for parents to be fairly discrepant from each other in parenting and yet both fall into the range of good (for example, one parent scores very high and the other scores just above the cut-off for "good parenting"), or both to fall into the range of poor, parenting practices. Of course, the range of discrepancy scores was restricted for the "both good" and "both poor" groups, compared with the range for the "mixed" group. No parents fell into the category of being "mixed" in their quality of parenting and yet low in discrepancy.

Parent-Child Relationship

When parents were both using poor parenting practices, but were also discrepant from each other, we found the highest levels of conflict between adolescents and their residential parents (see Figure 12.4). When at least one parent was using good parenting practices, discrepancies didn't appear to matter much with respect to residential parent-child conflict. Discrepant parenting in general was related to heightened levels of feeling caught between one's parents, particularly in the context of poor parenting by both parents or mixed-quality parenting (see Figure 12.5). There was no benefit from only one parent exercising good parenting in reducing loyalty conflicts. There was some benefit from both parents exercising good parenting—even if the parenting differed somewhat between the parents—but even more benefit from consistent parenting.

Adolescent Adjustment

Depression was lowest among those adolescents who had both highly consistent and good parents (see Figure 12.6). Depression was lower in

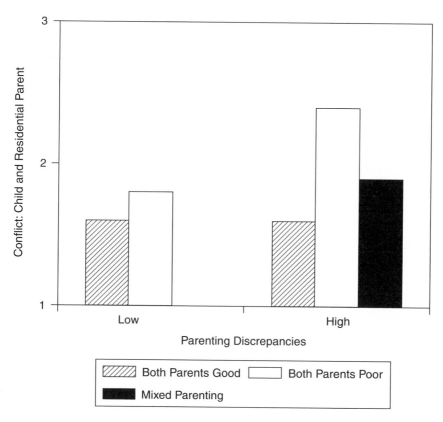

Figure 12.4 Conflict between residential parent and child as a function of parenting discrepancies and parenting quality. Means are adjusted for age and sex of adolescent and the average education of the two parents.

this group than in any other group, indicating that both discrepancies (even when both parents fall within the range of good parenting overall) and poor parenting are associated with increased levels of depression. With regard to deviance, however, good parenting on the part of both parents was the most important factor and discrepancies between parents were less important (see Figure 12.7). For overall deviance, and for school deviance and antisocial behavior, if both parents practiced good parenting—whether parents were similar to each other or not in the degree of good parenting—adolescents were involved in less deviant behavior than when both parents exercised poor parenting. The effects of mixed parenting (one parent good and one parent poor) fell between

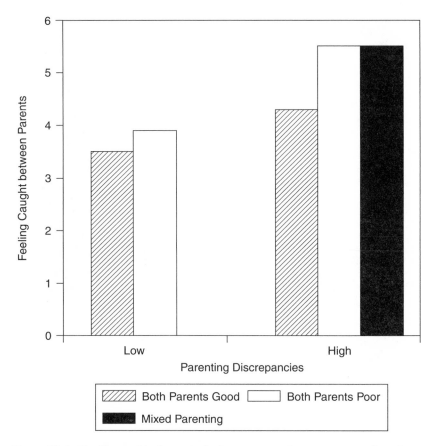

Figure 12.5 Feelings of being caught between one's parents as a function of parenting discrepancies and parenting quality. Means are adjusted for age and sex of adolescent and the average education of the two parents.

these two extremes, and only for antisocial behavior was having mixed-quality parenting significantly worse than having two "good" parents (consistent or not). Parenting, as defined by consistency and quality of parenting, was not related to school grades or school effort.

Summary

One might have expected that discrepancies in parenting would be fairly high among a group of divorced mothers and fathers. Our adolescents, however, did not perceive a high level of discrepancy. Adolescents in our

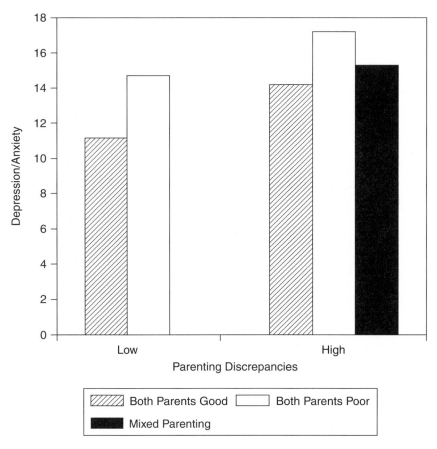

Figure 12.6 Depression/anxiety as a function of parenting discrepancies and parenting quality. Means are adjusted for age and sex of adolescent and the average education of the two parents.

sample reported a surprisingly high degree of similarity in how those parents went about managing their homes. No doubt because reports of both parents were obtained from the adolescents themselves, there is some reporting bias involved, with adolescents tending to see their parents as more similar than they really are. Further evidence of reporting bias comes from only adolescents' reports of interparental conflict (and not parents' own reports) being related to discrepancies in parenting. Even so, the degree of discrepancy between parents was much lower than we would have predicted.

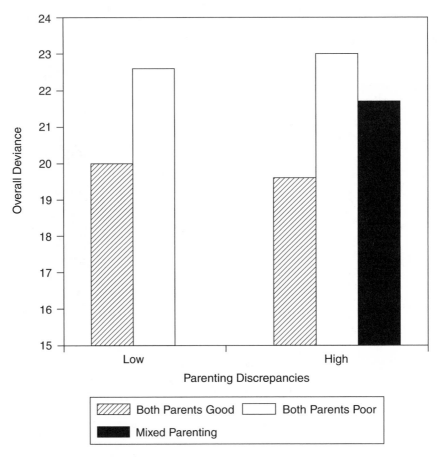

Figure 12.7 Overall deviance as a function of parenting discrepancies and parenting quality. Means are adjusted for age and sex of adolescent and the average education of the two parents.

Discrepancies between parents were lower in families where adolescents had high levels of contact with both parents than they were in families where contact with the nonresidential parent was low. This may indicate a drift toward less visitation in those situations where residential parents are unhappy with the parenting style of the nonresidential parent, or where adolescents find that discrepancies in parenting expectations make spending much time in the nonresidential home uncomfortable.

As we expected, inconsistency in parenting between homes was related to more negative parent-child relationships. In particular, discrepant parenting was related to higher levels of conflict between adolescents and their residential parents if the overall quality of the parenting in both homes was relatively poor. When parents differ in their expectations and rules for adolescents, adolescents are, no doubt, more likely to question or challenge the rules that they like least. In situations of divorce, this may lead to challenges of the residential parent in particular, given that most of the adolescent's time is spent with the residential parent, and residential parents are more likely than nonresidential parents to exercise more control and place more restrictions on the adolescent (see Chapter 10). The fact that this scenario only appeared to hold in situations of relatively poor parenting by both parents, however, indicates that good parenting on the part of one parent may be effective in stifling such challenges.

We also found that inconsistent parenting practices were related to a higher likelihood that children would feel caught between parents. As noted earlier, children may simply feel torn about the differing expectations, feeling that they have to act in different ways to please different parents. When parents differ in their standards, however, they may also engage in other kinds of behavior that leads to loyalty conflicts, for example, asking the child to carry messages to the other parent or interrogating the child about activities with the other parent or the standards maintained in the other household.

Inconsistent parenting was not linked to a greater tendency to use parents against each other, as we had thought it would be. The possible link between parenting differences and adolescent manipulation of one's parents seems so plausible that we are hesitant to discount it based on our results. More likely, our one-item measure ("How often do you use your parents against each other?") was not an adequate indicator of the tendency to manipulate parents.

Parenting discrepancies were, as expected, related to higher levels of adjustment problems—depression/anxiety and antisocial behavior, in particular. The link between discrepancies and depression/anxiety was explained by the fact that both residential parent-child conflict and feelings of being caught were higher when discrepancies were high, and parent-child conflict and feelings of being caught were both linked to depression. That feelings of being caught only mattered in the case of depression is consistent with results reported in Chapter 11 indicating that loyalty conflicts have their greatest impact on internalizing kinds of problems and less impact on externalizing problems.

In addition to evidence for the indirect effects of parenting inconsistency on adolescent adjustment, via parent-child conflict and feelings of being caught between one's parents, direct effects of inconsistency for some measures and some subgroups of adolescents were also found. For instance, inconsistency was a direct and strong predictor of antisocial behavior. Antisocial behavior represents some of the more extreme forms of misbehavior (destroying property, carrying weapons); the link between such forms of behavior and parenting discrepancies indicates either that disagreement between parents provides the inclination and opportunity for such extreme behavior or that, when adolescents participate in such behavior, parents are likely to differ in how they respond to it. In the latter case, we would expect that the differing reactions between parents cause them to become less effective in dealing with the adolescent's deviance.

Inconsistency in parenting also had direct associations with depression for girls and younger adolescents. This may reflect the fact that adolescent girls are more susceptible to depression in response to stress (Buchanan, Maccoby, and Dornbusch, 1992; Compas, 1987; Gore, Aseltine, and Colten, 1993; Petersen, Sarigiani, and Kennedy, 1991). Younger adolescents may have more emotional trouble with discrepant parenting because of their generally greater investment in the family. Older adolescents, however, have more conflict with their residential parent than younger adolescents as a result of discrepancies; thus younger adolescents may be internalizing the stress of parenting discrepancies while older adolescents may react, not by becoming sad or depressed or anxious directly, but by fighting about what they want or trying to use the inconsistencies to their advantage.

Inconsistency was also more strongly related to various forms of deviance (antisocial behavior, overall deviance) if the adolescent had low levels of contact with the nonresidential parent. We might have thought that parenting discrepancies would be more stressful under conditions of high levels of contact with each parent, because in such cases adolescents would be continually exposed to the differences. We are not sure what to make of this set of findings, except to note that both low visitation and discrepancies are negative factors for the adolescent. Although neither in itself was related to deviance as a measure of adjustment (see also Chapter 9), the existence of both may be detrimental for adolescents. Also, it may be that relatively high contact with both parents provides more opportunities for adolescents to learn their parents' different styles and adapt to the differences.

With regard to the interparental relationship and parenting discrepancies, we obtained mixed findings. Inconsistency was linked to more depression when parents were less hostile toward one another at T3. Yet inconsistency was related to more overall deviance and lower school performance if parents argued frequently (according to adolescents at T4). Why this particular pattern of results should appear is not clear.

Was consistency in parenting more important than absolute quality of parenting? No. In general, consistently poor parenting was of no benefit to adolescents. Furthermore, when considering deviance, consistent good parenting was no better for the adolescent than inconsistent good parenting. "Good parenting," as we measured it, means that parents are aware of their adolescents' activities, that parents stay involved in decision making concerning the adolescent while still allowing the adolescent to have quite a bit of input into those decisions, and that they generally have fair and consistent rules and routines in the home. Two parents who generally stay involved with their adolescents in these ways, even when the absolute level at which they do so differs, have adolescents who are unlikely to become involved in deviant activities.

Consistently good parenting did have some benefits over inconsistent parenting, even when both parents were generally good parents, with regard to adolescent depression. In this case, we see the potential benefits of experiencing consistent and good parenting, over and above inconsistent but good parenting. Consistently poor parenting, in line with what was said above, was not of significant benefit in reducing depression. The findings for depression are in line with those of Johnson and colleagues (1991), who found benefits for adolescents in what they called "congruent" authoritative ("good") parenting over both congruent permissive parenting (a less desirable parenting style) and incongruent parenting. When parents both fall into the range of what we would consider "good" parenting, but are still different from one another, this seems to take at least a modest emotional toll on the adolescent, even though it reduces the risk of deviance.

Of course, as we have acknowledged throughout this book, we cannot specify cause and effect with certainty. We have argued that parenting inconsistency can, for many reasons, lead to emotional and behavioral problems among adolescents. It is also possible, however, that more troubled adolescents are more difficult to parent, and therefore the two parents are more likely to come up with different ways of handling such children. Further research should investigate this question, using a longitudinal design to provide more insight into the processes taking place. In general, however, we found support for our hypotheses that inconsistency between households in parenting is associated with negative characteristics in family relationships, as well as with lower levels of adjustment among adolescents.

13

Conclusion

In this chapter we present our interpretation of the most important empirical findings from our study of adolescents four and a half years after their parents' separation. Before delving into the empirical results, however, we begin with an impression. The impression is that most of the adolescents we talked to appeared to be adjusting quite well to their family situation. For the most part, they talked easily and openly with us about their homes, their relationships, and their feelings. And most of the adolescents impressed us with their insight, understanding, and acceptance of the circumstances in their families. This impression should not be viewed as minimizing the pain that these children felt in the years immediately surrounding the estrangement of their parents, nor indeed the pain they sometimes still felt. Most studies have concluded that the first two years after divorce are the most difficult for children, and we intentionally chose to study a period when the children had had time to build a new life and to integrate their relationships with two parents who were no longer together. Thus we most certainly would have heard of more distress had we interviewed the adolescents earlier in the divorce process. And even after four and a half years, some adolescents were unhappy and still struggling with the breakup of their original family. What was remarkable, however, was that even in those instances in which adolescents communicated ongoing hardship or pain, they often did so in a way that indicated a mature understanding of the situation.

Our purpose in conducting this study, however, was not to assess the adjustment of these adolescents taken as a group. Rather, our central interest was to uncover the conditions under which adolescents functioned well or poorly after their parents divorced. It was the variability in adjustment among the adolescents in our sample that was of most interest to us: it provided us with the opportunity to study the circumstances and processes that are associated with more or less successful adjustment after divorce.

Adjustment in the Three Residential Arrangements

A central question for our study was whether the well-being of adolescents depended on where they lived—in other words, whether adolescents appeared to be better off when living with their mothers, with their fathers, or in a shared arrangement in which they spent substantial time in both parental households. Dual residence (also sometimes called joint custody) has been a particularly controversial arrangement. Its advocates have insisted that it offers great benefits to children by shielding them from the loss of either parent and by providing support from both parents. Its opponents have warned about the potential dangers of the instability involved in moving constantly from one home to another, the loyalty conflicts that would surely stem from maintaining close relationships with two mutually hostile parents, and the difficulty for parents in keeping track of youngsters who are away so much of the time. We have found, however, only minor differences among the residential groups, on the average, in adolescent adjustment. What differences there were favored the adolescents in dual residence, and indicated somewhat more adjustment difficulties among father-resident adolescents.

Does the similarity among residential groups mean that it hardly matters where or with whom an adolescent lives after parents divorce? Not at all. Parents came to their initial agreement about physical custody on the basis of their intimate knowledge of themselves and their children, usually attempting to put the children in the household they thought would provide the most supportive environment (Maccoby and Mnookin, 1992). Following these initial arrangements, there was considerable shifting of residence, with nearly a third of the sample moving from one residential arrangement to another during the four-and-a-half postdivorce years prior to our study. This means that families selected and reselected the arrangements they considered most suited to their family circumstances. Their choices appear to have been about equally good—from the standpoint of the well-being of their adolescent children—whether they ended up with mother, father, or dual residence. This does not mean that the residential choices were unimportant. If one arbitrarily assigned children to one of the three arrangements, without the benefit of any effort to match residence to individual family circumstances, there is no reason to believe that the differences in outcomes would still be as small as they have proved to be in our study.

The modest differences that we did find among residential groups are to some extent a reflection of self-selection into these groups. When there had been residential shifts, we asked the adolescents to tell us why the changes had occurred. Moves into mother residence, more often than moves into father or dual residence, occurred when one parent or the other relocated. When adolescents had moved into dual residence, they usually explained the move in terms of their missing one or the other parent, and the implication is that the parents responded to their children's wish to spend time with both parents by making the effort to maintain a dual-resident arrangement. Moves into father residence, by contrast, more often occurred because of family conflicts. Thus we have evidence that moves into mother or dual residence occur for more benign or positive reasons than do moves into father custody.

The implication is that over the course of the postdivorce period, fathers probably were taking into their households somewhat more troubled children—children who had had difficulty adapting to other residential arrangements—compared with families in which children moved into mother or dual residence. This conclusion is supported by the finding that adolescents currently living with their fathers who had shifted residential arrangements one or more times since the parental separation were more likely to have problems in adjustment than other father-resident adolescents. Instability of residence was linked to negative adjustment only for this one group.

We wanted to know whether there were factors, however, over and above self-selection, that might affect adolescent adjustment in each of the three residential groups. We expected that certain family processes would support adolescent adjustment and that others would weaken it. The question then was: were adolescents in the three residential groups being exposed to different living situations—different environmental inputs or different family processes in their primary residential households? And if so, did these differences in process account for any differences in adjustment among the residential groups? After describing some of the ways in which family processes were linked to adolescent adjustment, we will be in a position to see whether the processes linked to good or problematic outcomes were more prevalent in one residential group than another.

Life Situation, Family Processes, and Adolescent Adjustment

Life Stresses

The more life stresses experienced by the adolescents in the previous year, the more adjustment problems they had. The life stresses we assessed ranged from financial hardships, to losing a pet, to having a serious fight with a good friend. In line with other research on stress in general (Rutter, 1979; Simmons et al., 1987) and stress for children of divorce specifically (Amato, 1993), the total number of life stresses was a powerful and pervasive predictor of adjustment for adolescents in all residence arrangements.

Parents' Repartnering

For adolescents in sole-residence arrangements,[1] one of the more consistent predictors of good adjustment was having a remarried residential parent. In contrast, when the residential parent was living with a new partner to whom he or she was not married, adjustment was worse in a number of ways, particularly for boys. These findings are partly at odds with other research on adolescents, which has suggested that adolescents are more poorly adjusted in stepfamilies than they are in divorced families where a remarriage has not occurred (Ferri, 1984; Furstenberg, 1987; Hetherington and Clingempeel, 1992). For mother-resident adolescents, better adjustment in situations of remarriage was partly due to closer relationships between adolescents and remarried mothers. In addition, the better adjustment of mother-resident adolescents—and to some extent father-resident adolescents as well—in situations of remarriage occurred because remarried new partners were accorded more acceptance by the adolescents. Although it was easier for some adolescents to accept parents' new partners than for others, on average, acceptance was greater if the parent and new partner were remarried than if the parent and new partner were cohabiting or only dating on a regular basis. An adolescent's acceptance of a new partner, and of that person as an authority figure in the home, means that there are now two adults available for effective supervision, monitoring, and development of rapport with the adolescent. Other studies have indicated that the presence of two parents means higher levels of parental supervision for adolescents (Dornbusch et al., 1985; Hetherington, 1987), but results conflict concerning whether two parents necessarily provide a greater degree of protection against risky or unhealthy types of behavior than does the presence of only one (Dorn-busch et al., 1985; Steinberg, 1987). Our results suggest that the benefits of two parents, and any accompanying increases in supervision, for adolescents' behavior are more likely to emerge when the second adult is accepted by the adolescent. In situations where a new partner is simply cohabiting, the same degree of acceptance and authority is not accorded, and the same benefits in terms of adjustment do not accrue.

Interparental Conflict

Interparental conflict after divorce had much smaller direct relations to adolescent adjustment than we had expected on the basis of previous research (Amato, 1993; Emery, 1982; Johnston and Campbell, 1988). Yet recent reviewers of the research on marital conflict have noted that there is, in fact, variability in the impact of conflict, and that the task of researchers is to identify conditions under which, or individuals for whom, conflict has the most detrimental effects (Cummings and Davies, 1994; Depner, Leino, and Chun, 1992). Our data can begin to address this question.

Interparental conflict as reported by adolescents was more strongly related to adjustment than conflict as reported independently by parents over the first three and a half years since their separation. Of course, to some extent this may reflect a reporting bias on the part of adolescents; those adolescents who are not doing well may have a more negative outlook and report their parents' relationships as more negative than they really are. Instead or in addition, however, adolescents' reports may reflect the conflict to which the adolescent has been exposed (as distinct from the conflict that occurs between parents privately), a factor that others have identified as important in anticipating conflict's impact on the child (Cummings and Davies, 1994; Davies and Cummings, 1994).

Interparental conflict was also more likely to be related to poor adjustment for boys than for girls. Among boys, conflict was related both to higher levels of deviance and to higher levels of depression. Why boys should be more affected by conflict is not clear; our findings add more diversity to an already diverse body of literature on sex differences in response to conflict. Conflict was also more likely to predict negative adjustment for father-resident adolescents than for other adolescents.

Other research has suggested that conflict between parents can be especially detrimental for children who continue to spend time with both parents after divorce. Recommendations for policy have sometimes been made based on this assumption—that children should be encouraged to maintain contact with both parents unless those parents cannot get along. In our study, however, conflict between parents did not appear to affect children more negatively the more time they spent with each parent, with one potentially important exception. Adolescents who lived in dual residence were more strongly affected by interparental conflict in terms of their feelings of being caught between their parents. When parents were in high conflict, dual-resident adolescents were more likely to feel caught up in this conflict than were adolescents living primarily with either their mothers or their fathers. When parents were not in conflict, dual-resident adolescents were the group least likely to feel caught between their parents. Although feelings of being caught between one's parents were related to problems in adjustment (particularly depression), we did not find that dual-resident adolescents were especially prone to adjustment difficulties under situations of high interparental conflict. It seems that other factors intervene in determining the dual-resident adolescent's ultimate adjustment—for example, the benefits of maintaining close relationships with both parents in dual residence may offset the negative effects of conflict and loyalty problems even when parents are in high conflict.

Among sole-resident adolescents, we found no evidence that adolescents who visited the nonresidential parent frequently were more likely to suffer negative consequences of interparental conflict. Our results are different from those of several other studies (see, for example, Amato and Rezac, 1994; Hetherington, Cox, and Cox, 1978, 1982; Johnston and Campbell, 1988), most of which focus on preadolescent children (see Amato and Rezac, 1994, for an exception). On the one hand, adolescents may be better able than younger children to understand that they are not responsible for their parents' conflict (Wallerstein and Kelly, 1980), and thus may be more able to benefit from maintaining a relationship with the nonresidential parent. On the other hand, feelings of being caught between parents increased with age in our sample, which suggests that as children get older it may become more difficult in some respects to avoid becoming involved in interparental conflict. Thus it is unclear whether the age of our sample accounts to any extent for our failure to replicate the earlier findings. There are, in fact, a few studies other than our own that also provide no support for the hypothesis of worsened outcomes in situations of high interparental conflict and high visitation (for example, Crosbie-Burnett, 1991), and yet others suggest that high visitation may buffer the effects of high interparental conflict (Forehand et al., 1991). This mixture of findings in the literature suggests that the impact of visitation in high-conflict situations probably depends on yet other factors (for example, the extent to which parents use the child to carry messages or spy on the other home). Our own findings regarding dual-resident adolescents are evidence that multiple factors (amount of contact with each parent, degree of interparental conflict, and the adolescent's closeness to each parent) are in fact important.

Parent-Child Relationships and Parenting Style in the Residential Home

A great deal of previous research points to the importance for adolescents' adjustment of continued positive relationships with their parents. More specifically, adolescents, like younger children, benefit from warm, affectionate, responsive relationships with their parents. They also adjust better when their parents continue to make maturity demands—when they set clear and reasonable rules, maintaining expectations for good behavior while also allowing for growing input and negotiation on the part of the adolescent (see, for example, Baumrind, 1991a, 1991b; Eccles et al., 1993; Lamborn et al., 1991; Maccoby and Martin, 1983). Thus we expected positive adjustment to be associated both with parent-child closeness and with the extent of parental management and control, that is, with the degree to which parents were involved in setting limits and making decisions, as opposed to adolescents' being completely in control of such things, and the degree to which parents established reasonable and predictable household routines.

In general, our results supported these expectations. Of all of the aspects of the household context and family relationships that we considered, the affective closeness of the relationship between the residential parent and the child and the extent of management and control a parent exercised were the strongest and most consistent predictors of a range of adjustment indices. There were some qualifications, however. First of all, the benefits of close father-child relationships were somewhat weaker in father residence than in the other arrangements, and the benefits of parental management and control for girls were limited to certain aspects of that management (to monitoring, in particular). Why might good parenting on the part of a sole-resident father have less of an impact on the adolescents in his care than good parenting on the part of other residential parents? One reason may concern the nonresidential mother.

As we will discuss later, the adjustment of father-resident adolescents depended to a greater extent—relative to adolescents in other arrangements—on their continuing relationship with their nonresidential parent. Another reason, no doubt, is that father-resident adolescents are more likely to represent more difficult adolescents, from more difficult family circumstances. There may be other reasons as well. In any case, although there were still clear benefits to fathers' exercising warm, responsive, involved, demanding parenting—and sole-resident fathers should be encouraged to engage in this kind of parenting—the benefits appear to be moderated, more so than in other arrangements, by other factors.

A second important qualification is that the closeness of the relationship between the residential parent and the child, and the parent's management and control, were highly related to each other. The closer and more trusting the relationship between parents and adolescents, the more well managed and controlled was the household. In other words, when parents had good relationships with their adolescents, they were better able to stay in touch with the activities and concerns of their adolescents, discuss important matters with them concerning their decision making and behavior, and, no doubt, be accorded more respect and authority regarding rules and decisions. Of these two aspects of parenting, the degree to which a parent managed the household well and stayed involved in rule-setting and decision making was a stronger and more direct predictor of several aspects of adjustment, especially deviant kinds of behavior, than was closeness considered separately. When it comes to reducing the likelihood that adolescents will act out or will be susceptible to peer pressure to participate in such acts as cutting class or taking drugs, a parent's continued knowledge of and involvement in decisions concerning the adolescent's behavior play a highly important role. The closeness of the relationship, in many cases, played only an indirect role, in the sense that it facilitated such knowledge and involvement on the part of the parent.

Was a positive parent-child relationship (feeling close to the residential parent, engaging in activities together, and trusting and identifying with that parent) of primary importance for any aspect of adjustment, over and above the role of management and control? For mother-resident adolescents, closer mother-child relationships were associated with less depression and less school deviance (which reflects rather minor forms of deviance like class-cutting and being tardy). For father-resident adolescents, a closer father-daughter relationship was related to the use of compromise in peer conflicts by those girls and less substance use. There were thus some direct relations between closeness and adjustment, but the number of significant relations was smaller than we would have predicted.

Adolescents who felt disengaged from the residential home (didn't enjoy being there, tried to spend time away from the home or at least away from others in the home) were also more likely to show indications of poor adjustment. In particular, they were more likely to be depressed. It may be that depressed adolescents withdraw from the home, or that not feeling integrated into the home leads to depression. Either way, our data suggest that such signs of withdrawal from the family and home are a warning sign of emotional distress. Disengagement from the home was also linked to higher levels of deviance—especially antisocial behavior—among boys. As we noted earlier, continued parental supervision and monitoring during adolescence is of benefit with regard to "acting out" kinds of behaviors. Boys who withdraw from the home, and therefore do not have that supervision, are at risk for some of the more serious forms of deviant behavior.

In general, our data point to the importance of continued engaged and involved parenting after divorce. Hetherington and her colleagues have documented the "diminished parenting" that often takes place in the first year or two following divorce (Hetherington, Cox, and Cox, 1982). Certainly devoting the time and attention to children—even adolescent children—that they require is a difficult task for a parent who, after divorce, is usually working full time and parenting very much alone. Our data indicate, however, that at four and a half years after divorce, some parents are finding a way to maintain involved and vigilant parenting and some are not. These variations among primary residential parents depend hardly at all on the amount of time adolescents spend in each parent's home. In other words, some parents who have little or no "relief" from parenting by virtue of their adolescents' spending time with the other parent, as well as some parents whose adolescents spend a great deal of time out of their own home, find ways to stay responsive and involved with their adolescents. As difficult as such responsive parenting might be, our data indicate that it is one of the most important facilitators of adolescents' adjustment after divorce; parents' efforts in this area should have high payoffs.

Role Reversal

A concern that has been voiced about children of divorce is that they will be drawn into "playing parent" to their own parents. There is fear that parents, in the absence of a spouse with whom they can share their troubles, concerns, or joys, will turn to children as confidants. There is also concern about the danger that children will feel the need to help, or take care of, a parent who is lonely, discouraged, angry, helpless, frightened, or in any of a number of negative emotional states that can arise as a result of separation and divorce. To investigate this, we looked separately at the extent of parents' confiding in their adolescent children, and the adolescents' feelings of worry or needing to take care of that parent. Our findings did not indicate any negative ramifications of parental confiding. Among sole-resident adolescents, however, feeling worried about the residential parent or feeling that the parent needed to be cared for by the adolescent was related to negative adjustment indices. The critical factor appears to be whether the parent conveys that she or he is weak and vulnerable and needs the adolescent to be strong, to be the caretaker. Seemingly, there are parents who confide in their adolescents without having such an effect: either they confide about more positive things, or in confiding negative information they leave the child feeling that the parent is capable of coping with hardship. But the confiding in and of itself did not appear to be a problem.

The Nonresidential Parent: How Important Is Continuing Contact?

Early in the book we raised the issue of parental loss. It was reassuring for us to find that in our sample, few parents completely dropped out of their adolescents' lives. Most continued to have some kind of contact. Even so, there was a great deal of variability in the extent of that contact over the course of a year, with some nonresidential parents having very little and others having a great deal of contact. Was that variability in contact related to any indices of adolescent functioning? The level of visitation in and of itself turned out not to be important with respect to an adolescent's adjustment. Even adolescents who rarely or never saw their nonresidential parents were, on average, adjusting as well as adolescents who saw their nonresidential parents on a regular basis. Not surprisingly, however, adolescents who visited their nonresidential parents on a regular basis maintained closer relationships with those parents than did adolescents who rarely or never visited. What was more surprising was that the level of visitation required to sustain feelings of closeness was quite low: adolescents who visited their nonresidential parent for as little as two weeks in the summer felt about as close to that parent as did adolescents who visited regularly and frequently throughout the school year. Having at least a few weeks of contact each year, then, appeared to permit, but by no means guarantee, a close relationship with the nonresidential parent. Given the fact that we could document no negative effects of visitation, even in the face of continuing conflict between parents (as we will see below, visitation also did not interfere with the functioning of the residential home), the closeness that nonresidential parents and their children can sustain through visitation may be a goal worth pursuing in and of itself.

Furthermore, closeness with the nonresidential parent appears to have some beneficial effects on the adolescent—at least in the context of a close relationship with the residential parent. In fact, for father-resident adolescents, a good relationship with their mother appeared crucial: without a close relationship with their mother, a close relationship with their father was of little benefit. Even father-resident girls, whose relationships with their nonresidential mothers frequently appeared strained, benefited when the mother-daughter relationship remained close. For mother-resident adolescents, maintaining a close relationship with their father also had modest benefits, but the importance of the mother-child relationship did not depend on that continued closeness.

In neither mother nor father residence, however, did adolescents benefit by being close only to the nonresidential parent. The benefits of a close father-child relationship for mother-resident adolescents were too modest to make up for a loss in closeness to their mother. And the benefits of a close mother-child relationship for father-resident adolescents depended on being close to their father as well. For father-resident adolescents, then, it was especially important to maintain a good relationship with both parents: a poor relationship with either mother or father led to noticeable deficits in adjustment.

Interestingly, the ability and willingness of the nonresidential parent to remember special days (holidays, birthdays) was also linked to several aspects of better adjustment. The benefits of a nonresidential parent's remembering special days rivaled those of having a close relationship and superseded any other aspect of the relationship between the nonresidential parent and child. By remembering special days, the nonresidential parent communicates that the child is still important and not forgotten, regardless of how frequent the contact or how emotionally close the relationship between parent and child. Apparently the symbolic value of a parent's love and commitment has noticeable rewards with regard to adolescents' well-being.

Residence Differences in Life Situations
and Family Processes

We now return to the modest differences among the three residential groups in adolescent adjustment, and consider whether there were differences in the life situations, or family or household conditions, experienced by adolescents in these three groups that might help to account for the differences in adjustment. In doing so, we continue to keep in mind that there is not a great deal to be explained: the three groups were quite similar in adjustment. Still, on the average, dual-resident adolescents were doing somewhat better, and father-resident adolescents somewhat worse, and we have attempted to understand why this is so.

Dual-resident adolescents were a relatively advantaged group, in that their parents had more education and higher incomes than parents in the other groups. But their adjustment advantage remained after we controlled for parental socioeconomic status. We expected that dual-resident adolescents might be benefiting from greater cooperation between their parents, but these adolescents reported only slightly higher levels of cooperation, and there had been equivalent amounts of interparental conflict in the three residential groups since the divorce. What about the kind of control and organization that prevailed in the two parental households where dual-resident adolescents spent their time? We had expected that dual-resident adolescents might be worse off in this respect. We thought that life might be relatively unorganized and chaotic in households where children were moving in and out, and that it might be easier for dual-resident children to slip between the cracks of parental supervision. We found, however, that the households of dual-resident parents were as well organized as any others, and it appeared that all family members had adjusted to whatever patterns of alternation had been adopted for the children. As far as monitoring was concerned, dual-resident boys were somewhat less closely monitored than their sole-resident counterparts, but dual-resident girls were more closely monitored, and considering boys and girls together, the dual-resident adolescents did not appear to be advantaged in this respect.

What stands out for dual-resident adolescents is that they were able to maintain closer relationships with both parents than the other groups. Indeed, girls in dual residence felt closer to their fathers than did girls who actually lived with their fathers most of the time. Their closeness to both parents undoubtedly reflects some self-selection into the dual-resident group. That is, parents who maintained dual residence four and a half years after divorce were probably more child-centered and therefore more willing to make the extra effort that this arrangement entails. Parents who earlier tried dual residence but did not maintain it, or parents who never tried it, probably were less willing or able to set aside some of their personal concerns and goals for the sake of enabling their children to maintain a close relationship with the other parent. Furthermore, adolescents who moved into a dual-residence arrangement after initially being in sole custody commonly said they did so because they missed the less-seen parent. Dual residence is thus more likely to be implemented among families where parents and children are initially close; subsequently, the high levels of contact with both parents allow those close relationships to be maintained. Being able to maintain close relationships with two parents after a divorce, in turn, appears to benefit adolescents' well-being.

In general, dual-resident adolescents did not appear to be paying a price in terms of loyalty conflicts for their closeness to both parents. In fact, being close to both parents was, overall, linked with lower levels of loyalty conflicts. And when the parents of dual-resident adolescents were not in active conflict, those adolescents reported feeling caught between their parents less frequently than any other group. When their parents were still hostile and in conflict, these adolescents were more susceptible to feeling caught between their parents than other adolescents, although we did not find that the high levels of loyalty conflicts translated directly into their being the worst-adjusted group. The benefits of maintaining a close relationship with both parents appeared to soften the impact of torn loyalties even among dual-resident adolescents whose parents were highly conflicted. We must emphasize again at this point that our dual-resident families represent a small group of families whose dual-resident arrangements had survived over time or had been adopted voluntarily since the divorce. Our results concerning the well-being of adolescents in even the high-conflict families should not be construed to suggest that adolescents would benefit from court-imposed dual residence for parents who are highly hostile or in which the relationships between children and parents are not likely to be close or positive.

Why did we find somewhat more problems in adjustment among adolescents living with their fathers? For one thing, fathers in this group expressed relatively high levels of hostility toward their former spouses, and this was a source of distress for the adolescents in their care even more so than adolescents in other arrangements. Adolescents in father residence also reported less close relationships with their fathers than did adolescents in the other groups with their residential parents. The lower level of closeness to residential fathers was particularly true for the small group of girls who lived with their fathers. Similarly, as far as monitoring is concerned, it was once again the father-resident girls who were least likely to report that their fathers really knew about their interests, activities, and whereabouts. We return below to the special case of father-resident girls, but note here merely that the greater incidence of adjustment problems among father-resident adolescents can be traced, at least in part, to the higher number of cases in this group in which the adolescent felt emotionally alienated from the custodial parent and in which monitoring was weak.

Same-Sex Parents: Do Children Need Their Same-Sex Parent More?

Other researchers have claimed that it is optimal for children, when their parents divorce, to be in the custody of their same-sex parent, or at least to maintain a close relationship with that parent (Santrock and Warshak, 1979; Santrock, Warshak, and Elliott, 1982; Zaslow, 1989). In our study, we find only weak evidence to support this hypothesis, and it is limited to girls. When adolescents live with their mothers, we do not find that boys benefit more than girls from maintaining contact with a nonresident father—neither sex appeared to benefit significantly from such contact alone. Adolescents did benefit somewhat from a continuing relationships with nonresidential fathers if the relationship was a close, trusting one, but this benefit accrued equally to mother-resident boys and girls. In addition, the boys in our sample were not better adjusted when living with their fathers than when living with their mothers. If anything, the balance tipped slightly toward the advantages of mother residence for boys, although generally speaking, mother-resident and father-resident boys were very similar on our measures of adjustment. It might be thought that boys would have more interests in common with their fathers (for example, in sports) and that this would mean a greater compatibility between fathers and sons; there may be some truth to this, but we were surprised to find that all parents—mothers, fathers, stepmothers, and stepfathers—engaged in higher levels of joint activities with boys than with girls. There was no pattern of more joint activities for same-sex parent-child pairs.

The situation was somewhat different for girls. Out of our sample of 522 adolescents, only 38 were girls living with their fathers. Most of these girls (all but 9) had changed residences at least once since their parents had separated. In some ways, this group of girls represents a unique subgroup among the population of adolescents with divorced parents. They reported more adjustment problems than any other group (see Appendix Table B.6).[2] They felt less emotionally close to their residential parent and received less monitoring and supervision from their residential parent than did other groups. Some of the emotional distance between fathers and their resident daughters reflects processes that occur in families whether or not divorce has occurred. We know that in many families, fathers withdraw to some degree from interaction with adolescent daughters; at least, fathers feel less free to show physical affection toward daughters who are becoming physically mature. Some fathers have told us, too, that there are certain topics or activities that arise in parenting daughters (for example, helping them to braid their hair, discussing their choice of clothes, dealing with the physical changes of puberty) that don't come as naturally to fathers as they would to mothers (Maccoby and Mnookin, 1992). Mothers, by contrast, don't seem to encounter as many uncomfortable issues in raising adolescent boys.

The lower levels of emotional closeness in the father-daughter relationship were linked with lower levels of monitoring, which in turn predicted more problems among father-resident girls. Like all other adolescents, father-resident girls benefit from a parent's awareness of activities and behavior that can come from having a close relationship with that parent. We were surprised to find, however, that other aspects of parental management and control—specifically, curfews and parental involvement in decision making—were not as beneficial for this group of girls (see Chapter 6) as for other adolescents. Although we believe that these girls do benefit from their fathers' involvement and supervision, it would appear that there is something about their background or emotional state that makes certain controls more difficult for residential fathers to maintain and less effective when fathers do impose them.

Father-resident girls stood out, too, with respect to their relationship with their nonresidential mothers. For instance, they had more conflict with their mothers than did father-resident boys or than mother-resident children of either sex had with their nonresidential fathers. And although boys were closer to nonresidential mothers than to nonresidential fathers on several dimensions, this was not true of girls. Girls' relationships with nonresidential mothers were not especially warm, and they were conflictual. In addition, it was only among father-resident girls that closeness to father was unrelated to closeness to mother. For all other groups, a good relationship with one parent was predictive of—and may have facilitated—a good relationship with the other. Furthermore, the relationships between father-resident girls and their nonresident mothers appeared to be especially sensitive to the presence of ongoing interparental conflict. Although both boys and girls in both mother and father residence reported less close relationships with their nonresidential parents in situations of ongoing parental conflict, this was especially true of father-resident girls. These findings may indicate that the father's hostility toward the mother—which was especially high among sole-resident fathers—contributed to the problems between these girls and their mothers. It is still true, however, that when a father-resident girl was able to sustain a close relationship with her mother, this was especially beneficial. For example, a positive relationship with the nonresidential parent was associated with lower levels of deviance for father-resident girls only.

There are strong social norms leading to mother residence for children in divorcing families. It is unusual for children of either sex to live with their fathers, but especially unusual for girls to do so. It is not surprising, then, that father-resident girls should be different in important ways, because in many cases there would necessarily have been a special reason for their residential situation. Although it was not true of all father-resident girls, some had especially troubled relationships with their mothers; others had had trouble with a stepfather and had moved into the father's residence more to escape an unwelcome situation in the mother's household than out of any positive desire to be with their fathers. Boys, more often than girls, when they moved in with their fathers, did so because they wanted to be with them. And boys, by and large, sustained positive relationships with their nonresidential mothers. It would appear that a number of the father-resident girls in our sample were relatively alienated from both parents—more, at least, than the number of adolescents who were so alienated in other arrangements.

These findings have made us acutely aware that girls who live with their fathers after divorce are an important group to understand. They are relatively uncommon, so they are not an easy or representative group to study. However, we need more information about the circumstances under which they come to be in the custody of their fathers, and how the circumstances of living with their fathers and apart from their mothers influence their development.

The Impact of Parents' Repartnering on Home and Relationships

We have already noted that a residential parent's remarriage was associated with positive adjustment, and that cohabiting was associated with negative adjustment. We also looked at how a parent's involvement with a new partner affected relationships within the family as well as the degree of parental control and management. In terms of relationships between the ex-spouses, the earlier study of the parents of these adolescents noted that remarriage typically led either to a more disengaged or a more conflictual co-parenting style (Maccoby and Mnookin, 1992). In our study, the parent's stage of repartnering had little to do with the quality of the relationship between the two parents as the adolescents reported it.

Parent-child relationships did depend, however, on a residential parent's repartnering status, and this effect differed depending on whether it was a mother or a father who was involved with the new partner. Adolescents who lived with their mothers in either mother or dual residence had closer relationships with their mothers if either the mother was not involved in a new relationship at all or the mother was remarried. Previous research has demonstrated that mothers and preadolescent children (daughters in particular) often become very close when the mother is a single parent (Hetherington, 1993). Some of the problems that preadolescent girls have with remarriage have been attributed to interference with this close bond. Our data indicate, however, that the quality of the mother-child relationship with both sons and daughters may suffer most when mothers are in the earliest stages of repartnering: dating or living with a person to whom they are not remarried. It is, perhaps, in these stages of a new relationship that a mother reduces the time spent with her children most significantly, as she develops and establishes the new relationship. The fact that mothers were reported to be lower in management and control of the household during the dating stages of a relationship is further evidence for lowered maternal involvement with their children during this period. By the time they are remarried, mothers appear to be more settled in the new relationship and therefore able to spend more time with their children than they did in the earlier repartnering stages. In addition, by the time a mother remarries, her children may have had more time to accept this new partner and may see him as less threatening to their relationship with their mother.

Mothers' serious involvement with a new partner had another potential benefit. Adolescents were less likely to worry about, or feel the need to take care of, mothers who had a live-in partner (either remarried or not).

For both mothers and fathers, involvement with a new partner reduced the amount of confiding that that parent did with the opposite-sex adolescent. Mothers confided less in sons when they had a live-in new partner (cohabiting or remarried) and fathers confided less in daughters. The new partner, especially when available in the home on a daily basis, appears to take the place of an opposite-sex child as confidant. Of course, because our data were not longitudinal, we cannot rule out the possibility that parents who are less prone to confiding in their opposite-sex children are more likely to seek out or find a new partner. Further research is needed to clarify which of these processes takes place.

We found no evidence that the presence of a new partner interfered with adolescents' relationships with their nonresident biological parents. For adolescents living with their mothers (in sole or dual residence) there were no differences in the quality of the father-adolescent relationship depending on the mother's repartnering status. For adolescents living with their fathers (again, in sole or dual residence) the presence of a new partner was related to a better relationship between adolescents and their mothers. Our data thus provide no reason for nonresidential parents to fear the arrival of a new partner, at least when the new partner has been present for less than four years, as was the case in our study.

Integrating Life in Two Homes

As long as both parents are still alive, many children of divorce face the reality of being a part of two families. When they spend time in both households on a regular basis, they also face the task of actively integrating life in two separate homes. How is it that children integrate—or fail to integrate—life in two homes after divorce?

Our overriding impression was that there was no one way to handle visitation or transitions between homes that was ideal for all adolescents. Adolescents and their families appeared to be adapting equally well to many different forms of family life after divorce, whether with regard to residential arrangement or visitation schedules. For example, the amount of time spent in the nonresidential home had virtually no bearing on the relationships in or functioning of the residential home. We also found that when adolescents spent time with both parents, and especially when those parents were not in conflict, adolescents were able to sustain close relationships with both parents. Love is not a zero-sum game. Emotional ties to one parent do not subvert ties to the other parent.

We did identify two potential difficulties in integrating life in the two homes and two families, however. First, a majority of adolescents said that they at least sometimes experienced the feeling of being caught between their parents, and we found that the more loyalty conflicts the adolescents felt, the more depression they experienced, and the more likely they were to be involved in deviant behavior (although the link with deviance was less strong than the link with depression).

How can parents reduce the chances that adolescents will experience such torn loyalties? Above all, they can try to limit the amount of conflict in their relationship with the ex-spouse, and in the event that such conflict cannot be limited, they can take steps to make sure that their children are not drawn into it. For example, when ex-spouses communicate directly with each other about matters concerning their children or their ongoing parenting relationship, rather than passing messages through the children, this is of benefit to the children. Even when the issues seem harmless, having to carry messages from one parent to the other can be a stressful experience. Parents can also reduce the chances of stimulating loyalty conflicts in their children by refraining from asking questions about the other parent or other home—especially if those questions are motivated by jealousy or criticism of the other parent—and from derogating the other parent in the child's presence. In the end, parents must try to allow the child to develop and maintain a good relationship with the other parent if that is what the child wants, and the problems and hostilities within the marital relationship should be contained there as much as possible. Otherwise, children may react by withdrawing from one or both parents (children who felt most caught said they were not close to either parent; perhaps withdrawal from both relationships represents an attempt to relieve the stress of loyalty conflicts).

Of course, our data on loyalty conflicts are preliminary; our measures were limited, and our cross-sectional data preclude conclusions about cause and effect. Given the association between feelings of being caught and adjustment (especially depression), however, we believe this is an aspect of children's postdivorce experience that merits focused attention.

A second potential difficulty in integrating life in two homes arises when the two parents are inconsistent with respect to management and control. Inconsistent parenting has been identified as a risk factor for negative adjustment among children in nondivorced families (Block, Block, and Morrison, 1981; Stoneman, Brody, and Burke, 1989). Our data suggest that, after divorce, when parents' rules and expectations for the child are inconsistent, this can generate conflict between the residential parent and child as well as loyalty conflicts. Parent-child conflict and loyalty conflicts are particularly likely, in turn, to be associated with depression in the adolescent; in fact, they account for the relation between inconsistency and depression. Furthermore, inconsistent parenting by itself (regardless of any associations with parent-child conflict or loyalty conflicts) is linked to higher levels of antisocial deviant behavior on the part of the adolescent. Again, this finding merits further investigation to identify the extent to which inconsistencies allow antisocial behavior to emerge versus the extent to which inconsistencies emerge as a parental response to antisocial behavior in the child. In any case, it appears that adolescents do have difficulty—particularly emotional difficulty—when parents do not establish consistent routines and styles of control in the two postdivorce homes.

It is not an easy matter for divorced parents to maintain consistency between the two households. With the passage of time, there is a rapid drop-off in the frequency with which the two parents talk to one another about the children (Maccoby and Mnookin, 1992). At Time 1 of the initial study (about six months after parental separation), 68 percent of parents reported that they talked together about the children at least once a week; by Time 3 (three and a half years after separation), this proportion had dropped to 40 percent. Even as early as Time 1, only about half of the parents said that they were attempting to coordinate rules between the two households, and by Time 3, only about a third were doing so. As parents remarry and residential moves take place, it becomes ever more difficult to reach and sustain any explicit agreements about what adolescents' curfews should be, what decisions they can make on their own, where they may go after school or in the evenings, and how much supervision they require. More and more, it is a question of whether the two parents (and their new partners) happen to have the same kinds of values and standards, independent of each other. Yet consistency does benefit the children, and parents should be aware of its influence and attempt not to diverge too greatly from each other's standards if the children are spending time in both households. Among the families in our study, dual-resident parents were generally more successful at maintaining consistency than other parents, perhaps because they communicated with each other more often.

Summary

In general, we are encouraged by the results of our endeavor. Four and a half years after their parents had separated, many adolescents were functioning well and could talk to us frankly and articulately about their experiences as members of divorced families. Furthermore, our findings have allowed us to identify actions that parents can take to enhance their children's adjustment to the divorce. Some of these actions may not be easy. It requires effort and self-discipline not to disparage an ex-spouse; to maintain an involved, affectionate, supervisory parental role; to take steps to prevent children from feeling the need to move into a caretaking role; or to work out consistent rules and standards across homes in which the adolescent spends time. For parents who feel they must divorce, however, but who care deeply about their children's functioning, these achievements are possible.

Resolving Discrepancies in Reports
of New Partners

In the course of our study, we encountered discrepancies between siblings, and between adolescents and parents, in reports of the presence of new partners or the duration of new relationships. With regard to the *existence* of new partners, discrepancies between siblings were resolved as follows: (1) if the adolescents lived with different parents, we took the answer of the adolescent living with the parent in question; (2) if one adolescent gave information that clearly conflicted with earlier information given by one or both parents and one did not, we took the nonconflicting answer; and (3) if we could not resolve the discrepancy, we took the affirmative answer (for example, that the parent was remarried, was dating someone, or was living with someone). Although there were some disagreements between children and parents over the *existence* of new partners, we always took the adolescent's answer in such cases because of the possibility of change between the time of the last parent interview and the adolescent interview. Discrepancies about whether a parent was living with a new partner were also resolved in the adolescent's favor for the same reason. When parent and adolescent disagreed over the *remarriage status* of a parent, we coded the parent as remarried (if the adolescent said that the parent was remarried and the parent said that he or she was not remarried, the remarriage could have occurred since the parent interview; if the parent responded positively regarding remarriage but the adolescent answered negatively—yet identified the same new partner—we assumed that the parent knew best).

Disagreements between siblings or between parent and adolescent concerning the length of time the parent had been involved with or remarried to the new partner were resolved as follows:

•If the adolescent said that the new partner had been around for a long time (longer than parent's T3 interview) but the parent indicated no special new partner at T3, we counted this person as a new partner (as explained above), but categorized time of involvement as "1" (less than two years), even if the time given by the adolescent had been two years or longer.

•If the time period for which the adolescent said that the parent and new partner had been dating was longer than the time period since the parent's Time 3 interview but shorter than the time period since the parent's Time 2 interview, and the parent's interviews did not contradict this (in other words, the parent said he or she was not involved at T2 but was involved at T3), we categorized the couple's time of involvement based on the number of months the adolescent said this couple had been dating. If more than one adolescent was interviewed and their answers fell into different categories, we averaged (for two adolescents) or took the majority answer (for more than two adolescents).

•If the parent indicated that he or she was "seriously involved" or "dating one person frequently" at both Times 2 and 3, yet the adolescent gave the time of involvement as less than two years, we took the adolescent's answer since we could not discern from the parent's interview whether the new partners of Time 2 and Time 3 were the same.

•If the adolescent and parent disagreed on the time the couple had lived together (for remarried or cohabiting new partners), and we could tell by the names given that they were talking about the same new partner, we used the date given by the parent (for remarriage or start of time living together) to compute time. If the adolescent and parent were talking about different people, we took the adolescent's answer to reflect the most recent situation. If names weren't available, and the discrepancy in times given by parent and child was large enough to place the answers in different categories (with the adolescent giving a length of time as less than two years, and data from the parent indicating a relationship of two or more years), we took the adolescent's answer on the assumption that things could have changed within the year prior to our talking to the adolescent.

•If the adolescent said he or she did not know the length of a new relationship, we used parent information to compute the length. If there was no parent information, or if parent information was not specific enough, data were left as missing.

•If we had no information at all from parents, we took the adolescent's answer to be correct. Where there was more than one sibling and the answers conflicted, the same procedures for resolution as described above were used (in other words, taking the average or majority answer depending on the number of siblings).

•If we had information only from the ex-spouse of the parent whose new partner was at issue, and that information conflicted with information given by the adolescent, we took the adolescent's answer.

•With the exceptions listed above, disagreements between adolescent and parent at issue were resolved in favor of the parent, even in cases where we had information from the other parent that more closely agreed with the adolescent.

APPENDIX B

Supplementary Tables

Table B.1 Descriptive statistics for measures

Measure	Time measured	*n*	Mean	S.D.	Min.	Max.	Cronbach's alpha
Demographics							
Age of adolescent	4	522	14.1	2.5	10	18	N/A
Sex of adolescent	1	522	1.49	.50	1	2	N/A
Mother's education	1	519	5.1	1.3	2	8	N/A
Father's education	1	521	5.4	1.6	2	8	N/A
Mother's earnings	Average T1–T3	507	19,214	12,156	0	82,333	N/A
Father's earnings	Average T1–T3	495	43,871	28,296	0	204,976	N/A
Family size	1	522	2.3	.87	1	6	N/A
Mother's working hours	3	431	36.6	16.8	0	84	N/A
Father's working hours	3	377	46.2	12.3	0	85	N/A
Stability of Residential Arrangement	4	522	.68	.47	0	1	N/A
Life Stresses	4	522	4.9	2.6	0	14	N/A
Interparental Relationship							
Discord	2	361	4.6	2.0	1	10	.72
Discord	3	339	4.1	1.5	1.2	8.5	.69
Cooperative communication	2	369	4.6	1.7	1	8	.52
Cooperative communication	3	338	4.5	1.9	2	9.3	.56
Mother's hostility	1	349	5.6	2.1	1	10	N/A
Father's hostility	1	282	5.3	2.1	1	10	N/A
Mother's hostility	2	416	5.3	2.4	1	10	N/A
Father's hostility	2	324	5.1	2.6	1	10	N/A
Mother's hostility	3	447	5.1	2.3	1	10	N/A
Father's hostility	3	378	4.9	2.3	1	10	N/A
Parental arguing	4	514	2.0	.99	1	4	N/A
Parental cooperation	4	334	6.2	2.2	.80	10.49	.57
Parental agreement on child rearing	4	520	15.4	5.0	5	25	.83
Overall parental conflict[a]	T1–T3	381	99.5	11.2	75	131	.81
Parent-Child Relationship							
Closeness to mother	4	521	36.1	7.5	10	45	.89
Closeness to father	4	494	33.0	8.1	9	45	.90
Trust of mother	4	522	9.5	2.5	2	12	.70
Trust of father	4	518	8.6	3.0	2	12	.78
Identification with mother	4	520	7.2	2.3	2	10	.79

Table B.1 (continued)

Measure	Time measured	n	Mean	S.D.	Min.	Max.	Cronbach's alpha
Identification with father	4	520	6.4	2.5	2	10	.82
Joint activities with mother	4	468	4.2	1.9	0	8	N/A
Joint activities with father	4	390	4.2	2.2	0	8	N/A
Mother remembers special days	4	519	2.9	.35	1	3	N/A
Father remembers special days	4	518	2.7	.60	1	3	N/A
Eager to see mother	4	468	3.6	1.1	1	5	N/A
Eager to see father	4	468	3.4	1.2	1	5	N/A
Overall closeness to mother[b]	4	521	102.0	12.0	60	122	.80
Overall closeness to father[b]	4	491	98.2	13.4	61	122	.79
Average conflict with mother	4	444	1.8	.93	1	5	.83
Average conflict with father	4	312	1.7	.91	1	5	.89
Maximum conflict with mother	4	444	2.4	1.4	1	5	N/A
Maximum conflict with father	4	312	2.1	1.3	1	5	N/A
Disengagement from mother's home	4	486	7.1	2.4	3	14	.55
Disengagement from father's home	4	360	6.5	2.4	3	14	.57
Considered moving out	4	494	.38	.49	0	1	N/A
Both places feel like home	4	468	.27	.44	0	1	N/A
Mother confides	4	520	3.7	1.9	0	7	.74
Father confides	4	496	2.2	1.9	0	7	.76
Adolescent nurtures mother	4	522	3.2	1.6	0	6	.63
Adolescent nurtures father	4	522	2.5	1.7	0	6	.66
Feels caught between parents	4	522	4.8	2.9	0	12	.64
Uses parents against each other	4	499	1.5	.71	1	4	N/A

Table B.1 (continued)

Measure	Time measured	*n*	Mean	S.D.	Min.	Max.	Cronbach's alpha
Parental Control and Management							
Monitoring–mother	4	447	11.8	2.4	5	15	.75
Monitoring–father	4	315	10.8	2.6	5	15	.75
School night curfew–mother	4	423	2.2	2.0	0	6	N/A
School night curfew–father	4	212	1.9	1.9	0	6	N/A
Weekend night curfew–mother	4	459	3.5	2.6	0	8	N/A
Weekend night curfew–father	4	339	3.1	2.6	0	8	N/A
Adult home after school–mother	4	382	.48	.50	0	1	N/A
Adult home after school–father	4	198	.51	.50	0	1	N/A
Youth-alone decisions–mother	4	464	.45	.27	0	1	N/A
Youth-alone decisions–father	4	351	.42	.26	0	1	N/A
Youth decides–mother	4	464	.61	.26	0	1	N/A
Youth decides–father	4	351	.59	.25	0	1	N/A
Joint decisions–mother	4	464	.70	.44	0	1	N/A
Joint decisions–father	4	351	.73	.42	0	1	N/A
Household organization–mother	4	486	38.1	8.9	9	54	.79
Household organization–father	4	360	38.8	8.2	13	54	.74
Acceptance of rules–mother	4	487	19.0	3.8	5	25	.68
Acceptance of rules–father	4	368	18.7	3.8	5	25	.67
Chores–mother	4	486	26.3	5.8	11	43	N/A
Chores–father	4	360	23.3	6.4	11	44	N/A
Household management–mother[c]	4	444	100.1	10.7	68	121	.75
Household management–father[c]	4	301	100.0	10.2	69	121	.71
Adolescents' Satisfaction with Time Spent with Each Parent	4	521	6.9	2.6	1	10	N/A

Table B.1 (continued)

Measure	Time measured	*n*	Mean	S.D.	Min.	Max.	Cronbach's alpha
Adolescent Adjustment							
Depression/anxiety	4	522	15.2	7.0	0	30	.83
Overall deviance	4	522	21.8	5.7	16	46	.83
Substance use	4	522	7.9	3.3	6	24	.83
School deviance	4	521	7.2	2.5	4	16	.70
Antisocial behavior	4	522	5.7	1.2	5	13	.53
School grades	4	522	5.8	1.6	1	8	N/A
School effort	4	477	14.6	3.2	5	24	.55
Worst problem	4	522	111.3	14.9	83.7	168.1	N/A
Attacking conflict resolution style	4	522	1.6	.33	1	2.88	.67
Compromising conflict resolution style	4	522	2.6	.38	1.25	3	.58
Avoiding conflict resolution style	4	522	2.0	.33	1	3	.50
Enjoyment of activities	4	522	5.8	1.7	1	9	N/A
Closeness to same-sex friend	4	519	36.3	5.8	16	45	.79

N/A = Not applicable.

a. A composite combining several of the "interparental relationship" scales (discord at T2 and T3, cooperative communication at T2 and T3, and both mother's and father's hostility at T1 and T3). See Chapter 5 for further explanation.

b. A composite combining several of the "parent-child relationship" scales (closeness, trust, identification, and joint activities). See Chapter 5.

c. A composite combining several of the "parental control and management" scales (monitoring, school night curfew, weekend night curfew, youth-alone decisions, household organization, and acceptance of rules). See Chapter 5.

Table B.2   Age and school grade of the adolescent respondents ($N = 522$)

Age		Grade in school	
10½–11	19.7%	Fifth–sixth	26.5%
12–13	25.6	Seventh–eighth	23.2
14–15	21.5	Ninth–tenth	21.9
16–17	19.2	Eleventh–twelfth	17.9
18	14.0	Dropped out before	
	100.0%	completing high school	1.9
		Completed high school,	
		not now in school	2.3
		Taking college courses	6.3
			100.0%

Table B.3 Characteristics of the adolescents' parents

Characteristic	Mothers	Fathers
Highest Education Attained		
Eighth grade or less	1.0%	1.9%
Less than high school graduate	5.0	6.0
Graduated high school	27.3	22.3
Some college	39.7	28.0
College graduate	13.8	18.1
Some postgraduate education	5.2	5.8
Completed advanced degree	8.0	17.9
	100.0%	100.0%
	$n = (363)$	(364)
Working Hours at Time 3		
Not employed for pay	17.2%	6.2%
Under 30 hours per week	5.9	1.1
30–39 hours	11.3	2.2
40–44 hours	41.2	35.4
45 hours or more	24.4	55.1
	100.0%	100.0%
	$n = (320)$	(274)
Yearly Earnings at Time 3		
(for employed parents)		
Less than $10,000	8.8%	00.0%
$10,000–$19,999	41.3	10.6
$20,000–$29,999	30.0	14.2
$30,000–$39,999	12.9	24.8
$40,000–$49,999	4.7	17.9
$50,000 or more	2.3	32.5
	100.0%	100.0%
	$n = (317)$	(330)

Table B.4 Composition of the parental households[a]

Persons in household	Percentage of households including indicated person	
	Mothers' households	Fathers' households
Stepparent (married to natural parent)	31.6%	36.8%
Parent's new partner (unmarried)	15.4	18.7
Natural sibling	60.4	27.7
Stepsibling[b]	6.6	21.2
Half-sibling	8.5	9.3
Adult relative	6.6	7.7
Unrelated adult female	6.3	3.3
Unrelated adult male	2.7	6.9
Child of adolescent subject	.8	0.0
Child cousin	1.9	1.6
Unrelated child	1.6	1.1
Composition not known	.5	4.4

a. This table excludes cases of adolescents not living with either parent. Columns add to more than 100 percent because some households included persons in more than one category.

b. Children of unmarried but cohabiting new partners are included in the count of stepsiblings.

Table B.5 Adolescents' personal resources by residential arrangement and sex of adolescent[a]

Measure of personal resources	Mother residence		Dual residence		Father residence		F_{sex}	$F_{residence}$	$F_{interaction}$
	M	(n)	M	(n)	M	(n)			
Conflict resolution styles									
Attacking style (range: 1–3)[b]									
Boys	1.58	(168)	1.59	(32)	1.60	(62)	.16	1.43	.82
Girls	1.54	(197)	1.65	(19)	1.63	(38)			
Compromising style (range: 1–3)									
Boys	2.55	(168)	2.45	(32)	2.49	(62)	7.09**	1.13	.15
Girls	2.64	(197)	2.60	(19)	2.61	(38)			
Avoidant style (range: 1–3)									
Boys	1.94	(168)	1.88	(32)	2.02	(62)	.01	.20	1.93
Girls	1.96	(197)	1.96	(19)	1.90	(38)			
Enjoyment of activities (range: 1–10)									
Boys	5.9	(168)	5.4	(32)	6.2	(62)	.50	.74	1.50
Girls	5.7	(197)	5.7	(19)	5.6	(38)			
Closeness to same-sex friend (range: 9–45)									
Boys	34.7	(167)	35.4	(32)	35.3	(61)	17.68****	.89	.70
Girls	37.8	(197)	39.3	(19)	37.1	(37)			

a. All means are adjusted for age and sex of adolescent and average parental education.
b. The ranges given are possible, not actual, ranges.
$**p \leq .01.$ $****p \leq .0001.$

Table B.6 Adolescents' internalizing problems, externalizing problems, school adjustment, and "worst problem" by residential arrangement and sex of adolescent[a]

Measure of adjustment	Mother residence		Dual residence		Father residence		F_{sex}	$F_{residence}$	$F_{interaction}$	Significant differences
	M	(n)	M	(n)	M	(n)				
Internalizing Problems										
Depression/anxiety (range: 0–30)[b]										
Boys	14.0	(168)	13.0	(32)	13.3	(62)	12.59***	2.10	2.10	
Girls	16.5	(197)	14.0	(19)	18.5	(38)				
Externalizing Problems										
Substance use (range: 6–24)										
Boys	7.8	(168)	7.8	(32)	8.5	(62)	.64	3.77*,c	.25	F > M, D
Girls	7.6	(197)	7.2	(19)	8.5	(38)				
School deviance (range: 4–16)										
Boys	7.2	(168)	7.5	(32)	7.5	(62)	1.09	1.00	.03	
Girls	6.9	(196)	7.2	(19)	7.3	(38)				
Antisocial behavior (range: 5–20)										
Boys	5.9	(168)	6.2	(32)	6.0	(62)	21.59****	1.50	1.28	
Girls	5.3	(197)	5.2	(19)	5.6	(38)				

	Mean	(n)	Mean	(n)	Mean	(n)				
Overall deviance (range: 15–68)										
Boys	22.0	(168)	22.6	(32)	23.1	(62)	3.85+	3.58*	.46	F > M
Girls	20.9	(197)	20.6	(19)	22.7	(38)				
School Adjustment										
Grades (range: 1–8)										
Boys	5.6	(168)	6.1	(32)	5.4	(62)	2.14	2.87+,d	.43	F < D
Girls	6.0	(197)	6.2	(19)	5.6	(38)				
School effort (range: 2–24)										
Boys	14.2	(153)	14.2	(32)	14.7	(59)	1.07	.58	3.01+,e	
Girls	15.1	(176)	15.4	(17)	13.9	(35)				
"Worst Problem" (standardized)										
Boys	111.4	(168)	109.3	(32)	112.4	(62)	.09	5.39**	2.32+,e	F > M, D
Girls	110.2	(197)	104.5	(19)	116.9	(38)				

a. All means are adjusted for age and sex of adolescent and mid-parent education.
b. The ranges given are possible, not actual, ranges.
c. The effect weakens in random subsamples.
d. The effect gets stronger when residence effects are examined controlling for sex.
e. The effect drops out in three random subsamples.
$+p \leq .10$. $*p \leq .05$. $**p \leq .01$. $***p \leq .001$. $****p \leq .0001$.

Table B.7 Selected indices of family context by new-partner status

Demographic factor	No new partner	Dating	Cohabiting	Remarried	p
Residential Mothers[a]					
Mean age of adolescent	14.2	14.5	13.9	13.7	+
Mother's education[b]	5.5	5.2	5.2	5.0	+
Mother's earnings (T1–T3)[b,c]	20.7	22.6	18.7	19.7	n.s.
Mother's working hours (T3)[b]	40.8	40.8	30.4	33.2	***
Residential Fathers[d]					
Mean age of adolescent	13.9	14.7	14.1	13.3	+
Father's education[b]	5.4	5.8	4.7	5.6	n.s.
Father's earnings (T1–T3)[b,c]	44.1	37.1	44.2	57.2	+
Father's working hours (T3)[b]	44.9	39.7	48.6	49.5	*

Header spanning "No new partner / Dating / Cohabiting / Remarried": **New-partner status**

a. Included here are cases in which the adolescents lived with their mothers (in sole or dual residence).

b. Numbers are based on a sample of only one adolescent per family selected randomly.

c. In thousands of dollars per year. Based on average over T1, T2, and T3.

d. Included here are cases in which the adolescents lived with their fathers (in sole or dual residence).

$^{+}p = \leq .10$. $^{*}p = \leq .05$. $^{***}p = \leq .001$.   n.s. = not significant.

Table B.8 Relation of visitation levels to demographic characteristics

Demographic characteristic	Level of visitation				$F_{visitation}$
	Little or none (1)	Vacation only (2)	Moderate (3)	High (4)	
Mother-Resident Adolescents					
Maximum *n*	(116)	(63)	(75)	(93)	
Mean age of adolescents	14.5	14.0	14.1	13.1	6.50*** (4 < 1,2,3)
Percentage male	41.4	39.7	50.7	54.8	1.85
Mother's education[a]	4.9	5.1	5.2	5.3	1.15
Father's education[a]	5.0	5.8	5.3	5.6	2.39+ (1 < 2,4)
Mid-parent education[a]	5.0	5.4	5.3	5.5	2.14+ (1 < 4)
Percentage with mother remarried[a,b]	33.6	36.3	20.7	38.0	1.42
Percentage with father remarried[a,b]	38.8	49.3	28.8	33.9	1.37
Percentage who have been in same residence since divorce[b]	77.8	71.9	84.3	81.7	1.22
Father-Resident Adolescents					
Maximum *n*	(23)	(28)	(22)	(25)	
Mean age of adolescents	15.4	14.0	14.7	12.9	5.29** (4 < 1,2,3; 2 < 1)
Percentage male	56.5	60.7	59.1	76.0	.80
Mother's education[a]	4.4	5.0	4.4	4.7	1.65
Father's education[a]	4.9	5.9	5.2	4.8	3.10* (2 > 1,4)
Mid-parent education[a]	4.7	5.5	4.8	4.7	3.23* (2 > 1,3,4)
Percentage with mother remarried[a,b]	24.9	48.8	27.4	24.1	1.11
Percentage with father remarried[a,b]	22.5	46.6	34.4	50.6	1.10
Percentage who have been in same residence since divorce[b]	54.8	32.5	21.3	30.4	2.06

a. Values taken from a random sample where only one adolescent per family is represented.
b. Means are controlled for age and sex of adolescent and mid-parent education.
+$p \leq .10$.   *$p \leq .05$.   **$p \leq .01$.   ***$p \leq .001$.

Table B.9 Parent-adolescent relationships in three residential arrangements, by sex of adolescent[a]

Measure of parent-adolescent relationship	Mother residence		Dual residence		Father residence	
	M	(n)	M	(n)	M	(n)
Closeness to mother (range: 9–45)[b]						
Boys	37.3	(168)	37.4	(31)	**35.7**	(61)
Girls	35.9	(197)	39.4	(18)	**30.5**	(38)
Closeness to father (range: 9–45)						
Boys	**33.5**	(151)	35.7	(32)	35.6	(62)
Girls	**31.1**	(186)	37.8	(19)	32.6	(38)
Trust of mother (range: 2–12)						
Boys	9.8	(168)	10.0	(31)	**9.6**	(62)
Girls	9.3	(197)	10.1	(18)	**8.0**	(38)
Trust of father (range: 2–12)						
Boys	**8.4**	(168)	9.5	(32)	9.8	(61)
Girls	**8.1**	(194)	9.6	(19)	9.5	(38)
Identification with mother (range: 2–10)						
Boys	7.6	(168)	8.3	(31)	**7.3**	(61)
Girls	7.0	(196)	7.8	(18)	**5.4**	(38)
Identification with father (range: 2–10)						
Boys	**6.5**	(168)	7.7	(32)	7.0	(62)
Girls	**5.8**	(195)	7.5	(19)	6.8	(38)
Joint activities with mother (range: 0–11)						
Boys	4.1	(162)	4.9	(31)	**4.2**	(41)
Girls	4.3	(184)	3.9	(16)	**3.4**	(27)
Joint activities with father (range: 0–11)						
Boys	**4.2**	(113)	5.1	(32)	5.0	(62)
Girls	**3.5**	(126)	4.4	(17)	4.0	(36)
Average conflict with mother (range: 0–5)						
Boys	1.9	(162)	1.6	(31)	**1.5**	(30)
Girls	1.9	(184)	1.8	(16)	**2.2**	(14)

Table B.9 (continued)

Measure of parent-adolescent relationship	Mother residence		Dual residence		Father residence	
	M	(n)	M	(n)	M	(n)
Average conflict with father (range 0–5)						
Boys	**1.6**	(89)	1.6	(32)	1.9	(62)
Girls	**1.5**	(74)	1.7	(17)	1.8	(36)
Maximum conflict with mother (range: 0–5)						
Boys	2.5	(162)	2.1	(31)	**1.8**	(30)
Girls	2.6	(184)	2.4	(16)	**2.8**	(14)
Maximum conflict with father (range: 0–5)						
Boys	**1.9**	(89)	2.1	(32)	2.4	(62)
Girls	**1.8**	(74)	2.3	(17)	2.5	(36)
Disengagement from mother's household (range: 3–14)						
Boys	7.2	(168)	6.9	(31)	**5.6**	(44)
Girls	7.4	(197)	5.9	(18)	**7.2**	(21)
Disengagement from father's household (range: 3–14)						
Boys	**6.0**	(106)	7.0	(32)	7.2	(62)
Girls	**5.9**	(101)	6.1	(19)	7.8	(38)
Mother confides (standardized; actual range: 0–7)						
Boys	3.7	(168)	4.0	(31)	**3.4**	(61)
Girls	3.8	(197)	3.8	(18)	**3.3**	(37)
Father confides (standardized; actual range: 0–7)						
Boys	**2.1**	(152)	3.2	(32)	3.0	(62)
Girls	**1.7**	(187)	3.2	(19)	2.2	(38)
Adolescent nurtures mother (standardized; actual range: 0–6)						
Boys	3.4	(168)	2.8	(31)	**2.9**	(62)
Girls	3.3	(197)	3.2	(18)	**3.0**	(38)

Table B.9 (continued)

Measure of parent-adolescent relationship	Mother residence		Dual residence		Father residence	
	M	(n)	M	(n)	M	(n)
Adolescent nurtures father (standardized; actual range: 0–6)						
Boys	**2.4**	(168)	2.3	(32)	2.8	(62)
Girls	**2.5**	(197)	2.9	(19)	2.7	(38)
Mother remembers special days (range: 1–3)						
Boys	2.93	(168)	2.91	(31)	**2.89**	(61)
Girls	2.91	(195)	3.00	(18)	**2.71**	(38)
Father remembers special days (range: 1–3)						
Boys	**2.63**	(167)	2.74	(32)	2.85	(61)
Girls	**2.63**	(195)	3.00	(19)	2.83	(38)
Eagerness to see mother (range: 1–5)						
Boys	3.5	(146)	3.6	(31)	**3.7**	(58)
Girls	3.7	(173)	3.5	(16)	**3.5**	(36)
Eagerness to see father (range: 1–5)						
Boys	**3.4**	(146)	3.3	(32)	3.4	(58)
Girls	**3.3**	(173)	3.2	(17)	3.6	(36)

Note: Means for nonresidential parents are presented in boldface.

a. Means are adjusted for age of adolescent and the appropriate form of parental education (mother's education when comparing relationships with mother, father's education when comparing relationships with father) by entering these variables as covariates in the analysis.

b. Unless otherwise noted, range of scores indicates possible, not actual, range.

Table B.10 Parental management and control in three residential arrangements, by sex of adolescent[a]

Measure of parental management/control	Mother residence		Dual residence		Father residence	
	M	(n)	M	(n)	M	(n)
Monitoring by mother (range: 5–15)[b]						
Boys	11.7	(162)	11.6	(31)	**10.9**	(32)
Girls	12.1	(184)	12.6	(16)	**9.9**	(15)
Monitoring by father (range: 5–15)						
Boys	**10.3**	(88)	11.4	(32)	11.9	(61)
Girls	**10.1**	(79)	12.2	(17)	10.9	(36)
Youth alone–mother (range: 0–1)						
Boys	.46	(162)	.51	(31)	**.46**	(44)
Girls	.41	(184)	.37	(16)	**.51**	(20)
Youth alone–father (range: 0–1)						
Boys	**.42**	(103)	.50	(32)	.44	(62)
Girls	**.40**	(99)	.38	(17)	.41	(36)
Youth decides–mother (range: 0–1)						
Boys	.62	(162)	.70	(31)	**.64**	(44)
Girls	.58	(184)	.51	(16)	**.67**	(20)
Youth decides–father (range: 0–1)						
Boys	**.60**	(103)	.70	(32)	.61	(62)
Girls	**.55**	(99)	.50	(17)	.57	(36)
Joint decisions–mother (range: 0–1)						
Boys	.68	(162)	.57	(31)	**.68**	(44)
Girls	.76	(184)	.79	(16)	**.63**	(20)
Joint decisions–father (range: 0–1)						
Boys	**.73**	(103)	.60	(32)	.70	(62)
Girls	**.77**	(99)	.82	(17)	.72	(36)
School night curfew–mother (range: 0–6)						
Boys	2.1	(162)	2.4	(30)	**2.1**	(17)
Girls	2.2	(184)	2.2	(16)	**1.9**	(9)

Table B.10   (continued)

Measure of parental management/control	Mother residence		Dual residence		Father residence	
	M	(*n*)	*M*	(*n*)	*M*	(*n*)
School night curfew–father (range: 0–6)						
Boys	**2.1**	(37)	2.5	(28)	1.8	(62)
Girls	**1.6**	(38)	1.8	(12)	1.9	(35)
Weekend night curfew–mother (range: 0–8)						
Boys	3.5	(162)	3.9	(28)	**3.3**	(43)
Girls	3.6	(184)	2.8	(15)	**3.5**	(20)
Weekend night curfew–father (range: 0–8)						
Boys	**3.2**	(98)	4.2	(31)	3.2	(62)
Girls	**2.7**	(95)	3.0	(17)	3.3	(35)
Household organization–mother (range: 9–54)						
Boys	38.6	(168)	40.4	(31)	**39.6**	(44)
Girls	36.9	(197)	40.8	(18)	**37.4**	(21)
Household organization–father (range: 9–54)						
Boys	**39.4**	(106)	40.4	(32)	39.3	(62)
Girls	**37.8**	(101)	40.2	(19)	37.4	(38)
Chores–mother (range: 11–48)						
Boys	27.6	(168)	25.6	(31)	**22.1**	(44)
Girls	26.5	(197)	25.8	(18)	**23.9**	(21)
Chores–father (range: 11–48)						
Boys	**21.4**	(152)	24.4	(32)	27.5	(62)
Girls	**21.3**	(187)	23.9	(19)	26.2	(38)
Acceptance of rules–mother (range: 5–25)						
Boys	19.2	(168)	19.1	(31)	**19.4**	(44)
Girls	18.9	(197)	19.6	(18)	**18.2**	(22)
Acceptance of rules–father (range: 5–25)						
Boys	**19.2**	(109)	18.8	(32)	18.8	(62)
Girls	**18.3**	(106)	19.3	(19)	17.8	(38)

Table B.10 (continued)

Measure of parental management/control	Mother residence M	Mother residence (n)	Dual residence M	Dual residence (n)	Father residence M	Father residence (n)
Adult home after school–mother (range: 0–1)						
Boys	.46	(145)	.41	(30)	**.59**	(14)
Girls	.50	(168)	.45	(14)	**.17**	(7)
Adult home after school–father (range: 0–1)						
Boys	**.62**	(37)	.52	(27)	.44	(57)
Girls	**.66**	(35)	.44	(11)	.36	(31)

Note: Means for nonresidential parents are presented in boldface.

a. Means are adjusted for age of adolescent and the appropriate form of parental education (mother's education when comparing relationships with mother, father's education when comparing relationships with father) by entering these variables as covariates in the analysis.

b. Range of scores indicates possible, not actual, range.

Table B.11 Results of multivariate regression predicting parenting discrepancies

Predictor variables	Parenting discrepancies b	Parenting discrepancies β
Constant	1.16	
Female	.10	.07
Parental education	.04	.07
Frequency of parental arguing (T4)	.06	.08
Parental cooperation (T4)	−.07****	−.23
Contact with nonresidential parent (T4)	−.12**	−.17
Education × arguing (T4)	−.07*	−.11
Education × cooperation (T4)	.03*	.11
Total R^2 = .12, F = 7.08****		

$*p \leq .05.$ $**p \leq .01.$ $****p \leq .0001.$

NOTES

1. Introduction

1. An additional factor that has been emphasized as important in understanding the effects of divorce is economic stress. Even among fairly affluent families, divorce can mean economic stringency. Families currently spend a much higher proportion of their incomes on housing than was the case twenty-five or more years ago. At present, supporting two residences is substantially more costly than supporting one, and the postdivorce standard of living of one or both parents must reflect this fact. For some families, one or both parents simply live less well, and perhaps must work longer hours. For other families, however, one or both households will fall below the poverty line. Most commonly, it is the mother's household—usually including the children—that becomes impoverished. Although economic factors, per se, are not a central focus of this book, we take these and related factors into account as we examine the importance of the other more interpersonal factors.

2. The processes whereby parents negotiate their custodial decisions are described and analyzed in Mnookin et al. (1989) and in Maccoby and Mnookin (1992).

3. In Study 1, "residence" and "residential arrangement" were used to describe a child's physical custody arrangement, which in a number of cases was not the same as the custody arrangement specified in the divorce decree. We continue the practice of using "residence," rather than "custody," when we are referring to the adolescents' physical custody arrangements.

4. See the early work of Wallerstein and Kelly (1980) and Hetherington and colleagues (for example, Hetherington, Cox, and Cox, 1982). More recent evidence and reviews of the growing body of research may be found in Hetherington and Clingempeel (1992) and in Emery (1988).

2. Methods

1. The findings from these parent interviews are reported in Maccoby and Mnookin (1992).
2. Detailed information about how each scale was constructed can be obtained from the first author.

3. The Adolescents

1. Maccoby and Mnookin (1992) report similar findings for the overall sample from which our adolescents were drawn. For example, Study 1 children who were under age six when their parents separated were more likely to lose contact with nonresidential fathers over time than children six years and older. Thus our adolescent sample was drawn from those age groups most likely to maintain or increase contact with nonresidential fathers over time (see Maccoby and Mnookin, 1992, p. 180, Figure 8.6).
2. We did compare the adjustment of our adolescents with adolescents of comparable age from another large study of adolescents in the same geographic area (Dornbusch et al., 1991; Steinberg et al., 1991). The comparison adolescents had answered the same questions concerning depression/anxiety and deviance that our adolescents answered, except that they answered using a written questionnaire. We found that our adolescents were more depressed and anxious than the comparison group from nondivorced families, and similar in depression to a comparison group from divorced families. Adolescents in our study, however, reported lower levels of deviance than either the divorced or nondivorced comparison samples, leading us to believe that the method of data collection influenced reporting of deviance.
3. The means and ranges for each of the scales we discuss in the following section are among those recorded in Appendix Table B.1.
4. Schoenbach and colleagues (1983) asked a junior high school sample (twelve- to fifteen-year-olds) questions similar to ours, but focusing on "the last week" rather than "the past month." They found that between 10 percent and 20 percent of the early adolescent sample experienced a variety of symptoms of depression "a lot of the time" or "most of the time," while over 50 percent experienced them "rarely or none of the time."
5. Two-fifths said that their most heated discussion with their mothers in the last two weeks had been "pretty angry," "very angry," or "extremely angry." Fewer (30 percent) reported conflicts of this intensity with fathers.

4. Adolescent Adjustment

1. The difference in father's earnings between dual residence and father residence did not quite reach statistical significance but, as Table 4.1

shows, was almost as substantial as the difference between dual residence and mother residence.

2. We realized that using the average across the two parents as a control may not have adequately accounted for differences in the residential parent's resources across arrangements. In addition, controlling for education—although more strongly related to residence than income—may not have captured the income differentials completely. Thus, in additional analyses, we compared adjustment scores across residential arrangements, controlling for both income and education of the residential parent, thus statistically equating residential mothers' and residential fathers' socioeconomic status. Because of the difficulty in defining a "residential parent" for adolescents in dual residence, dual-resident adolescents were excluded from some of these analyses; in others, we continued to use average parental education as the measure of education for dual-resident adolescents. In general, controlling for the residential parent's resources made little difference in the results. In the couple of instances where results changed slightly, we note this fact in the appropriate section of the text.

3. Controlling for residential parent's income and education (rather than average parental education) strengthened the residence difference.

4. The standardized score ($M = 100, S.D. = 16$) for each of these scales was summed to create the "worst problem" score.

5. The difference between mother- and dual-resident adolescents was significant at $p \leq .10$.

5. Life in the Residential Home

1. For analyses of residence differences concerning factors that were measured at the child or family level (in other words, there was only one measure of the construct for each adolescent respondent; examples are the number of life stresses and the amount of cooperation between parents), we compared all three residential groups in one analysis. However, when we examined residence differences in aspects of context or family functioning that were measured separately for each parent or each parent's household (constructs for which each adolescent could potentially have two scores, one for mother's home and one for father's home; examples include the number of people living in each household, the adolescent's closeness to each parent, and the level of monitoring in each home), we made three sets of comparisons. First, we compared households of mothers for adolescents in mother versus dual residence and households of fathers for adolescents in father versus dual residence. Then we excluded dual-resident households and directly compared homes of the residential parent for adolescents in mother and father residence.

2. Analyses for contextual factors were conducted with and without controlling for the demographic factors identified in Chapter 4 as linked to residence (age and sex of adolescent, education of parent). Adding controls never changed the results substantially. Because we were less interested in reasons for any differences in context than we were in whether such differences in fact existed, we discuss results obtained without controls.

3. The overall equation predicting father's hostility at Time 3 (using sex and age of adolescent and father's education, as well as residence) was not significant. The main effect of residence, however, was significant, and the differences among means for this main effect were consistent with the differences described for hostility measured at the other time points, and with what we would have predicted given the circumstances under which fathers often get custody. Thus we consider the results obtained at Time 3 as significant and meaningful.

4. However, over all ages (not just among the adolescents), according to the parents' own reports of the closeness of their predivorce involvement with the children, fathers who obtained sole physical custody were not more closely involved than other fathers before the parental separation.

5. Although the contrast between dual- and sole-resident fathers was not significant, the magnitude of the difference between means was the same as that for the significant contrast between dual- and sole-resident mothers.

6. Linking Home Life and Adjustment

1. Details about the derivation of these scores can be obtained from the first author.

2. For boys in mother residence, girls in mother residence, and boys in father residence, we used a modified hierarchical regression procedure whereby variables in the "context" set were entered first, followed by variables in the "interparental" relationship set, then variables in the "parent-child relationship" and "parental control and management" sets (see Cohen and Cohen, 1983, for a description of hierarchical regression using sets of variables). Yet even in the larger groups (for example, mother-resident boys) we did not have enough cases to legitimately enter all variables representing all four sets of constructs. We therefore used a "modified" procedure, as follows. Given that there is a strong theoretical basis for expecting that context variables influence process variables, rather than vice versa, we first entered the set of context variables. Any context variables that were not significant in predicting adjustment when just the context set was entered were dropped from subsequent analyses. In other words, our first analysis considered all context variables in

predicting each adjustment variable, but when we moved to include the interparental relationship set, we controlled only for those context variables that had been statistically significant in the first analysis, with the exception that age of adolescent was retained in all analyses. (The initial analysis of context variables was done both including and excluding parental working hours. Because including parental working hours reduced the number of cases available for analysis significantly, we only proceeded on the basis of the analysis including working hours if in fact working hours was a significant predictor of the adjustment measure in question. If working hours was not a significant predictor, we proceeded with further steps based on the analysis excluding working hours.) Entry of "interparental relationship" variables was done in three different ways: entering only the parent-reported variable (T3 maximum hostility or the parental conflict composite), entering just the two adolescent-reported (T4) measures of the relationship as a set, and entering parent-reported and adolescent-reported variables together as a set. If both parent-reported and adolescent-reported measures were significant predictors of a particular adjustment outcome (and the variables as a set added significant variance to the prediction at hand), both were retained for further analysis. If only the parent report or only the adolescent report added significant variance to the prediction of the adjustment measure, just that measure (or set, in the case of the adolescent-reported measures) was retained. In a similar fashion, we then entered the "parent-child relationship" set and the "parental control and management" set, both separately and together, controlling for context variables that had been significant, and any interparental relationship sets that had added significant variance to the context variables. In the description of results, we focus on whichever equation provided the best prediction of the adjustment measure at hand.

Note that this analysis strategy does not test explicitly for interactions of the predictor variables with sex or residence. When it appeared from the by-group analyses that a predictor of adjustment was different for boys and girls, or for mother- and father-resident adolescents, we then tested for interactions by entering multiplicative terms into a regression equation that included all of the main effect predictors that had been significant for each group separately.

3. In Table 6.2, we show the correlations of parent's new partner status with "worst problem" with only the adolescent's age and residential parent's education controlled. The predictive power of the residential parent's new partner status—for both presence of a stepparent and presence of an unmarried new partner—was stronger, however, when the other contextual variables (set 1) were controlled in regression analyses.

4. The presence of a cohabiting new partner was linked to attacking conflict

resolution, substance use, overall deviance, school grades, and "worst problem" for both mother- and father-resident boys; the links to attacking conflict resolution, antisocial behavior, and school effort were strongest for father-resident boys; and the link with school deviance was strongest for mother-resident boys.

5. The association between the presence of a cohabiting new partner and adolescent adjustment is no longer significant, although the residual correlations are in the same direction as before.

6. Table 6.2 shows significant relations between parent-child conflict and "worst problem," but these do not hold up in multivariate analyses when other aspects of the parent-child relationship are also included.

7. The relations were not statistically significant for father-resident girls, but were similar in magnitude to the relations for mother-resident girls.

8. This association was only significant for mother-resident girls, but went in the same direction for mother- and father-resident boys.

9. We examined the correlations separately for younger and older girls because we noted that when we correlated household management with "worst problem" without partialling the adolescent's age, the correlation went in the predicted direction.

10. The correlations between "worst problem" and the different components of household management for the fourteen father-resident girls who were fifteen or older were not significant, and several were close to zero.

11. Given the weakness of most direct associations between parent-child closeness and adolescent adjustment among father-resident adolescents, this interpretation may have less validity for this group. Even among father-resident adolescents, however, father-child closeness was highly related to the father's household management. The father's management, in turn, was clearly related to better adjustment among boys living with their fathers, and most likely related to better adjustment of girls as well (with the caveats already noted in the text).

12. The colinearity between measures for the two parents meant that when they were entered together in a multiple regression, the highest first-order correlation would absorb the variance common to both, and the beta coefficient for the second parent's scores was drastically reduced, or indeed in many instances switched signs, leading to a very misleading picture of the role of the parent with the initially lower correlation.

13. The links between the affective quality of the parent-child relationship and household management for the very small group of dual-resident girls were different in some ways from those in every other group. For example, the correlation between the averaged (across parents) scores for "household management" and "overall closeness" was .05 for these girls, making them the only group in which these two constructs were not

significantly and positively associated. However, the two main components of each of these composites—parent-child emotional closeness and
parental monitoring—were, in fact, positively and significantly correlated ($r = .52$). It turns out that other aspects of "overall closeness" and
"household management" were negatively related for these girls (for
example, more closeness was related to later curfews; more joint activities between parent and child were related to feelings that rules were less
fair and consistent). It appears that among this small group of girls, it is
still the case that close relationships facilitate more effective monitoring,
but that this relation is not apparent when we use the "overall closeness"
and "household management" composites.

7. Adaptation to New Partners

1. This strategy means that we had many fewer new partnerships to study
for fathers (a maximum of 151 cases) than we had for mothers (a maximum of 417). When we subdivided our sample by residence, sex of
adolescent, and our fourfold grouping of new-partner status, cell sizes
became quite small in some instances, especially for the father-resident
group. For example, there were only eighteen adolescents—nine boys
and nine girls—living with their fathers in sole or dual residence whose
fathers had a cohabiting partner. Cell sizes dropped even further when
some of the cases did not provide data on certain questions of interest,
or when we attempted to check our results in random subsamples using
only one sibling per family. We dealt with these issues by first subdividing
our cases by our four categories of new-partner status and sex of adolescent, and noting how or whether these subgroups differed with respect
to family process. We also, however, contrasted the remarried group with
the other three new-partner groups combined, and contrasted the families in which a new partner was living in the home (cohabiting or remarried) with the other two new-partner groups combined.

Throughout this chapter, analyses predicting "child-level" variables (in
other words, variables on which siblings in the same family could differ)
were first conducted using all adolescents, despite the fact that a parent's
new-partner status (the independent variable) was the same for all siblings in a family. Because siblings may differ in their reaction to the same
new-partnering situation, we felt that analyses using the full sample were
appropriate, especially given the low cell sizes that resulted in some of
the analyses using random subsamples. We did, however, follow the
procedure outlined in Chapter 2 for checking results in random subsamples where only one adolescent per family was represented, and thus any
results that did not hold up in subsamples are noted or considered
nonsignificant.

2. Mother's education was used as the control when examining mother's new-partner status, and father's education for father's new-partner status, with a few exceptions. When using measures of one parent's new-partner status to predict the relationship between adolescents and the other biological parent, we used the other parent's education as the control if it was related to the outcome measure of interest. New-partner status was not related to the number of children of the marriage, to the number of moves that adolescents had made from one household to the other, or to the number of life stresses adolescents had encountered. These factors, therefore, did not need to be controlled in the analyses of new-partner status and family processes.

3. In two random subsamples contrasting all four repartnering groups, and in the whole-sample analysis contrasting those who had live-in new partners (both cohabiting and remarried) with those who didn't, there was a significant repartnering status by sex interaction.

4. In a comparison of remarried versus nonremarried mothers, there was a trend-level interaction of mother's remarriage and sex of adolescent, indicating a tendency for girls to feel closer to their fathers if the mother was remarried than if she was not. There was also a trend-level relation between the mother's remarriage and lower levels of disengagement from the father's home for both sexes.

5. The differences for boys in closeness to their fathers were significant only for the original closeness composite, not for "overall closeness," although it is apparent in Figure 7.3 that the stated trend exists for "overall closeness" as well.

6. On several measures of the parent-adolescent relationship, we also found that adolescents, especially girls, experienced better relationships with their fathers when they did not have a new partner living in the home (there was no new partner or only regular dating) than when they did (the father was remarried or cohabiting with the new partner).

7. There was a significant sex by new-partner status interaction when contrasting the group that had live-in new partners (remarried or cohabiting) with the group that did not have such partners.

8. Household management was also high among dating fathers, particularly when we used the full sample of adolescents. But in all subsamples of adolescents where we used only one adolescent per family, selected randomly, the level of management in the "dating only" group was reduced and was not significantly higher than the household management of fathers who had no new partner or a cohabiting new partner. Also, the level of management in the "dating only" group was reduced to the level of the "no new partner" group when we took into account the fewer working hours among fathers in the "dating only" group. Thus the most robust finding was the difference in management between

remarried fathers and fathers with no new partner or a cohabiting new partner.

9. Although when all four groups were contrasted with one another the effect of father's repartnering status on "adult home after school" was not significant, there was a significant difference on this variable between remarried fathers and the other three groups combined.

10. When adolescents are quoted, their ages are identified only as "early adolescent" (ages ten to thirteen), "mid-adolescent" (ages fourteen to sixteen), and "late adolescent" (ages seventeen to eighteen) in order to further conceal their identity. Gender or residence may be omitted for the same reason.

11. The interaction of age and sex of adolescent is not significant, but post-hoc t-tests indicate that there is a sex difference in the acceptance of mother's new partner's authority only for thirteen- and fourteen-year-olds.

12. There was a significant interaction of closeness to the residential parent and sex of the adolescent when predicting acceptance of the new partner's authority in the following instances: predicting acceptance of the new father for mother- and dual-resident adolescents combined, and predicting acceptance of the new mother for father-resident adolescents alone. The sex difference did not apply to dual-resident adolescents' acceptance of a new mother's authority.

13. The three scales with negative correlations are of course not independent of one another, and so must be taken together in indicating a weak negative trend.

14. When we repeated these analyses using the adolescent's closeness to the parent's new partner, rather than acceptance of the new partner's authority, the results were in the same direction, but somewhat weaker.

15. The relation between remarriage and adjustment was somewhat weaker in the analyses presented in Table 7.8 than in the analyses reported in Chapter 6. The change in magnitude of the relations among the father- and dual-resident adolescents is due to the somewhat different subset of adolescents used in Chapter 6 and in the present analyses. If dual-resident adolescents are excluded from the current analyses, the associations between father's remarriage and the adjustment indices are stronger. Among the mother- and dual-resident group, however, the findings indicate that the better adjustment of adolescents with a stepfather is partially a result of the fact that these adolescents have closer relationships with their mothers. As we noted in Chapter 6, the positive effects of parental remarriage are attenuated when the affective quality of the residential parent-child relationship is considered.

16. With regard to compromising conflict resolution, accounting for acceptance of the authority of the new partner reduced the importance of

remarriage itself. In addition, although acceptance of the new partner's authority was not a significant predictor of compromising, the relation between acceptance and compromise was as large for the acceptance of new mothers as it was for the acceptance of new fathers. Thus if there had been larger numbers of adolescents living with their fathers in sole or dual residence, we might have found the relation between acceptance of the new mother's authority and compromising in conflict situations to be significant.

9. Visitation

1. If regression analyses were required, we dummy coded the visitation scale to represent the different categories of interest, unless we had determined that the scale did bear a linear relation to the variable under study.
2. The residence difference was significant using all subjects but was of borderline significance in random samples.
3. These correlations are partialed for sex of adolescent and average parent education.
4. The differences in means for the father-resident adolescents are not significant, but are roughly the same magnitude as the differences for mother-resident adolescents.

10. Life in the Nonresidential Home

1. When using all subjects in our sample, there was a trend-level interaction between residence and sex, indicating that average conflict with mother did not differ by residential arrangement for girls, but that for boys, conflict was highest in mother residence. The interaction was not significant in random subsamples, although the means went in the same direction.
2. Dual-resident adolescents were excluded from analyses comparing only nonresidential parents, because dual-resident adolescents do not have a nonresidential parent.
3. Although the statistical results indicated that adolescents of both sexes reported more trust in nonresidential mothers than nonresidential fathers, the means clearly show that the effect is carried by boys.
4. Statistical tests generally did not reveal that boys and girls differed in the *difference between* relationships with residential fathers and nonresidential mothers; however, the means for some of the measures suggest that girls' relationships with each parent were less similar than those of boys (see the means for trust, conflict, and remembering special days). In each of these cases, the evidence indicates a somewhat troubled relationship

between girls and their nonresidential mothers, at least in comparison to the relationship between boys and nonresidential mothers.

5. When mother- and father-resident adolescents were analyzed separately, the difference between conflict with the residential parent and nonresidential parent was significant for mother-resident adolescents and not significant for father-resident adolescents. However, in analyses incorporating residential arrangement, the interaction between residence and type of parent was not significant.

6. The adjustment indices were regressed on each characteristic of the nonresidential parent–child relationship, controlling for that same characteristic of the adolescent's relationship with the residential parent. Age of adolescent was also accounted for in each analysis. Dual-resident adolescents were excluded from these analyses.

7. We also explicitly tested for interactions between gender of adolescent, residential arrangement, and relationships with the nonresidential parent as this set of factors related to adolescent adjustment. The analyses used were stepwise regressions, in which main effects were entered in the first step, all two-way interactions in a second step, and the three-way interaction in the third step.

8. In only two instances was there an indication of a link, and these emerged only in random subsamples and for specific subgroups of the sample.

9. Statistically, the relation between eagerness to see the nonresidential parent and adolescent deviance was significant for all father-resident adolescents, but an examination of the relations separately for boys and girls makes it clear that the effect is carried by girls.

10. The correlations for father-resident girls are no longer negative if we use only the component of "overall closeness" that we have called "emotional closeness," although they are still close to zero.

11. The analyses used were stepwise regressions, with adjustment measures as the dependent variables, and the following sets of predictor variables: (1) main effects of overall closeness to the residential parent and overall closeness to the nonresidential parent; (2) two-way interactions, including the central one of closeness to residential parent by closeness to nonresidential parent; and (3) the three-way interaction of closeness to residential parent by closeness to nonresidential parent by residential arrangement.

12. Analyses using categorical versions of parent-child "overall closeness" indicated that the adjustment of adolescents who experienced low closeness in their relationships with both father and mother was not different from that of adolescents who experienced low closeness to father but high closeness to mother.

13. Analyses using categorical versions of parent-child "overall closeness" indicated that the difference in adolescent adjustment between experi-

encing a close relationship with both parents and experiencing a close relationship with only the mother was not significant. In addition, these analyses indicated that the adjustment of adolescents who experienced low closeness in their relationships with both their mother and their father was not different from that of adolescents who experienced low closeness with their mother but high closeness with their father.

14. "Worst problem" was predicted with a dummy variable indicating dual (1) versus sole (0) residence, controlling for age and sex of adolescent, average parental education, and the sum of closeness to two parents.

15. These remaining analyses in this chapter use, as the predicted variable, the "emotional closeness" component of the "overall closeness" composite that included emotional closeness, activities, trust, and identification.

16. The significance of the effects of parental conflict (and any interactions of conflict with sex, residence, or sex and residence) on closeness to the residential parent or the nonresidential parent were tested using stepwise multiple regression. The dependent variable in these regressions was either closeness to the nonresidential parent or closeness to the residential parent. The independent variables were age of adolescent, sex of adolescent, residential arrangement (mother versus father), interparental conflict (step one); two-way interactions between sex of adolescent and conflict, residential arrangement and conflict, and sex of adolescent and residential arrangement (step two); and the three-way interaction of sex, residential arrangement, and conflict (step three).

17. The interaction of sex and nonresidential parent's hostility was significant when using all cases but not in random subsamples. The three-way interaction of sex, residence, and nonresidential parent's hostility was significant using all cases and marginally significant in random subsamples, but the correlation between hostility and closeness to the nonresidential mother remained strong for father-resident girls.

18. The effect for girls in father residence was significantly greater than that for any other group of adolescents for hostility of the residential parent and frequency of parental arguing, and nonsignificant but of the same pattern for T3 discord and T3 cooperative communication.

19. Any apparent differences in the magnitude of the relation between the interparental relationship and closeness to the nonresidential parent between boys and girls in mother residence were not statistically significant, with the exception of cooperation at T4.

20. For hostility of residential parent, the interaction with age was significant at $p \le .05$; for hostility of nonresidential parent, the interaction was significant at $p \le .10$.

21. We explicitly tested whether the difference in the association between the interparental relationship and closeness to the residential versus nonresidential parent was significant. Overall there was a differential

effect of interparental conflict on closeness to the residential versus the nonresidential parent for residential parent hostility, nonresidential parent hostility, and frequency of parental arguing. The differential negative impact of the nonresidential parent's hostility only emerged when the hostility measure was dichotomized, and is not evident using the correlational analysis depicted in Table 10.2. Among adolescents in father residence, however, T3 cooperation, residential parent hostility, nonresidential parent hostility, and T4 frequency of arguing had their greatest negative impact on closeness to nonresidential mothers for girls: only for girls in father residence was the impact of interparental conflict on closeness to the nonresidential parent consistently greater than it was on closeness to the residential parent.

22. The interactions of closeness to the nonresidential parent, interparental conflict, and residential arrangement were tested using stepwise multiple regression. In the first step, the main effects of age, sex, residential arrangement, closeness to the nonresidential parent, and interparental conflict were entered. In the second step, all two-way interactions were entered, including the interaction of central interest, closeness to the nonresidential parent by interparental conflict. Finally, in the third step, the three-way interaction of closeness by conflict by residential arrangement was entered.

23. See Chapter 6 for a more detailed discussion of the importance of mother-child closeness. It was noted there that some of the effects of closeness on adjustment are indirect, mediated by the mother's monitoring of her adolescent's activities and whereabouts.

11. Feeling Caught between One's Parents

1. Feelings of being caught were predicted, in an analysis of variance, by residence, sex of adolescent, and the interaction of residence and sex, with age of adolescent and parental education as controls. In Buchanan, Maccoby, and Dornbusch (1991), we reported that residence was essentially unrelated to feelings of being caught, because we did not control for parental education in that instance. Although parental education was not significantly related to feelings of being caught ($r = .06$, $p > .10$), it was related to residential arrangement (see Chapter 4); analyses employing parental education as a control were therefore conducted for exploratory purposes. We found, in fact, that this control did increase the magnitude of the differences between residence groups, although the significance of the difference was reduced to trend level ($p \leq .10$) in random samples.

2. Regression analyses were used to address this question. Feelings of being caught were predicted with age of adolescent, sex of adolescent, one of

the co-parenting measures, a dummy variable indicating whether the adolescent was in dual residence or in sole residence (either mother or father), and the interaction of being in dual residence with the co-parenting measure. Only the parent-reported measures of co-parenting were used in these analyses.

3. Although there was not a significant relation of feeling caught to parents' new-partner status when the four separate groups were compared, a two-group comparison of remarried mothers with those not remarried showed significantly higher levels of feeling caught in the nonremarried group. Feelings of being caught were also significantly lower in mother's households that had a new partner in the home (whether remarried or only cohabiting) than in those without a new partner.

4. This correlation is partialed for age of adolescent and sex of adolescent.

5. This correlation is partialed for age of adolescent and sex of adolescent.

6. In all of these analyses, we controlled for age and gender of the adolescent, as well as residential arrangement.

12. Inconsistency in Parenting

1. These four discrepancy scores loaded above .60 on a single factor, in a factor analysis of discrepancies in seven aspects of household management and control (in addition to the four noted, assignment of chores, school-night curfews, and weekend-night curfews were included). These four highly related discrepancy scores were standardized before averaging to create the parental discrepancy composite. A constant was added to bring all scores above zero.

2. See also Chapter 6, where we noted that the high correspondence between adolescents' reports of parent-child relationships and parental control and management in the two homes precluded using indicators of family process in both homes together in analyses predicting adolescent adjustment.

3. A significant linear progression was indicated in regression analyses treating the contact measure as a continuous variable.

4. This involved testing two-way interactions between the various demographic, contact, and interparental relationship variables. Individual interactions that remained significant at $p \leq .10$ in analyses controlling for all significant main effects were entered into a multiple regression analysis predicting parental discrepancy, with all significant main effects and interactions entered simultaneously. Subsequently, the model was re-run eliminating all nonsignificant predictors except sex, which remained as a control in all analyses. Interactions involving contact were tested by treating the contact variables as categorical as well as continuous variables. Because results of the two types of analyses were similar, we report

only the results of analyses in which contact was treated as a continuous variable.

5. When parents had higher levels of education, a higher frequency of arguing was not related to more discrepancies in parenting, and lower levels of cooperation were not as strongly related to more discrepancies in parenting.

6. The control variables were composites of the level of monitoring, youth-alone decision making, household organization, and consistency and fairness of rules in mother's and father's homes.

7. To address these questions, each of the adjustment measures (depression, antisocial behavior, and "worst problem") was predicted, in turn, with a full set of factors, including (a) parent-child relationship factors (feelings of being caught, conflict with the residential parent); (b) parenting discrepancies, and interactions of parenting discrepancies with background variables that were significant predictors of either the adjustment index or relationship factors; and (c) background variables that had been shown earlier to be related to parental discrepancies. Only those interaction terms that remained significant at $p \leq .10$ when controlling for all background factors related to discrepancy were included in the full models predicting adjustment. If an interaction term does not appear in the model, the reader may assume that it was not significant.

8. Evidence that "feeling caught" and "parent-child conflict" mediated the relation between parenting discrepancies and depression/anxiety was provided by examining the link between parenting discrepancies and depression/anxiety with and without the hypothesized mediators in the model. Without "feeling caught" and "parent-child conflict" in the model, discrepancies were significantly related to depression ($\beta = .16$, $p < .01$). With these two variables in the model, the link between discrepancies and depression was no longer significant ($\beta = .07$).

13. Conclusion

1. We could not test this for dual-resident adolescents, given the low numbers of individuals in the remarried and cohabiting groups.

2. As noted in Chapter 4, in statistical terms the residence differences indicating poorer adjustment applied equally to both boys and girls; however, the difference is generally larger for girls, and father-resident girls have the highest mean on the "worst problem" scale.

REFERENCES

Abarbanel, A. 1979. Shared parenting after separation and divorce: A study of joint custody. *American Journal of Orthopsychiatry, 49,* 320–329.

———— 1993. Children's adjustment to divorce: Theories, hypotheses, and empirical support. *Journal of Marriage and the Family, 55,* 23–38.

Amato, P. R., and B. Keith. 1991. Parental divorce and the well-being of children: A meta-analysis. *Psychological Bulletin, 110,* 26–46.

Amato, P. R., and S. J. Rezac. 1994. Contact with nonresident parents, interparental conflict, and children's behavior. *Journal of Family Issues, 15,* 191–207.

Aponte, J. J., and J. M. Van Deusen. 1981. Structural family therapy. In A. S. Gurman and D. P. Kniskern, eds., *Handbook of family therapy,* pp. 310–360. New York: Brunner/Mazel.

Barber, B. L., and J. S. Eccles. 1992. Long-term influence of divorce and single parenting on adolescent family- and work-related values, behaviors, and aspirations. *Psychological Bulletin, 111,* 108–126.

Barber, B. L., and J. M. Lyons. 1994. Family processes and adolescent adjustment in intact and remarried families. *Journal of Youth and Adolescence, 23,* 421–436.

Baron, R. M., and D. A. Kenny. 1986. The moderator-mediator variable distinction in social psychological research: Conceptual, strategic, and statistical considerations. *Journal of Personality and Social Psychology, 51,* 1173–1182.

Baumrind, D. 1991a. Effective parenting during the early adolescent transition. In P. A. Cowan and M. Hetherington, eds., *Family transitions,* pp. 111–163. Hillsdale, N.J.: Lawrence Erlbaum Associates.

———— 1991b. The influence of parenting style on adolescent competence and substance use. *Journal of Early Adolescence, 11,* 56–95.

Block, J. H., J. Block, and P. F. Gjerde. 1986. The personality of children prior to divorce: A prospective study. *Child Development, 57,* 827–840.

Block, J. H., J. Block, and A. Morrison. 1981. Parenting agreement-disagreement on child-rearing orientations and gender-related personality correlates in children. *Child Development, 52,* 965–974.

Bowlby, J. 1973. *Attachment and loss,* vol. 2, *Separation.* New York: Basic Books.

Braver, S. L., S. A. Wolchik, I. N. Sandler, B. S. Fogas, and D. Zvetina. 1991. Frequency of visitation by divorced fathers: Differences in reports by fathers and mothers. *American Journal of Orthopsychiatry, 61,* 448–454.

Bray, J. H. 1991. Psychosocial factors affecting custodial and visitation arrangements. *Behavioral Sciences and the Law, 9,* 419–437.

Bray, J. H., and S. H. Berger. 1990. Noncustodial father and paternal grandparent relationships in step-families. *Family Relations, 39,* 414–419.

———— 1993a. Developmental issues in StepFamilies Research Project: Family relationships and parent-child interactions. *Journal of Family Psychology, 7,* 76–90.

———— 1993b. Nonresidential family-child relationships following divorce and remarriage. In C. E. Depner and J. H. Bray, eds., *Nonresidential parenting: New vistas in family living,* pp. 156–181. Newbury Park, Calif.: Sage.

Buchanan, C. M., J. S. Eccles, and J. B. Becker. 1992. Are adolescents the victims of raging hormones: Evidence for activational effects of hormones on moods and behavior at adolescence. *Psychological Bulletin, 111,* 62–107.

Buchanan, C. M., E. E. Maccoby, and S. M. Dornbusch. 1991. Caught between parents: Adolescents' experience in divorced homes. *Child Development, 62,* 1008–1029.

———— 1992. Adolescents and their families after divorce: Three residential arrangements compared. *Journal of Research on Adolescence, 2,* 261–291.

Camara, K. A., and G. Resnick. 1988. Interparental conflict and cooperation: Factors moderating children's post-divorce adjustment. In E. M. Hetherington and J. D. Arasteh, eds., *Impact of Divorce, Single Parenting, and Stepparenting on Children,* pp. 169–195. Hillsdale, N.J.: Lawrence Erlbaum Associates.

Chase-Lansdale, P. L., A. J. Cherlin, and K. E. Kiernan. 1995. The long-term effects of parental divorce on the mental health of young adults: A developmental perspective. *Child Development, 66,* 1614–1634.

Cherlin, A. J., and F. F. Furstenberg. 1994. Stepfamilies in the United States: A reconsideration. In J. Hagan and K. Cook, eds., *Annual Review of Sociology,* vol. 20, pp. 359–381. Palo Alto, Calif.: Annual Reviews.

Cherlin, A. J., F. F. Furstenberg, P. L. Chase-Lansdale, K. E. Kiernan, P. K. Robins, D. R. Morrison, and J. O. Teitler. 1991. Longitudinal studies of effects of divorce on children in Great Britain and the United States. *Science, 252,* 1386–1389.

Clingempeel, W. G., E. Brand, and R. Ievoli. 1984. Stepparent-stepchild relationships in stepmother and stepfather families: A multimethod study. *Family Relations, 33,* 465–473.

Clingempeel, W. G., and S. Segal. 1986. Stepparent-stepchild relationships and the psychological adjustment of children in stepmother and stepfather families. *Child Development, 57,* 474–484.

Cohen, J., and P. Cohen. 1983. *Applied multiple regression/correlation analysis for the behavioral sciences.* Hillsdale, N.J.: Lawrence Erlbaum Associates.

Collins, W. A., and G. Russell. 1991. Mother-child and father-child relationships in middle childhood and adolescence: A developmental analysis. *Developmental Review, 11,* 99–136.

Compas, B. E. 1987. Stress and life events during childhood and adolescence. *Clinical Psychology Review, 7,* 275–302.

Crosbie-Burnett, M. 1991. Impact of joint versus sole custody and quality of co-parental relationship on adjustment of adolescents in remarried families. *Behavioral Sciences and the Law, 9,* 439–449.

Cummings, E. M., and P. Davies. 1994. *Children and marital conflict: The impact of family dispute and resolution.* New York: Guilford Press.

Davies, P. T., and E. M. Cummings. 1994. Marital conflict and child adjustment: An emotional security hypothesis. *Psychological Bulletin, 116,* 387–411.

Deal, J. E., C. F. Halverson, Jr., and K. S. Wampler. 1989. Parental agreement on child-rearing orientations: Relations to parental, marital, family, and child characteristics. *Child Development, 60,* 1025–1034.

Depner, C. E., E. V. Leino, and A. Chun. 1992. Interparental conflict and child adjustment: A decade review and meta-analysis. *Family and Conciliation Courts Review, 30,* 323–341.

Dornbusch, S. M., J. M. Carlsmith, S. J. Bushwall, P. L. Ritter, H. Leiderman, A. H. Hastorf, and R. T. Gross. 1985. Single parents, extended households, and the control of adolescents. *Child Development, 56,* 326–341.

Dornbusch, S. M., R. Mont-Reynaud, P. L. Ritter, Z. Chen, and L. Steinberg. 1991. Stressful events and their correlates among adolescents of diverse backgrounds. In M. E. Colten and S. Gore, eds., *Adolescent stress: Causes and consequences,* pp. 111–130. Hawthorne, N.Y.: Aldine de Gruyter.

Dornbusch, S. M., P. L. Ritter, P. H. Leiderman, D. F. Roberts, and M. J. Fraleigh. 1987. The relation of parenting style to adolescent school performance. *Child Development, 58,* 1244–1257.

Duncan, G. J., and S. D. Hoffman. 1985. Economic consequences of marital instability. In M. David and T. Smeeding, eds., *Horizontal equity, uncertainty, and well-being,* pp. 427–469. Chicago: University of Chicago Press.

Dunn, J. 1990. *Separate lives: Why siblings are so different.* New York: Basic Books.

Eagly, A. H., and V. J. Steffen. 1986. Gender and aggressive behavior: A meta-analytic review of the social psychological literature. *Psychological Bulletin, 100,* 309–330.

Eccles, J. S., C. Midgley, A. Wigfield, C. M. Buchanan, D. Reuman, C. Flanagan, and D. MacIver. 1993. Development during adolescence: The impact of stage/environment fit on young adolescents' experiences in schools and families. *American Psychologist, 48,* 90–101.

Emery, R. E. 1982. Interparental conflict and the children of discord and divorce. *Psychological Bulletin, 92,* 310–330.

——— 1988. *Marriage, divorce, and children's adjustment.* Newbury Park, Calif.: Sage Publications.

Espenshade, T. J. 1979. The economic consequences of divorce. *Journal of Marriage and the Family, 41,* 615–625.

Fauber, R., R. Forehand, A. M. Thomas, and M. Wierson. 1990. A mediational model of the impact of marital conflict on adolescent adjustment in intact and divorced families: The role of disrupted parenting. *Child Development, 61,* 1112–1123.

Ferri, E. 1984. *Stepchildren: A national study.* Windsor, Berkshire, U.K.: NFER-Nelson Publishing Co.

Flanagan, C., J. Schulenberg, and A. Fuligni. 1993. Residential setting and parent-adolescent relationships during the college years. *Journal of Youth and Adolescence, 22,* 171–189.

Funder, K. 1991. Children's constructions of their post-divorce families: A family sculpture approach. In K. Funder, ed., *Images of Australian families,* pp. 73–87. Melbourne: Longman-Cheshire.

Furman, W., and D. Buhrmester. 1985a. Children's perceptions of the personal relationships in their social networks. *Developmental Psychology, 21,* 1016–1024.

——— 1985b. Children's perceptions of the qualities of sibling relationships. *Child Development, 56,* 448–461.

Furstenberg, F. F. 1987. The new extended family: The experience of parents and children after remarriage. In K. Pasley and M. Ihinger-Tallman, eds., *Remarriage and stepparenting: Current research and theory,* pp. 42–61. New York: Guilford Press.

——— 1990. Coming of age in a changing family system. In S. S. Feldman and G. R. Elliott, eds., *At the threshold: The developing adolescent,* pp. 147–170. Cambridge, Mass.: Harvard University Press.

Furstenberg, F. F., Jr., S. P. Morgan, and P. D. Allison. 1987. Paternal participation and children's well-being after marital dissolution. *American Sociological Review, 52,* 695–701.

Furstenberg, F. F., Jr., C. W. Nord, J. L. Peterson, and N. Zill. 1983. The life course of children of divorce. *American Sociological Review, 48,* 656–668.

Furstenberg, F. F., Jr., and G. Spanier. 1984. *Recycling the family: Remarriage after divorce.* Beverly Hills, Calif.: Sage.

Galambos, N. L., H. A. Sears, D. M. Almeida, and N. L. Kolaric. 1995. Parents' work overload and problem behavior in young adolescents. *Journal of Research on Adolescence, 5,* 201–224.

Ganong, L. H., and M. Coleman. 1984. The effects of remarriage on children: A review of the empirical literature. *Family Relations, 33,* 389–406.

Garmezy, N., A. S. Masten, and A. Tellegen. 1984. The study of stress and competence in children: A building block for developmental psychopathology. *Child Development, 55,* 97–111.

Gilligan, C. 1982. *In a different voice: Psychological theory and women's development.* Cambridge, Mass.: Harvard University Press.

Gjerde, P. F. 1986. The interpersonal structure of family interaction settings: Parent-adolescent relations in dyads and triads. *Developmental Psychology, 22,* 297–304.

——— 1988. Parental concordance on child-rearing and the interactive emphases of parents: Sex-differentiated relationships during the preschool years. *Developmental Psychology, 24,* 700–706.

Glover, R. J., and C. Steele. 1989. Comparing the effects on the child of post-divorce parenting arrangements. *Journal of Divorce, 12,* 185–201.

Goldstein, J., A. Freud, and A. J. Solnit. 1979. *Beyond the best interests of the child.* New York: Free Press.

Gore, S., Aseltine, R. H., Jr., and Colten, M. E. 1993. Gender, social-relational involvement, and depression. *Journal of Research on Adolescence, 3,* 101–125.

Grief, J. B. 1979. Fathers, children, and joint custody. *American Journal of Orthopsychiatry, 49,* 311–319.

Groves, R. M., and R. L. Kahn. 1979. *Surveys by telephone: A natural comparison with personal interviews.* New York: Academic Press.

Gunnoe, M. L. 1994. Noncustodial mothers' and fathers' contributions to the adjustment of adolescents in stabilized stepfamilies. Paper presented in J. Bray, chair, Family transitions and adolescent adjustment: Impact of divorce, remarriage, and repartnering. Symposium conducted at the biennial meetings of the Society for Research in Adolescence, San Diego. February.

Hartup, W. W., D. C. French, B. Laursen, M. K. Johnston, and J. R. Ogawa. 1993. Conflict and friendship relations in middle childhood: Behavior in a closed-field situation. *Child Development, 64,* 445–454.

Heider, F. 1958. *The psychology of interpersonal relations.* New York: John Wiley.

Hess, R. D., and K. A. Camara. 1979. Post-divorce family relationships as mediating factors in the consequences of divorce for children. *Journal of Social Issues, 35,* 79–96.

Hetherington, E. M. 1987. Family relations six years after divorce. In K. Pasley and M. Ihinger-Tallman, eds., *Remarriage and stepparenting today: Research and theory,* pp. 185–205. New York: Guilford.

——— 1993. An overview of the Virginia Longitudinal Study of Divorce and Remarriage with a focus on early adolescence. *Journal of Family Psychology, 7,* 39–56.

Hetherington, E. M., and W. G. Clingempeel. 1992. Coping with marital transitions: A family systems perspective. *Monographs of the Society for Research in Child Development, 57.*

Hetherington, E. M., M. Cox, and R. Cox. 1978. The aftermath of divorce. In J. H. Stevens, Jr., and M. Matthews, eds., *Mother-child, father-child relations,* pp. 149–176. Washington, D.C.: NAEYC.

——— 1982. Effects of divorce on parents and children. In M. E. Lamb, ed., *Nontraditional families,* pp. 233–288. Hillsdale, N.J.: Erlbaum.

Hill, J. P., and G. N. Holmbeck. 1986. Attachment and autonomy during adolescence. *Annals of Child Development, 3,* 145–189.

Hyde, J. S. 1984. How large are gender differences in aggression? A developmental meta-analysis. *Developmental Psychology, 20,* 722–736.

Ihinger-Tallman, M. 1988. Research on stepfamilies. In W. R. Scott and J. Blake, eds., *Annual Review of Sociology,* vol. 14, pp. 25–48. Palo Alto, Calif.: Annual Reviews.

Irving, H. H., M. Benjamin, and N. Trocme. 1984. Shared parenting: An empirical analysis utilizing a large data base. *Family Process, 23,* 561–569.

Johnson, B. M., S. Shulman, and W. A. Collins. 1991. Systemic patterns of parenting as reported by adolescents: Developmental differences and implications for psychosocial outcomes. *Journal of Adolescent Research, 6,* 235–252.

Johnston, J. R., and L. E. G. Campbell. 1987. Instability in family networks of divorced and disputing parents. In E. J. Lawler, ed., *Advances in group processes,* vol. 4, pp. 243–269, Greenwich, Conn.: JAI Press.

——— 1988. *Impasses of divorce: The dynamics and resolution of family conflict.* New York: Free Press.

Johnston, J. R., M. Kline, and J. M. Tschann. 1989. Ongoing post-divorce conflict in families contesting custody: Effects on children of joint custody and frequent access. *American Journal of Orthopsychiatry, 59,* 576–592.

Kalter, N., and J. Rembar. 1981. The significance of a child's age at the time of parental divorce. *American Journal of Orthopsychiatry, 51,* 85–100.

Kelly, J. B. 1993. Current research on children's postdivorce adjustment: No simple answers. *Family and Conciliation Courts Reviews, 31,* 29–49.

King, V. 1994. Nonresident father involvement and child well-being. *Journal of Family Issues, 15,* 78–96.

Kline, M., J. M. Tschann, J. R. Johnston, and J. Wallerstein. 1989. Children's adjustment in joint and sole physical custody families. *Developmental Psychology, 25,* 430–438.

Kurdek, L. A. 1987. Children's adjustment to parental divorce: An ecological perspective. In J. P. Vincent, ed., *Advances in family intervention, assessment, and theory,* vol. 4, pp. 1–31. Greenwich, Conn.: JAI Press.

Kurdek, L. A., D. Blisk, and A. Siesky, Jr. 1981. Correlates of children's long-term adjustment to their parents' divorce. *Developmental Psychology, 17,* 565–579.

Lamb, M. E., J. H. Pleck, E. L. Charnov, and J. A. Levine. 1987. A biosocial perspective on paternal behavior and involvement. In J. B. Lancaster, J. Altman, A. S. Rossi, and L. R. Sherrod, eds., *Parenting across the lifespan: Biosocial dimensions.* New York: Aldine de Gruyter.

Lamborn, S. D., N. S. Mounts, L. Steinberg, and S. M. Dornbusch. 1991. Patterns of competence and adjustment among adolescents from authoritative, authoritarian, indulgent, and neglectful families. *Child Development, 62,* 1049–1065.

Levy, B., and C. Chambers. 1981. The folly of joint custody. *Family Advocate, 3,* 6–10.

Luepnitz, D. A. 1982. *Child custody: A study of families after divorce.* Lexington, Mass.: Lexington Books/D. C. Heath and Company.

———— 1986. A comparison of maternal, paternal, and joint custody: Understanding the varieties of post-divorce family life. *Journal of Divorce, 9,* 1–12.

Lutz, P. 1983. The stepfamily: An adolescent perspective. *Family Relations, 32,* 367–375.

Maccoby, E. E. 1990. Gender and relationships. *American Psychologist, 45,* 513–520.

———— 1995. Divorce and custody: The rights, needs, and obligations of mothers, fathers, and children. In G. Melton, ed., *The individual, the family, and social good: Personal fulfillment in times of change,* Nebraska Symposium on Motivation, vol. 42, pp. 135–172. Lincoln: University of Nebraska Press.

Maccoby, E. E., C. E. Depner, and R. H. Mnookin. 1990. Coparenting in the second year after divorce. *Journal of Marriage and the Family, 52,* 141–155.

Maccoby, E. E., and C. N. Jacklin. 1974. *The psychology of sex differences.* Stanford, Calif.: Stanford University Press.

Maccoby, E. E., and J. Martin. 1983. Socialization in the context of the family: Parent-child interaction. In P. H. Mussen, ed., *Handbook of child psychology,* vol. 4, *Socialization, personality, and social development,* pp. 1–102. New York: John Wiley and Sons.

Maccoby, E. E., and R. H. Mnookin. 1992. *Dividing the child: Social and legal dilemmas of custody.* Cambridge, Mass.: Harvard University Press.

McCormick, M. C., K. Workman-Daniels, J. Brooks-Gunn, and G. J. Peckham. 1993. When you're only a phone call away: A comparison of the information in telephone and face-to-face interviews. *Developmental and Behavioral Pediatrics, 14,* 250–257.

Miller, P. M., D. L. Danaher, and D. Forbes. 1986. Sex-related strategies for coping with interpersonal conflict in children aged five and seven. *Developmental Psychology, 22,* 543–548.

Minuchin, S. 1974. *Families and family therapy.* Cambridge, Mass.: Harvard University Press.

Mnookin, R. H., E. E. Maccoby, C. R. Albiston, and C. E. Depner. 1989. Private ordering revisited: What custodial arrangements are parents negotiating? In S. D. Sugarman and H. H. Kay, eds., *Divorce reform at the crossroads,* pp. 37–74. New Haven, Conn.: Yale University Press.

Montemayor, R. 1983. Parents and adolescents in conflict: All families some of the time and some families most of the time. *Journal of Early Adolescence, 3,* 83–103.

Montemayor, R., and J. R. Brownlee. 1987. Fathers, mothers, and adolescents: Gender-based differences in parental roles during adolescence. *Journal of Youth and Adolescence, 16,* 281–291.

Mussen, P., and N. Eisenberg-Berg. 1977. *Roots of caring, sharing, and helping.* San Francisco: W. H. Freeman.

Natriello, G., and S. M. Dornbusch. 1984. *Teacher evaluative standards and student effort.* New York: Longman.

Nelson, R. 1989. Parental hostility, conflict, and communication in joint and sole custody families. *Journal of Divorce, 13,* 145–157.

Neugebauer, R. 1989. Divorce, custody, and visitation: The child's point of view. *Journal of Divorce, 12,* 153–168.

Nolen-Hoeksema, S., and J. S. Girgus. 1994. The emergence of gender differences in depression during adolescence. *Psychological Bulletin, 115,* 424–443.

Noller, P. 1994. Relationships with parents in adolescence: Process and outcome. In R. Montemayor, G. R. Adams, and T. P. Gullotta, eds., *Personal relationships during adolescence,* pp. 37–77. Thousand Oaks, Calif.: Sage Publications.

Oppawsky, J. 1989. Family dysfunctional patterns during divorce—from the view of the children. In C. A. Everett, ed., *Children of divorce: Developmental and clinical issues,* pp. 139–152. Binghamton, N.Y.: Haworth Press.

Parke, R. D., and B. R. Tinsley. 1981. The father's role in infancy: Determinants of involvement in caregiving and play. In M. E. Lamb, ed., *The role of the father in child development,* pp. 429–457. New York: John Wiley and Sons.

Pasley, K., and M. Ihinger-Tallman, eds. 1987. *Remarriage and stepparenting: Current research and theory.* New York: Guilford Press.

Patterson, G. R. 1982. *Coercive family process.* Eugene, Ore.: Castalia.

Pearson, J., and N. Thoennes. 1990. Custody after divorce: Demographic and attitudinal patterns. *American Journal of Orthopsychiatry, 60,* 233–249.

Petersen, A. C., P. A. Sarigiani, and R. E. Kennedy. 1991. Adolescent depression: Why more girls? *Journal of Youth and Adolescence, 20,* 247–271.

Peterson, J. L., and N. Zill. 1986. Marital disruption, parent-child relationships, and behavior problems in children. *Journal of Marriage and the Family, 48,* 295–307.

Rosemond, J. K. 1994. Helping children with the before and after of divorce. *Hemispheres,* May: 99–103.

Russell, G., and A. Russell. 1987. Mother-child and father-child relationships in middle childhood. *Child Development, 58,* 1573–1585.

Rutter, M. 1979. Protective factors in children's responses to stress and disadvantage. In M. W. Kent and J. E. Rolf, eds., *Primary prevention of pathology: Social competence in children.* Hanover, N.H.: University Press of New England.

Rutter, M., P. Graham, O. F. D. Chadwick, and W. Yule. 1976. Adolescent turmoil: Fact or fiction? *Journal of Child Psychology and Psychiatry, 17,* 35–56.

Santrock, J. W. 1970. Paternal absence, sex typing, and identification. *Developmental Psychology, 2,* 262–274.

Santrock, J. W., and R. A. Warshak. 1979. Father custody and social development in boys and girls. *Journal of Social Issues, 35,* 112–125.

Santrock, J. W., R. A. Warshak, and G. L. Elliott. 1982. Social development and parent-child interaction in father custody and step-mother families. In M. E. Lamb, ed., *Nontraditional families.* Hillsdale, N.J.: Lawrence Erlbaum Associates.

Santrock, J. W., R. A. Warshak, C. Lindberg, and L. Meadows. 1982. Children's and parent's observed social behavior in stepfather families. *Child Development, 53,* 472–480.

Schoenbach, V. J., B. H. Kaplan, E. H. Wagner, R. C. Grimson, and F. T. Miller. 1983. Prevalence of self-reported depressive symptoms in young adolescents. *American Journal of Public Health, 73,* 1281–1287.

Seltzer, J. A. 1991. Relationships between fathers and children who live apart: The father's role after separation. *Journal of Marriage and Family, 53,* 79–101.

Sessa, F. M., and L. Steinberg. 1991. Family structure and the development of autonomy during adolescence. *Journal of Early Adolescence, 11,* 38–55.

Shiller, V. M. 1986a. Joint vs. maternal physical custody for families with latency age boys: Parent characteristics and child adjustment. *American Journal of Orthopsychiatry, 56,* 486–489.

——— 1986b. Loyalty conflicts and family relationships in latency age boys: A comparison of joint and maternal custody. *Journal of Divorce, 9,* 17–38.

Simmons, R. G., R. Burgeson, S. Carlton-Ford, and D. A. Blyth. 1987. The impact of cumulative change in early adolescence. *Child Development, 58,* 1220–1234.

Simring, S. 1984. Joint custody best alternative when ex-spouses are hostile:

New research. *Marriage and divorce today: The professional newsletter for family therapy practitioners, 9,* 1.

Smollar, J., and J. Youniss. 1985. Parent-adolescent relations in adolescents whose parents are divorced. *Journal of Early Adolescence, 5,* 129–144.

Steinberg, L. 1987. Single parents, stepparents, and the susceptibility of adolescents to antisocial peer pressure. *Child Development, 58,* 269–275.

Steinberg, L., N. S. Mounts, S. D. Lamborn, and S. M. Dornbusch. 1991. Authoritative parenting and adolescent adjustment across varied ecological niches. *Journal of Research on Adolescence, 1,* 19–36.

Steinman, S. B. 1981. The experience of children in a joint-custody arrangement: A report of a study. *American Journal of Orthopsychiatry, 51,* 403–414.

Stolberg, A. L., and P. M. Cullen. 1983. Preventive interventions for families of divorce: The divorce adjustment project. In L. A. Kurdek, ed., *New Directions for Child Development,* no. 19, *Children and Divorce,* pp. 71–82. San Francisco: Jossey-Bass.

Stoneman, Z., G. H. Brody, and M. Burke. 1989. Marital quality, depression, and inconsistent parenting: Relationships with observed mother-child conflict. *American Journal of Orthopsychiatry, 59,* 105–117.

Sweet, J. A., and L. L. Bumpass. 1987. *American families and households.* New York: Russell Sage Foundation.

Vaughn, B. E., J. H. Block, and J. Block. 1988. Parental agreement on child-rearing during early childhood and the psychological characteristics of adolescents. *Child Development, 59,* 1020–1033.

Wallerstein, J. S., and S. Blakeslee. 1989. *Second chances: Men, women, and children a decade after divorce.* New York: Ticknor and Fields.

Wallerstein, J. S., and J. B. Kelly. 1980. *Surviving the breakup: How children and parents cope with divorce.* New York: Basic Books.

Warshak, R. A., and J. W. Santrock. 1983. The impact of divorce in father-custody and mother-custody homes: The child's perspective. In L. A. Kurdek, ed., *New Directions for Child Development,* no. 19, *Children and Divorce,* pp. 29–46. San Francisco: Jossey-Bass.

Werner, E. E., and R. S. Smith. 1982. *Vulnerable but invincible: A study of resilient children.* New York: McGraw-Hill.

Whitehead, B. D. 1993. Dan Quayle was right. *Atlantic Monthly, 271,* 47–84.

Whiting, B. B., and J. W. M. Whiting. 1975. *Children of six cultures: A psychocultural analysis.* Cambridge, Mass.: Harvard University Press.

Youniss, J., and J. Smollar. 1983. *Adolescent relations with mothers, fathers, and friends.* Chicago: University of Chicago Press.

Zaslow, M. J. 1988. Sex differences in children's response to parental divorce: 1. Research methodology and post-divorce family forms. *American Journal of Orthopsychiatry, 58,* 355–378.

——— 1989. Sex differences in children's response to parental divorce: 2.

Samples, variables, ages, and sources. *American Journal of Orthopsy-chiatry, 59,* 118–141.

Zill, N. 1988. Behavior, achievement, and health problems among children in stepfamilies: Findings from a national survey of child health. In E. M. Hetherington and J. Arasteh, eds., *The impact of divorce, single parenting, and stepparenting on children.* Hillsdale, N.J.: Erlbaum.

INDEX

Adjustment, adolescents in our sample: 37–42, 253–254; as related to acceptance of new partner, 135–138, 140, 256–257; as related to visitation with nonresidential parent, 181–184; as related to loyalty conflicts, 226–230; as related to inconsistency in parenting, 240, 241–243, 244–246, 249. *See also specific indices of family relationships and family functioning, including* Residential arrangement

Adjustment, children of divorce: 4–7

Age of adolescents: in sample, 9, 16, 26–27; as factors in residence and visitation, 46, 166; as factor in acceptance of new partners, 126–127, 140; and feelings about visitation, 168, 174; and impact of visitation, 179, 181; and impact of interparental conflict, 208, 258; and loyalty conflicts, 219, 221, 258; and impact of inconsistency in parenting, 241, 250

Analysis strategies, 19–20, 25, 46, 48–49, 81–84, 98, 110–111, 136, 161–162, 193, 206, 239

Authoritarian parenting, 94–95. *See also specific indices of parenting, including* Closeness, child and residential parent, *and* Household management

Authoritative parenting, 94–95. *See also specific indices of parenting, including* Closeness, child and residential parent, *and* Household management

Birth order, of adolescents in sample, 27

Chores, 97–98, 192

Closeness, child and nonresidential parent: and residential parent's repartnering status, 114–116, 118–119, 132–134, 139–140, 270; and adolescent adjustment, 146–147, 193, 198, 199–200, 201–205, 210–212, 213, 263; and level of visitation, 176–179, 185–186, 208, 262–263; and sex of nonresidential parent, 188–189, 212; and impact of residential parent's repartnering on loyalty conflicts, 226. *See also* Closeness, parent-child

Closeness, child and residential parent: and residential arrangement, 70, 71–72, 264, 265–266; and adolescent adjustment, 90–91, 93–96, 101–102, 103, 105–106, 146, 201–205, 259–261, 263; and parent's repartnering status, 113–114, 116–117, 139, 269; and acceptance of parent's new partner, 131–132, 140; and closeness to nonresidential parent, 146, 200–201; and visitation with nonresidential parent, 180. *See also* Closeness, parent-child

Closeness, parent-child: measure, 24; in sample, 41, 67–70; as related to parent's residential status, 187–188, 212; and loyalty conflicts, 223–224, 231. *See also* Closeness, child and nonresidential parent; Closeness, child and residential parent

Cohabitation. *See* Remarriage and repartnering

Conflict and cooperation, interparental: and adolescent adjustment, 5, 89–90,

306.874
B918

92116

LINCOLN CHRISTIAN COLLEGE AND SEMINARY

3 4711 00093 7864